THE RADICALIZATION OF
THOMAS JEFFERSON

THE RADICALIZATION OF THOMAS JEFFERSON

CICERO PRESS

Publisher: Cicero Press
Contact: ciceropud1@gmail.com

ISBN 978-1-7327747-9-7

Edited by:
Cover & book design: Jim Shubin, BookAlchemist.net
Cover photo: Public Domain

First publication 2019

Dedication

In loving memory of Dr. Leonard Marsak, my intellectual father, Ph.D. adviser, and friend at the University of California at Santa Barbara. Dr. Marsak was one of those rare professors who had both the talent and interest to inspire a generation of students with a love of learning. His presence was felt throughout the writing of this book.

Acknowledgements

I began this study so long ago it is doubtful my friends and colleagues remember the encouragement and help they offered me over the past fifteen years. I want to acknow-ledge the painstaking work of my first copy editor, Kathryn Barbour who, eight years ago, edited and formatted the first draft of my manuscript.

I am deeply indebted to Professor Richard Matthews for his extraordinary assistance and sage advice over a period of several months in the re-writing and editing of my original manuscript. I also want to thank Professor Joyce Appleby for her review of my book and Professor Klaus Fischer who graciously wrote the foreword to it. I am also grateful for the inspirational support of my friend John Fetto, who labored beside me in a café while writing his novel, and to my good friend John Kling who helped with the editing of my final draft. I would be remiss if I did not thank my wife, Gayle, for her encouragement and enthusiastic support for this work.

CONTENTS

FOREWORD

by Klaus P. Fischer

In this new and exciting book on Thomas Jefferson, Clark Chelsey provides fresh insights into Jefferson's accom-plishment as one of the leading philosophical geniuses of the Enlightenment. Jefferson was a man of letters, an eighteenth-century philosophe in the best sense of the word. He was immensely curious about everything and he left a voluminous literary legacy that is still being gathered and assessed. In addition, few American presidents have received so much attention as the sage of Monticello. A huge scholarly literature now exists on Jefferson, but few historians have focused on the man's central philosophical vision and how it developed and matured over significant phases of his life. This effort to find a unifying field theory has now been accomplished by Clark Chelsey, who has spent decades in search of the quintessential Jefferson.

Chelsey goes about the task of penetrating to the center of Jefferson's vision by applying the tools of a trained intellectual historian who is sure of his method and the sources he uses. He traces what Arthur O. Lovejoy called the resonant "unit ideas" of Jefferson's age—natural rights, liberty, equality, government by consent of the governed, checks and balances, free enterprise, property rights—and connects them to their social origins, showing how Jefferson grappled with these concepts at a time of earth-shaking events. Jefferson lived through world-altering upheavals in his lifetime. Not only was he one of the most important founding fathers of an entirely new political experiment in history—the founding of a democratic Republic —but he also served his new nation as one of the most influential preceptors of civic responsibility in a democracy. All of this came at a time of three converging revolutions in history: the democratic revolution in America and France, the Scientific Revolution, and the beginning of the Industrial Revolution. Chelsey manages to trace the living fabric of Jefferson's ideas through these turbulent changes and how Jefferson modified, refined, and increasingly radicalized them in a coherent and systematic way. It is this approach, as indicated by the title, that makes the book such a fresh and original contribution to historical scholarship.

One important aspect of Chelsey's position is that Jefferson was as indebted to French intellectual thought as he was to English traditions. He spent five years as minister to France (1784-1789), where he met French philosophers, notably Destutt de Tracy, Condorcet and DuPont de Nemours, and read their writings. He witnessed the coming of the French revolution and advised the National Assembly in crafting its Declaration of the *Rights of Man and Citizen*. He owed as much to Montesquieu and Rousseau as he did to Locke or Hume. For some time, Jefferson saw the Jacobins as pure Republicans and applauded their focus on civic virtue.

For Jefferson the French revolutionary spirit became

a benchmark for judging not only the authenticity of one's republicanism but also the direction or evolution of democracy in America. Although Jefferson later admitted that his enthusiasm for the Jacobins had blinded him to their violent excesses, especially during the Reign of Terror, he retained from them a strong strain of egalitarianism that never left him. At the same time, he was acutely aware that there is always a tension between liberty and equality, and that excessive emphasis on one tendency at the expense of the other may have detrimental consequences for a democracy that claims to cherish them both. After all, what are the respective roles of liberty, equality, and fraternity, given the fact that they are not all coequal?

In reading Chelsey's work, it appears that for Jefferson the empire of liberty was more important than the empire of equality. The epicenter of his thought was individual liberty in conformity with republican principles. He distrusted centralized power, and for good reason once we remember that he was living in an age of royal absolutism. Government governs best if it governs least and always if it is consonant with rational moral laws and divided powers. Real power should be located in the people, preferably on the local (ward) level because it is at the local level that real participatory democracy can flourish. The key to Jefferson's political philosophy is found in two resonant concepts: self-government and popular sovereignty. If these should ever be threatened by an abusive central government, Jefferson revealed himself as one of the few radical democrats of the so-called American Revolution because he would have been the first to call for armed resistance and the overthrow of petty tyrants. The only remedy against oppression was the institutionalization of civic virtue and providing citizens with educational and practical experience in the art of politics.

In responding to Jefferson's critics that Jefferson's world is no longer ours, and that his political thought is therefore obsolete, Chelsey rightly reminds us that historical contingencies do not invalidate elements in Jefferson that transcend the purely temporal since they express truths about what is universal in human nature. Even granting the obvious fact that we now live in a postmodern technological world, Jefferson's belief in the possibility of creating ward republics and more intimate democratic villages was not an idle dream but is now closer to reality than it was in his own day because we have the technological means to bring people together in electronic villages that can make direct democracy feasible. The relevance and intellectual depth of Jefferson is therefore as relevant as it was over two hundred years ago. Chelsey's book is an important reminder of this fact.

PREFACE

Like so many of Thomas Jefferson's contemporaries and historians who have written brilliantly about his philosophy and the founding of the American republic, I was seduced by Jefferson's fertile imagination, "felicity of expression," and prodigious work in so many fields of human inquiry. The breadth and depth of Jefferson's knowledge and the central role he played as an architect of American democracy have been a source of fascination for me for over forty years

I first began this work as a graduate student at the University of California at Santa Barbara in 1971. In graduate courses with Alexander DeConde, George Dangerfield, and Morton Borden, I studied the collected writings of Thomas Jefferson and what seemed like hundreds of books and articles about him, while pursuing my studies on the French Enlightenment with my graduate adviser, Leonard Marsak, Professor of European Intellectual History. After almost two years of research and writing, I had the rueful awakening that the French philosophers' contribution to Jefferson's philosophy, although significant in science, economics and politics, did not sufficiently account for Jefferson's republicanism or his concept of human nature. I abandoned my study of Jefferson and decided instead to write my Ph.D. dissertation on Dugald Stewart, a Scottish philosopher I found referenced in an exchange of letters between Jefferson and Adams.

After completing my dissertation, *Dugald Stewart: Historian of the Enlightenment*, I left the university in 1976 and did not return to my study of Jefferson until the late 1980s. I had found in the writing of my earlier dissertation on the Scottish moral sense tradition a concept of human nature very different from the political liberalism and individualistic philosophy of John Locke. It struck me that Jefferson's republicanism and his faith in democracy was predicated on his belief in a moral sense in man, that is, man's instinctual sense of justice and duty toward others.

I began rewriting my original manuscript on Jefferson and the French Philosophes, incorporating new insights into it from my study on Scottish moral sense philosophy when I discovered two major works on the Scottish influence on Jefferson's philosophy, Richard Matthews' *The Radical Politics of Thomas Jefferson* and Garry Wills' *Inventing America*. Their analysis, in some respects, resembled my own. Wills had explored the moral and scientific culture of the Scottish Enlightenment and the similarities between Scottish philosophers, like Thomas Reid and Francis Hutcheson, and Jefferson's democratic and egalitarian philosophy, while Matthews seized on the radical implications of Scottish moral sense theory in Jefferson's political philosophy. I had some disagreements with their analyses, but since their works captured so much of what I was thinking and writing I put my study aside once again.

I continued with my studies over the next ten years, reading and rereading Jefferson's writings and an ever-growing number of books and articles on Jefferson's political, economic and moral philosophy. It eventually occurred to me that many of the debates between liberal and republican interpretations of Jefferson's philosophy did not account for the influence of the French philosophers and, even more importantly, Jefferson's experiences in revolutionary France. I recalled my own experiences during the anti-war movement in the late sixties and the impact it had on a generation of students demonstrating in the streets and on college campuses throughout the country. Students who had been content to study the required reading in their courses were suddenly reading Karl Marx, Herbert Marcuse and the Frankfurt School, and Sartre's existentialism. They questioned the legitimacy of state power and the capitalistic system, and began to imagine a world free of exploitation, war and famine, a world with endless possibilities for human creativity.

I began to wonder if Jefferson, having lived through the early stages of the French Revolution, conversing with the French philosophes in their most celebrated salons in Paris, was immune to the revolutionary climate of opinion in Paris or if instead he was deeply and profoundly affected by the events he witnessed in France. I began to study, once again, his letters and correspondence during his ministry to France and his observations of Hamilton and the Federalists upon his return from France. It became apparent to me that Jefferson's experiences in France during the French Revolution did in fact have a major impact on his philosophy and policies, changing the way he thought about America's revolutionary past, the republican and liberal theories of the English and the Scots, and the contest for political power in the United States. This is a study of that transformative time in Jefferson's life and its subsequent effects.

Introduction
Jefferson and the French Enlightenment

The French Revolution, the most "momentous event in human history," Jefferson wrote in 1789, was the turning point for the radical reevaluation of his philosophical beliefs. "In the same manner," Jurgen Habermas writes, "the Americans model had been a catalyst for French self-understanding, so now the American could discern the revolutionary aspect of the foundation of their own government in the mirror of the French Revolution."[1] Jefferson's travels through France and England, his friendships with the French philosophes, and, as importantly, the revolutionary climate of opinion in France transformed his understanding of science, economics, politics, and moral philosophy. Jefferson did not abandon his earlier principles and beliefs, but his personal observations and experiences in the highly stratified society of monarchical France deepened and broadened his understanding of the challenges facing democratic societies and the principles and measures required to maintain and strengthen them in a world hostile to the principle of equality and the rights of man. Jefferson became, like the French philosophes, an enemy of inequality and a champion of democratic egalitarianism.

When Jefferson arrived in Paris in 1784, the intellectual giants of French culture—Montesquieu, Voltaire, Rousseau, Denis Diderot, D'Alembert, Helvetius, Francois Quesnay—had died, and a new generation of intellectuals had taken their place in the cultural life of Paris. The generation of Montesquieu and Voltaire were the first of three overlapping generations in the French Enlightenment. They "grew up while the writings of Locke and Newton were still fresh and controversial."2 The second generation Buffon, Rousseau, Diderot, Condillac, Helvetius, and d'Alembert-"fueled the fashionable anticlericalism and scientific speculations of the first generation into a coherent modern view of the world."3 The third generation of philosophes, principally Holbach, Beccaria, Turgot, Condorcet, de Tracy and J.B. Say "moved into scientific mythology and materialist metaphysics, political economy, legal reform, and practice politics."4

As minister to the Court of Louis XVI, Jefferson was about to discover something he could not even have imagined when his journey first began in Boston, how much his feelings and thoughts would change because of the events he would witness in France and the people he would meet during his five years residency in Paris. He would become, not merely a compassionate witness to the social turmoil and political upheaval unfolding before him in Paris, but a passionate participant, sharing his thoughts and experiences as an American revolutionary with the French who were seeking a new path forward for the French nation.

Jefferson's generation of *philosophes* did not accept Dr. Pangloss' advice in Voltaire's Candide that we should cultivate our own gardens and not concern ourselves with the mayhem around us. The new generation of *philosophes* sought to right the wrongs in French society. They could no longer ignore, as others had, the injustices of the French monarchy, the poverty and abject misery of the peasantry, and the privileges of the Church and aristocracy. John Adams, as America's minister to England, witnessed and experienced the same injustices as Jefferson, the social inequality and class divisions in the English society but, like Dr. Pangloss, chose to ignore them. Jefferson was not as dispassionate about what he saw in France and England as Adams, and unlike Adams, he felt at home in the company of the radical *philosophes* whose philosophy he embraced without reservation.

Nothing could have prepared Jefferson for what he was about to see in the streets of Paris. A city with a population estimated between six hundred thousand to one million, roughly ten to twelve times larger than Philadelphia, America's largest city. There were more inhabitants in the city of Paris than in the state of Virginia, America's richest, largest in territory, and oldest British colony in North America. Jefferson's native state of Virginia, with a population he estimated at 567,614, was also largely rural, with very few towns."6

Paris presented a dramatically different scene from what he was accustomed to seeing in the American colonies. "You lost much, he wrote to William Short in 1785,

by not attending the Tedeum at Notre Dame yesterday. It bids defiance to description. I will observe to you in general that there were more judges, ecclesiastics and Grands seigneurs present, than Gen. Washington had of simple souldier in his army, when he took the Hessians at Trenton, beat the British at Princeton, and hemmed up the British army at Brunswick a whole winter.[7]

"I believe I may say with truth," Abigail reported that Mr. Jefferson saying about this occasion in her diary,

there were millions of people...as many people in the streets as there were in the State of Massachusetts, or any other of the States. Every house was full—every window and door, from the bottom to the top...Mr. Jefferson...supposed there were as many people in the streets as there were in the State of Massachusetts, or any other of the States. Every house was full-every window and door, from the bottom to the top. All this was to pay homage to the birth of the Duke of Normandy.[8]

Jefferson had never seen, and probably never even imagined a city as fascinating and frenetic as the city of Paris.

For the first time in his life, Jefferson was living in a rarefied cosmopolitan environment where every day he could meet and talk on equal terms with men and women who shared his own wide-ranging interests."[9] Jefferson had found "his true calling in this vital, unpredictable city in transition, aroused by its aesthetic and intellectual life, its climate of experiment and change, and is magnetic, heightened possibilities."[10] He seemed "to breathe with perfect satisfaction," Henry Adams observed, "nowhere except in the liberal, literary, scientific air of Paris in 1789."[11]

"Behold me at length on the vaunted scene of

Europe," he wrote to Charles Bellini in September, 1785,

"you are perhaps curious to know how this new scene has struck a savage of the mountains of America...Here it seems that a man might pass a life without encountering a single rudeness. In the pleasures of the table they are far before us because with good taste they unite temperance. They do not terminate their most sociable meals by transforming themselves into brutes. I have never seen a man drunk in France. Were I to proceed to tell you how much I enjoy their architecture, sculpture, painting, music, I should want for words. It is in these arts they shine."[12]

Jefferson enjoyed the city's new opera houses, theaters, broad boulevards and public spaces and the attractions of the duke d'Orleans new shopping mall, the Palais Royal.

He especially liked Beaumarchais's Le Mariage de Figaro and the Death of Socrates by David. He joined the fashionable chess club, the Salon des Echecs, above the Café de Foi, and, expressed to a friend from Richmond, Virginia the conveniences of having "cafes of all kinds, billiard halls, magic lantern shows, bookstalls...peddlers selling bawdy political satires...Courtesans and street walkers moved easily through the crowds disguised as countesses."[13]

Jefferson was particularly impressed with the architecture in France. "Here I am," he wrote to Madame de Tesse, the aunt of Lafayette, gazing at the Maison quarree, like a lover at his mistress."[14] He was "violently smitten," he told her "with the hotel de Salm and used to go to the Thulieres almost daily to look at it."15 The Maison quarree of Nimes," he wrote to James Madison, was "one of the most beautiful and precious morcel of architecture left us by antiquity...You see I'm not ashamed, as its object is to improve the taste of my countrymen, to increase their reputation, to reconcile them the respect of the world and procure them its praise."16

He was fond of visiting book stores in Paris, devoting "every afternoon I was disengaged, for a summer or two, in examining all the principal bookstore, turning over every book with my own hand, and putting by everything which related to America, and indeed whatever was rare and valuable in every science."17 "Books, really good," he said, "acquire a just reputation in that time, and so become known to us, and communicate to us all their advances in knowledge."18

It is critically important to learn the French language, he told his nephew, Peter Carr, "because the books which will be put into your hands when you advance into Mathematics, Natural Philosophy, etc. will be mostly French, these sciences being better treated by the French than the English writers."19 In the sciences, he wrote, "their literati [are] half dozen years before us and communicate to us all their advances in knowledge."20 Jefferson was aware that Paris, and not London, had become the intellectual center of Europe and the world. The city of Paris, so different from his native state of Virginia, and from the literary and scientific culture of the United States, nourished Jefferson's intellectual curiosity and passion for knowledge.

Jefferson also admired the manners of the French people. "I am much pleased," he wrote to Eliza House Trist, Aug. 18, 1785, with the people of this country. The roughness of mind is so thoroughly rubbed off with them that it seems as if one might glide thro'a whole life without a justle. Perhaps too their manners may be the best calculated for happiness to a people in their situation...."[21]

Jefferson's praise of the manners and geniality of French people was, at the same time, a veiled criticism of the coarse behavior of his fellow Virginians. To Chastellux, who had traveled through Virginia while Jefferson was in Paris, Jefferson shared his thoughts about "the character of the several states."[22] In the southern states he said, "they are fiery, voluptuary, indolent, unsteady, independent, zealous for their own liberties, but trampling on those of others, generous, candid, without attachment or pretention to any religion but that of the heart."[23]

Jefferson did not hold his fellow Virginians, or Southerners in the highest regard. There were obviously some good character traits, their independence, candor and generosity, but much else needed improvement. "He wished his countrymen, "without sacrificing too much the sincerity of language (would) adopt just so much of European politeness as to be ready to make all those little sacrifices of self which really render European manners amiable and relieve society from the disagreeable scenes to which rudeness often exposes it."[24] Jefferson's head and heart found a home in Paris.

Intellectual life in Paris was very different from what he experienced in the United States. "Although Philadelphia was the literary as well as the political capital of America, nothing proved the existence of a highly intellectual society."[25] "The tavern," Henry Adams wrote, "was the club and the forum of political discussion; but for those who sought other haunts, and especially women, no intellectual amusement other than what was called belles-lettres existed to give a sense of occupation to an active mind."[26]

In France, Jefferson would find many haunts for his "spacious and encyclopedic" mind, especially in the celebrated salons of Paris where France's most eminent philosophers, scientists, writers, artists and economists congregated. The French literati frequented the salons because they

were dependent for fame and fortune on the patronage of the...salons. Even if one was a philosopher...one was forced to look for a patron and perhaps a pension. Only the very famous could hope to earn the favour of Frederick the Great or Catherine of Russia; the rest remained at the mercy of society hostesses....[27]

Even those writers with secure incomes "depended upon the salon for success; the future of a book was largely determined by its reception in the leading drawing-rooms where the cultural aristocracy of Europe forgathered to discuss, applaud or condemn."[28] Montesquieu's election, d'Alembert's secretaryship and many of the *philosophes* appointed to academic chairs were owing to the social patronage of the women who controlled the intellectual life of France in the eighteenth century."[29]

Jefferson was fortunate to be introduced to Parisian salons by Benjamin Franklin, a man whose reputation, John Adams wrote, "was more universal than that of Leibniz or Newton, Frederick (the Great) or Voltaire, and his character more beloved than any or all of them."[30] "Jefferson inherited two of Franklin's devoted friends, Madame Houdetot and Madame Helvetius, who gave him entrée to the Paris salon. Jefferson visited the salons of Madame Corny, Madame d'Houdetot, Jean Jacque Rousseau's lover, memorialized in Rousseau's Sophie of the *Confessions*, Madame de Tesse, Madame Helvetius, the widow of a noted atheist-materialist philosopher, and the beloved of Benjamin Franklin, and Madame Necker.

Jefferson made his "more valuable contacts at the salon of Madame Helvetius which Franklin called 'l'Academie des Belles Letters d'Auteuil. The men of literature and learning, Franklin wrote, "attached themselves to Madame as straws to amber. "Auteuil always seemed to Jefferson a delicious village, and Madame Helvetius the most delicious spot in it."31 It was in Madame Helvetius' salon that the most radical of the French *philosophes* and scientists congregated to discuss literature, philosophy, economics and the science of man and of government. At Madame Helvetius' salon, Jefferson became friends with Destutt de Tracy, J.B. Say; Pierre Cabanis. Madame de Stael, the daughter of Madame Necker, the Abbe Morellet, the Count de Volney, Duke de la Rochefoucald-Liancourt, the Baron von Grimm, Brissot de Warville, Marquis de Condorcet, Marquis de Lafayette, among others who became "leaders of the intellectual...life of Paris in the 1780's and later prominent in the early phases of the Revolution."32 Before their deaths, d'Alembert, Diderot, and d'Holbach were also habitual attendees of Madame Helvetius' salon.

Among those at the salon who had the greatest influence on Jefferson's understanding of science and economics in this period were Cabanis, de Tracy, and J.B. Say. Cabanis was the leading figure in the field of physiological psychology in Paris; Tracy commanded the respect of the French *philosophes* in the social sciences; and Say assumed the leadership of the French Smithians, the French school of economics. Jefferson was so impressed with Tracy that he later translated and edited Tracy's *A Commentary and Review of Montesquieu's Spirit of Laws and his A Treatise on Political Economy.* Say was so friendly with Jefferson that, after the fall of Napoleon and the Bourbon restoration in 1814, he asked Jefferson how much he would have to pay to buy a cotton farm in Charlottesville, near Jefferson's estate, Monticello.[33] These philosophes, as a group, were committed, as was Jefferson after his conversations and studies with them, to laissez-faire economics, materialism and democratic egalitarianism.

"In his role as American ambassador, Jefferson enjoyed a front row seat to the unfolding drama as France lurched, step by step, toward revolution. He attended the first meeting of the Estates General at Versailles in May...followed the debates closely, attending the meetings at Versailles almost daily in May and June."[34] Jefferson was not an impartial observer of French society and the French Revolution; he was actively engaged in the political debates and discussions of the French revolutionaries.

On August 25, 1789, at the request of Lafayette, Jefferson secretly hosted a meeting at the Hotel Langeac, his permanent residence during his ministry to France, for eight of the leading French liberal deputies of the National Assembly whose political differences were threatening a schism in the Patriot party. Jefferson blatantly violated diplomatic code in drafting a "ten-point document" or Charter of Rights on May 2, 1789 which "called for the abolition of all pecuniary privileges and exemptions enjoyed by the nobility, civilian rule over the military, equal treatment under the law, and the modified version of freedom of the press...He conveyed his draft to Lafayette in June 1789. The charter he wrote served as the "basis for the Declaration of Rights that Lafayette presented to the National Assembly the following month."[35] Jefferson later recalled that the discussions held at his residency were "truly worthy of being placed in parallel with the finest dialogues of antiquity, as handed down to us by Xenophon, by Plato, and Cicero. (The next day he apologized to Louis XVI's minister of foreign affairs, for their extraordinary diplomatic impropriety."[36]

Jefferson, like the French philosophes, experienced what Jonathan Israel defines as a "revolution of the mind," a structural shift before 1789 that "has been broadly missed because it was an intellectual transformation, bringing that huge cultural shift, the essential revolution, that preceded the revolution of fact."[37] This intellectual shift was caused, in part, by

the growth of cheap commercial lending libraries (that) allowed many to read extensively who did not possess the financial resources sufficient to build up a large private collection of books. Coffee houses offered newspapers and journals and some of the latest books for the use of customers, for the price of a cup of coffee. Booksellers' shops sometimes also offered light refreshments and a small circulating library for the use of patrons.[38]

The "revolution of the mind" was also made possible "by profound changes in the social position of writers and publishers. Writers of all countries were often collectively described as belonging to an idealized Republic of Letters."[39] "The books most widely read in the Enlightenment were often written by men and women, collectively called Grub Street by Darnton, "whose names are never mentioned in the canon of great Enlightenment thinkers," but who contributed, more forcibly than the literary elites, such as Voltaire and Diderot, "to the breakup of the Old Regime in France and the opening of a revolutionary situation at the close of the century."[40]

Like the elite writers, they believed in the "equality between all those involved in the Republic of Letters, the values of cosmopolitanism, (and) the idea that knowledge and its producers acted across political boundaries...."[41] We do not have any accounts by Jefferson of his encounters with these writers in the cafes, or of any exchanges between them, but it is undoubtedly something he witnessed during his daily walks through the streets of Paris "examining all the principal bookstores."

Philosophers in the Enlightenment may have thought of themselves as a family, with common loyalties and a common world view, willing to close ranks when one of their own came under governmental or ecclesiastical censure, or worse, imprisonment for their philosophical beliefs, but they were also aware of deep philosophical divisions between them. There was not one Enlightenment in France, England and America, but two— one moderate, and the other radical. The

moderate enlightenment was... not open to repudiating the existing hierarchical structure of society or portray society as it had evolved as inherently defective, oppressive, and systematically unjust, and hence wrongly organized for the purpose of advancing human happiness.[42]

Moderate enlightenment thinkers like Adam Ferguson, repudiated "the thought of Diderot, d'Holbach, Claude Adrien Helvetius, the marquis de Condorcet, and such British and American radicals as Paine, Jebb Barlow and Robert Coram."[43] Ferguson compared radical enlightenment thinkers to

that of an ambitious architect who inspires to tear down the entire edifice of institutions and then rebuild it from scratch on purely rational principles. The basic structure of government, law, and administration, as he and his Scottish colleagues and allies Hume, Kames, Smith, William Robertson, and Thomas Reid ...saw it—should remain always in place. [44]

The Radical Enlightenment Thinkers, like the Marquis de Lafayette, Condorcet, Destutt de Tracy, Pierre Cabanis, among many others, all friends of Jefferson, "were relentless," as he was, "in proclaiming reason as the sole guide, rejecting tradition as a source of authority and denouncing the existing order more or less in toto."[45] Whereas the Moderate Enlightenment postulated

a balance between reason and tradition and broadly supporting the status quo...the Radical Enlightenment conflated "body and mind into one, reducing God and nature to the same thing, excluding all miracles and spirits separate from bodies, and invoking reason as the sole guide in human life, jettisoning tradition.[46]

The radical French philosophes, like Jefferson, "sought to base theories about society on the principle of equality, and separated philosophy, science, and morality entirely from theology, grounding morality... on secular criteria only and especially the principle of equality."[47] Unlike the moderates in France, England and the United States, who were "content to work within one country... the radical enlightenment...by contrast, developed as an active force on both sides of the Atlantic...."[48] "The Radical Enlighteners were enemies of the hereditary principle as applied to land, high office, wealth and rank... The principle of equality was for them the foundation of any democratic social theory."[49] The radical enlightenment writers also had more confidence in reason, science and the progress of the human mind.

"One of the questions you know on which our parties took different sides," Jefferson later recalled to John Adams

was on the improvability of the human mind, in science, in ethics, in government, etc. Those who advocated reformation of institutions, pari passu, with the progress of science, maintained that no definite limits could be assigned to that progress. The enemies of reform, on the other hand, denied improvement, and advocated steady adherence to the principles, practices and institutions of our fathers, which they represented as the consummation of wisdom and acme of excellence, beyond which the human mind could never advance.[50]

Jefferson shared with his friend Condorcet "an uncompromising faith in human progress...with an almost theological intensity."[51] "Everything tells us,"

Jefferson wrote," that we are bordering the period of one of the greatest revolutions of the human race...The present state of enlightenment guarantees that it will be happy."[52]

Jefferson's optimism and faith in the future of mankind, however, did not blind him to the social political and economic inequities and injustices suffered by the great majority of people in saw in his travels through England and France. "In spite of the mildness of their governors," he wrote, "a genial climate, and fertile soil, the people are ground to powder by the vices of the form of government."[53] "Of twenty millions of people supposed to be in France," he wrote, "I am of opinion there are nineteen millions more wretched, more accursed in every circumstance of human existence, than the most conspicuously wretched individual of the whole United States."[54] He agreed with the truth of Voltaire's observation "that every man here must be either hammer or the anvil."[55]

In England, he observed, the aristocracy" has the laws and government in their hands, have so managed" the (laboring class) as to reduce them...below the means of supporting life, even by labor."[56] In the United States, on the other hand,

> Most (of) the laboring class possess property, cultivate their own lands, have families, and from the demand for their labor are enabled to exact from the rich and the competent such prices as enable them to be fed abundantly, clothed above mere decency, to labor moderately and raise their families.[57]

The wealthy in the United States, unlike the English aristocrats, "know nothing of what the Europeans call luxury. They have only somewhat more of the comforts and decencies of life than those who furnish them."[58] Jefferson was even concerned that American students studying and traveling to England and other European countries may acquire "a fondness for European luxury and dissipation and contempt for the simplicity of his own country."[59] A fascination "with the privileges of the European aristocrats," he says, may lead them to "a partiality for aristocracy or monarchy," and an abhorrence of the equality the poor enjoys with the rich in our own country.[60]

Jefferson's observations and experiences during his residency and travels through France radicalized him. In this atmosphere of political discontent and social upheaval, Jefferson seized upon a doctrine he believed would solve, not only France's problems, but serve as a guiding principle for all democratic societies, a doctrine that fully embraced the principles of democratic egalitarianism—The Earth Belongs In Usufruct to the Living, and not the Dead.

His doctrine "The Earth Belongs In Usufruct to the Living, and not the Dead," also represents a paradigmatic shift in Jefferson's political, constitutional and economic thought. He rejected Montesquieu's reasoning and arguments about republican forms of government in the *Spirit of Laws*, arguments he repeated and enshrined in his own draft of the Virginia state constitution. He now disagreed with Montesquieu's argument that political liberty is best secured by a system that checks and balances regional interests, social orders and economic classes to avoid the threat posed by unpropertied masses eager to trample on the rights of private property, a belief shared by moderates in the United States, England and France. Jefferson believed, against the moderates, that all laws and constitutions, even the right to own property have a limited duration. This was a major departure, not only from Montesquieu, but also from the teachings of Coke and Blackstone, whose legal opinions and writings formed the basis for the legal education of America's revolutionary generation.

In the salon of Madame Helvetius, Jefferson also learned from the French economists, Destutt de Tracy and J.B. Say the economic theories of Adam Smith. He retained a preference for the agricultural class, as did Adam Smith, but he recognized the fallacies in the reasoning and economic arguments of the physiocrats' arguments he once favored before his departure to France. He saw in the teachings of Tracy and Say an economic philosophy that would foster and encourage economic growth for the great mass of the American people while preventing, at the same time, the maldistribution of wealth into the hands of the few. Jefferson judged the success of an economic program, not only by the wealth it produces, "the wealth of a nation," but by the more equitable distribution of that wealth among all classes of society. Jefferson used the economic reasoning and arguments of Say and Tracy against the programs and policies of Alexander Hamilton, especially those pertaining to the contraction of debts and the establishment of a national bank.

Jefferson's political, economic and moral philosophy was influenced by, and grounded in, his scientific worldview. Science in the Enlightenment was not limited to its methods, practices and discoveries alone; it was paradigmatic of the structure of all knowledge in this period. Natural philosophers in the eighteenth century believed that science was the engine for the political, moral and social amelioration of mankind.

Jefferson was an avid student of the new science. He embraced Newton's rules of reasoning in the natural sciences and Bacon's principle of induction. His early scientific papers and letters, in fact, reflect his indebtedness to English science. During his ministry to France, however, Jefferson's philosophy of science reflects a radically different perspective from that of other eminent scientists and leaders in America, England and Scotland. His associations with radical philosophers in France and the upheaval of the French Revolution radically transformed his thinking and, especially his philosophy of science.

Jefferson now embraced the scientific materialism of the French school. He did not accept metaphysical or spiritual explanations for man, nature or God. Even his definition of God, which has gone unnoticed by historians, was not a Newtonian God, but the God of Descartes, the Fabricator of all things from matter and motion. God was not a spiritual being, but a material being that thinks.

Under the influence of the French materialists, Jefferson also redefined and reinterpreted the meaning of the moral faculty in man. The moral sense, Jefferson later wrote to John Adams, is an "instinct, that the moral sense is as much a part of our constitution as that of feeling, seeing, or hearing; as a wise creator must have seen to be necessary in an animal destined to live in society; that every human mind feels pleasure doing good to another...."[61]

Jefferson rejected all attempts by moralists in the Enlightenment to attribute man's moral conduct to principles of self-love, sympathy, utilitarian standards of pain and pleasure, or God. He was especially critical of the most dominant theory of morality in the eighteenth century, expressed by Helvetius, that self-interest or egoism is the basis of man's nature. Self-interest, Jefferson believed, echoing the teachings of Scottish moral sense philosophers, was "the sole antagonist of virtues, leading us constantly by our propensities to self-gratification in violation of our moral duties to others."[62]

Jefferson was opposed to the idea that we act virtuously because "good acts give us pleasure," and "withdraw us from pain." If "these good acts give us please," he reasons, "but how happens it that they give us pleasure? Because nature hath implanted in our breasts a love of others, a sense of duty to them, a moral instinct, in short, which prompts us irresistibly to feel and to succor their distresses."[63]

The Creator, he argues, would indeed been a bungling artist, had he intended man for a social animal, without planting in him social dispositions. It is true they are not implanted in every man, because there is no rule without exception; but it is false reasoning which converts exceptions into the general rule."

Jefferson's belief in the moral sense was the basis of his conviction that man could live together peacefully and securely without the intrusive hand of government. He was not as fearful as Hamilton, Madison and Adams that man's selfish instincts posed a threat to society. The moral sense in man, he believed, instinctively prompted men to promote the good of others and to sacrifice for the common good. The moral instinct was a natural, instinctive check against the selfish instincts.

Jefferson never wavered in his belief that there was a moral sense in man, but his understanding of that moral sense did. The moral sense in man was, like the Creator, and not surprising because it was implanted in man by God, a physical sense, inseparable from the body, with the power of thought, of distinguishing between right and wrong, justice and injustice. It was not, as the Scottish moral sense philosophers defined it, a faculty of reason, distinct from the body. Man's moral sense became the moral and scientific foundation of Jefferson's political and economic egalitarianism.

The French Revolution, French culture, science and philosophy, were catalysts for Jefferson's reinterpretation of the past and his understanding of the future. When Jefferson left Paris in 1789 he had a new perspective of American society, one that was quite different from other national leaders in the United States; it was a French perspective of America's political culture in the 1790's and a negative vision of a possible "European" future for America if it did not learn from Europe's present.

The promise of a republican France fueled Jefferson's hopes that, as an ally of the United States, France could be trusted to protect America's interests and rights against the hostilities of the British monarchy. When he recognized, in the late 1790's, and not long after his election to the presidency, that Napoleon had seized power in France, Jefferson was forced to reevaluate his theories and policies, adjusting them to meet new realities at home and abroad. The failure of the French Revolution became one of the major contributing causes of his nationalism.

Jefferson was an enemy of inequality, favoring the interests of the majority against the interests of the few. He judged political ideologies and economic programs and measures on their compatibility with his democratic egalitarianism. If certain economic policies favored one class at the expense of another, contributing to the concentration of wealth and power in the hands of the few, or, if certain laws denied all white male citizens their equal rights and unfettered participation in the counsels of government, he was against it. Clearly, his egalitarianism did not extend to women, African Americans, and Native Americans, who were denied their civil liberties and too many even their lives.

We cannot understand Jefferson's thinking if we limit our inquiries to a specific document or event, such as the Declaration of Independence or the American Revolution. It is necessary to understand the specific meaning of a particular text or event in the context in which it was inscribed in history, but those same texts, events and ideas have a life beyond their birth, a meaning or meanings reborn in the light of new experiences and challenges. Jefferson's thinking was dynamic and not static, born and reborn, interpreted and reinterpreted by Jefferson himself in the ever-changing environment of the eighteenth and early nineteenth centuries.

Jefferson's ideas and thoughts transcend the immediacy of his own life, speaking to new generations of citizens about the events and ideas that confront them today, in this country and others, just as the past spoke to Jefferson about his present and the future of the American republic at a formative period in American history. It is ultimately through this dialogue of the past, present and future that we begin to penetrate the mind behind the words of Thomas Jefferson and its relevance to our present day.

CHAPTER 1

THE EMPIRICISM AND MATERIALISM OF THOMAS JEFFERSON

During a dinner with John Adams and Alexander Hamilton, Jefferson later recalled an incident that took place in the office of the State Department. On the walls was "a collection of the portraits of remarkable men, among them were those of Bacon, Newton and Locke. Hamilton asked me who they were. I told him they were my trinity of the three greatest men the world had ever produced, naming them. He paused for some time: 'the greatest man that ever lived was Julius Caesar.'"[1]

Jefferson's recollection of this occasion signifies two important aspects of his thought. First, that his was a passion for science, knowledge and truth while Hamilton's was a love of power, glory, and fame. And secondly, Jefferson's recognition of the Enlightenment's indebtedness to the scientific revolution of the seventeenth century. The Enlightenment's dreams and aspirations, he knew, were incomprehensible without the intellectual labors of Francis Bacon, Sir Isaac Newton and John Locke.

Natural philosophers in the eighteenth century rejected the rationalism of Leibniz, Spinoza and

Descartes, the metaphysics of Plato, the scholasticism of Aristotle and the Christian theology of the Church Fathers. Their interests instead turned toward a naturalistic, mechanistic and mathematical description of man, nature and society. John Locke enthusiastically claimed that "the works of Nature everywhere sufficiently evidence a Deity," and if God could be known from his works, his creation, there was evidently no need to consult the Bible to discover man's true nature and purpose on earth. Enlightenment philosophers "did not cease to bow down and worship they only gave another form and a new name to the object of worship: (they) deified Nature and denatured God."[2] "Reason changed from methods of formal logic to those of the natural sciences, and the laws of reason became identical with the laws of nature..."[3]

Enlightenment philosophers generally agreed with David Hume

that all the sciences have a relation greater or less, to human nature; and that however wide any of them may seem to run from it, they still return back by one passage or another. Even Mathematics, natural Philosophy, and Natural Religion, are in some measure dependent on the science of Man; since they lie under the cognizance of men, and are judged by their powers and faculties.[4]

Philosophers may have expressed radically different views about man's nature, but they believed with Hume that the science of man is "the only solid foundation for the other sciences, so the only foundation we can give to this science itself must be laid on experience and observation."[5]

In the writings of Bacon, Newton and Locke, eighteenth century philosophers discovered a method of inquiry and a philosophy by which to interpret and understand nature's laws. Bacon's method of induction, Locke's empiricism and epistemology, and Newton's principles of natural philosophy and his discovery of infinitesimal calculus became the psychological and philosophical foundation for the Enlightenment's faith in reason and in the future progress of man.

Science advances, Jefferson understood, with "each generation succeeding to the knowledge acquired by all those who preceded it, adding to it their own acquisitions and discoveries, and handing the mass down for successive and constant accumulation... indefinitely."[6]

"The insights we gain from scientific inquiry," he was confident,

have rendered the elements themselves subservient to the purposes of man, have harnessed them to the yoke of his labors, and effected the great blessings of moderating his own, of accomplishing what was beyond his feeble force, and extending the comforts of life to a much enlarged circle, to those who have known its necessaries only....[7]

Only a "bigoted veneration for the supposed superlative wisdom of their fathers, and the preposterous idea, that they are to look backward for better things, and not forward" keeps men chained to a state of "barbarism and wretchedness."[8]

The benefits of science, however, were not limited to scientific discoveries and technological achievements alone, important and convincing as they were in the fields of chemistry, medicine, zoology, physiology, magnetism and electricity in the eighteenth century; science was also a cultural force that extended its reach and influence on the arts, manners, and morals of a people. The eighteenth century, Jefferson wrote to Adams:

witnessed the sciences and arts, manners and morals, advanced to a higher degree than the world had ever before seen. And might we not go back to the era of the Borgia, by which time the barbarous ages had reduced national morality to its lowest point of depravity, and observe that the arts and sciences, rising from that point, advanced gradually thro'all the 16th, 17th and 18th centuries, softening and correcting the manners and morals of man? I think we may add, to the great honor of science and the arts, that their natural effects is, by illuminating public opinion, to erect it into a Censor, before which the most exalted tremble from their future, as well as present fame.[9]

Jefferson's education in science and mathematics began at William and Mary College in 1760 where he was first made aware of the scientific tradition in Europe by his Professor of Mathematics, William Small. "It was my great fortune," he later wrote in his *Autobiography*, "and what probably fixed the destinies of my life, that Dr. Small of Scotland, was then Professor of Mathematics, a man profound in most of the useful branches of science...and from his conversations I got my first views of the expansion of science, and of the system of things in which we are placed."[10]

It was also during his studies with Dr. Small that Jefferson was introduced to the writings of Bacon, Newton and Locke. Jefferson's fascination with natural philosophy continued after graduation and in 1780 he was elected a member of the American Philosophical Society with George Washington, Marbois and Reverend James Madison.[11] A year later he was elected a Councilor and began his study of his native state of Virginia, later published in France as his *Notes on the State of Virginia*. It was in Jefferson's Notes that we first see, in a comprehensive way, the influence of Bacon and Newton on his philosophy of science.

Sir Francis Bacon warned Enlightenment philosophers that veneration we have for the Ancients is misguided, and that the knowledge we have derived from the Greeks "is but the boyhood of knowledge, and has the characteristic property of boys: it can talk, but it cannot generate; for it is fruitful of controversies but barren of works."[12] If we are to advance our knowledge of the world, therefore, we must pay close attention to concrete facts, the material objects that lie before our senses. It is only by scrupulously examining the facts before us that we can hope to apprehend the truth. We must abandon the ancient's preoccupation with deductive, philosophical reasoning and return to the facts themselves. Man, armed with the new science, was no longer a spectator in the universe, but the master of nature.

Bacon considered the proper domain of science to be the study of "agriculture, cookery, chemistry, dyeing, the manufacture of glass, enamel, sugar, gunpowder, artificial fires, paper and the like." In short, science was to be useful to man and this required, in turn, that scientists examine those natural objects that would have the greatest benefit to mankind. Scientists would also have to learn to temper their theories with evidence and admit nothing but on the faith of their eyes and experiments.

Natural scientists, Bacon insisted, must be cognizant of the dangers posed by, what he called the "Idols." There are four classes of Idols, the first of which is the "Idols of the Tribe." This is the belief that man is the measure of all things. But man's perception, Bacon says, is "a false mirror which, receiving rays irregularly, distorts and discolors the nature of things by mingling its own nature with it."[13]

The second class of "Idols" is the "Idols of the Cave," the idols of the individual man. We are imprisoned within our own minds by the peculiarities of our own nature. Our education, conversations, and life experiences predispose us to interpret nature from a partial and incomplete point of view.[14]

Then there are the "Idols of the Marketplace," "formed by the intercourse and association of men with each other."[15] In their discourse with each other men tend to use words incorrectly, borrowing the language of the vulgar, words "overrule the understanding, and throw all into confusion, and lead men...into numberless empty controversies and idle fancies."[16]

Lastly, the "Idols of the Theater" are those which "have immigrated into men's minds from the various dogmas of philosophies, and also from the wrong laws of demonstration."[17] What the new science demands of natural philosophers is to divide apparently simple events into their more elementary elements and then reconstructing them with respect to their laws. It is in this way we arrive at a true understanding of the event itself. Jefferson studiously applied Bacon's recommendations for the new science of induction when he addressed Buffon's arguments in his *Notes on the*

State of Virginia.

Jefferson's *Notes on the State of Virginia*, the only book he ever wrote, was a reply to a request by Marbois, the Secretary to the French Minister in America, who, in 1780, sent twenty-two questions to state governors and prominent Americans inquiring about the population, geography, geology, the Indians, laws, religion, economy, the military and history of the states. Jefferson prepared detailed answers, not only to Marbois' queries, but to other topics of a more general and philosophical nature. Jefferson's Notes contains his studies and observations on the environment in Virginia, its flora and fauna and mineral resources, as well as Jefferson's early attitudes towards the laws and constitution, religion, slavery and the aborigines of his native state of Virginia.

In his *Notes*, Jefferson listed the assumptions of Buffon and other French naturalists about the American species and climate. "The opinion advanced by the Count de Buffon is 1. That the animals common both to the old and new world are smaller in the latter. 2. That those peculiar to the new, are on a smaller scale. 3. That those which have been domesticated in both have degenerated in America; and 4. That on the whole it exhibits fewer species."[18]

In Query VI of his *Notes*, Jefferson refutes Buffon's argument that animals in the New World are diminutive in size compared to those in Europe. An animal existed in the New World, he says, much larger than the elephant. However, Jefferson rejects the notion that the tusks and bones of this animal were those of an elephant. From the 30th degree of South latitude," he says,

to the 30th degree of North, are nearly the limits which

nature has fixed for the existence and multiplication of the elephant known to us. Proceeding thence northwardly to 36 degrees, we enter those assigned to the mammoth. The center of the Frozen zone then may be the Achme of their vigour, as that of the Torrid is of the elephant. Thus nature seems to have drawn a belt of separation between these two tremendous animals...to have assigned to the elephant the regions South of these confines, and those North to the mammoth, founding the constitution of the one in her extreme of heat, and that of the other in the extreme of cold.[19]

"Whatever animal we ascribe to these remains," he continues, "it is certain such a one has existed in America, and that it has been the largest of all terrestrial beings." It is contrary to the laws of nature, he admonishes Buffon,

that nature is less active, less energetic on one side of the globe than she is on the other. As if both sides were not warmed by the same genial sun; as if a soil of the same chemical composition, was less capable of elaboration into animal nutriment; as if the fruits and grains from the soil and sun, yielded a less rich chyle, gave less extension to the solids and fluids of the body, or produced sooner in the cartilages, membranes, and fibres, that rigidity which restrains all further extension, and terminates animal growth. The truth is, that a Pigmy and a Patagonian, a Mouse and a Mammoth, derive their dimensions from the same nutritive juices...What intermediate station they shall take may depend on soil, on climate, on food, on a careful choice of breeders. But all the manna of heaven would never raise the Mouse to the bulk of the Mammoth.[20]

To refute Buffon's charges that the domestic animals

in America are smaller compared to those found in Europe, Jefferson prepared tables comparing "The Quadripeds of Europe and America, presenting them to the eye in three different tables, in one of which shall be enumerated those found in both countries; in a second those found in one country; in a third those which have been domesticated in both."[21] After a careful, methodical review of quadrupeds on both continents, Jefferson informs Buffon, that by his own admission, "the beaver, the otter, the shrew mouse, though of the same species, are larger in America than Europe," and the bear is of the same size in Europe and America."[22] Jefferson's comparative tables also demonstrate that "the lynx, badger, red fox, and flying squirrel, are the same in America as in Europe...(and) The bones of the Mammoth which have been found in America, are as large as those found in the old world."[23]

Buffon's analysis, he says, admitted of no exceptions. Jefferson found many exceptions to Buffon's scientific observations. When he compared the "weights if actually known and stated in the third table...we may conclude," he said,

on probable grounds, that, with equal food and care, the climate of America will preserve the races of domestic animals as large as the European stock from which they were derived; and consequently that the third member of Mons. de Buffon's assertion, that the domestic animals are subject to degeneration from the climate of America, is as probably wrong as the first and second were certainly so.[24]

It was evident, Jefferson reasoned, that it does not

matter

whether the bulk and faculties of animals depend on the side of the Atlantic on which their food happens to grow, or which furnishes the elements of which they are compounded? Whether nature has enlisted herself as a Cis or Trans-Atlantic partisan? I am induced to suspect, there has been more eloquence than sound reasoning displayed in support of this theory....25

"It would be erring therefore against the rule of philosophy," he instructs Buffon, "which teaches us to ascribe like effects to like causes should we impute the diminution in size in America to any imbecility or want of uniformity in the operations of nature."26

In reaching these conclusions, the influence of Bacon and Newton are obvious. He refers to Newton's second rule of reasoning in natural philosophy that we are to assign "like effect to like causes." and Bacon's admonition to "admit nothing but on the faith of eyes, or at least of careful and severe examination; so that nothing is exaggerated for wonder's sake...."27

Inveighing against the fantasies of Buffon, Jefferson said that "a patient pursuit of facts, and cautious combination and comparison of them, is the drudgery to which man is subjected by his Maker, if he wishes to obtain sure knowledge."28 Jefferson suspected that this was "one of those cases where the judgment has been seduced by a glowing pen...."29 Nevertheless, Jefferson graciously said of Buffon's *Histoire Naturelle* that it was a wonder there was even "something in the great work to correct."

Bacon was the prophet of the new science and, like so

many natural philosophers in the eighteenth century, an amateur scientist. Newton's discovery of the law of universal gravitation, however, placed him above every scientist who ever lived. "Placed alongside Newton," Jefferson wrote, "every human character must appear diminutive."[30] Newton's discovery of the law of universal gravitation became paradigmatic of the sciences in general, and its acceptance by Enlightenment natural philosophers carried with it a belief in the unity of the sciences; that is, the assumption that the physical and moral sciences were based on, and subject to, the same invariable laws. Since the law of gravitation could be applied to both celestial and terrestrial phenomena, it was assumed that the laws of the physical universe were also applicable to man and society. "Human nature," Jefferson wrote, "is the same on every side of the Atlantic, and will be alike influenced by the same causes."[31]

Natural scientists in the eighteenth century believed that "natural law was simultaneously what is, because it is a regularity of nature, and what ought to be, because it is an unfailing guide to right action; it was a description and prescription at the same time...."[32] "To the extent that the laws of nature were to be discovered by experimentation and observation, they were purely descriptive. They revealed the ordered relations of phenomena and subjected them to rule. They revealed what is, but not what ought to be."[33]

Newton's philosophy had two aims and objectives. The first was "the development of mathematical laws and principles and their application to problems of rational mechanics, a name given by Newton himself to the subject of forces and the motions which they produce;" it embraced a number of subjects which we now call physics. The second aim of the *Principia*, the full title of the *Principia* was the *Mathematical Principles of Natural Philosophy*, was "the elaboration of the system of the world according to the principles of rational mechanics and the law of universal gravitation," or what Laplace later called "celestial mechanics."[34]

Jefferson's understanding of *Newton's Mathematical Principles of Natural Philosophy* was evident in his "Plan for Establishing Uniformity in the Coinage, Weights, and Measures of the United States" in 1790. There was, at that time, no uniform standard for measurement in America or Europe; a foot in London was not the same foot in Paris. Jefferson originally proposed

the latitude of 38 degrees, as that which should fix our standard, because it was the median latitude of the United States..." but when he became aware of a proposition in the National Assembly of France "to take that of 45 degrees as being a middle term between the equator and both poles, and a term which consequently might unite the nations of both hemispheres....[35]

He chose the French proposal, which, he noted, required the use of the second pendulum for 45 degrees of latitude, according to Sir Isaac Newton's computation...."[36] Jefferson's Newtonian solution was an example of how mathematics can bridge differences between countries, uniting, in this case, the United States with the "nations of both hemispheres."

If the law of universal gravitation explained the

relationship between the earth and the planets in the universe, Locke's *Essay on Human Understanding* explained how man comes to know of himself and the world outside of him. "Locke, perhaps more than anyone else," Carl Becker observed,

made it possible for the eighteenth century to believe what it wanted to believe: namely, that in the world of human relations as well as in the physical world, it was possible for men to correspond with the general harmony of Nature; that since man, and the mind of man, were integral parts of the work of God, it was possible for man, by the use of his mind, to bring his thought and conduct, and hence the institutions by which he lived, into a perfect harmony with the Universal Natural Order.[37]

Not until Locke's two-volume study, *Essay Concerning Human Understanding*, were the philosophers able to see the full relationship between man and his environment. "Locke has unfolded to man," Voltaire wrote, "the nature of human reason as a fine anatomist explains the powers of the body." "Taking physics as its model, Locke's science of nature treated mind on the analogy of Newtonian matter...Elementary ideas, identical in origin with elementary sensations, make the term of that analysis which would know only operations. These particular ideas drop into the mind through the five funnels of sense. There they bound, rebound, and combine like the corpuscles of which they are counterparts. In this kinetic theory of the intellect, the association of ideas is the counterpart of the law of universal attraction."[38]

"You can count on your fingers," Helvetius wrote,

"the people who have not read, thumbed and admired him...I can call to mind no thinker who exerted a profounder influence on the minds of his contemporaries than did he."[39] It belongs to Locke "the idea that there is nothing that is innate in the mind; that our abstract ideas, our reason itself, are derived from the sensations the mind records and its reactions thereto."[40]

In his *Essay* Locke argues that it is through sensation the senses convey into our minds several distinct perceptions of things, and thus we come by the ideas of yellow, heat, cold, and all those things we call sensible qualities. By reflection Locke means the notice which the mind takes of its own operations. Once the senses have conveyed the sensible qualities of things outside of us, the mind, through reflection, compares, relates, analyzes and dissects its sense impressions to form ideas and general concepts. Thus, external objects furnish the mind with the ideas of sensible qualities while the mind furnishes the understanding with ideas of its own operations. Accordingly, there is nothing in our mind which did not come in one of these two ways.

In a celebrated letter by Molyneux, Locke was asked: "Suppose a man born blind, and now adult, and taught by his touch to distinguish between a cube and sphere of the same metal. Suppose then the cube and sphere were placed on a table, and the blind man made to see: query, whether by his sight, before he touched them, could he distinguish and tell which was the globe and which the cube?"[41]

Locke's opinion, of course, was that the blind man could not distinguish by sight what he was able to distinguish by touch alone. Many other experiments were conducted along these lines with the results that formerly blind individuals could not identify the objects which they knew by touch when they were able to see. To identify objects of sight, then, it was necessary to have sight.

This was further proof for the empiricists, and especially Locke, that man receives all of his ideas from his senses; man's mind was a tabula rasa, a blank tablet, devoid of innate ideas. Man's understanding of nature, the universe, and of himself, consequently, is shaped and conditioned by his environment. Locke's empiricism and epistemology proved to be the decisive blow against the rationalism of the system-builders in the eighteenth century.

Locke's psychology and epistemology, however, fell short of declaring man a physical machine, reducing man's inner state of reflection to his sensory apparatus. French philosophers were not convinced with Locke's argument and hammered away at this last vestige of independence Locke attributed to reflection. The French *philosophes* broadened, radicalized and extended Locke's psychology to its logical outcome and declared that all of man's inner qualities, the internal operations of the mind, have their true origin in sensation, and sensation alone. Locke may have denied the existence of innate ideas, but he maintained the fiction of the innate operations of the mind. According to the French philosophers, comparing, observing, understanding and relating ideas, one to the other, is no different than seeing and hearing. What Locke referred to as reflection is only a transformed sensation acquired through experience and learning with no clear line of demarcation between them. Each phase of mental activity simply combines and melds into another.

During his ministry to France, from 1784 to 1789, Jefferson conversed with, and studied the writings of the leading scientists and philosophers in France and adopted their materialist interpretation of Locke's epistemology. Jefferson's understanding of the operations of the human mind, that is, the limits and scope of man's knowledge of nature, the universe and of human nature itself, was transformed by the reasoning and scientific research of French scientists and philosophes.

The new science of Bacon, Newton and Locke was heralded in France by Voltaire, Diderot, D'Almbert, D'Holbach, Helvetius, among other luminaries. Voltaire said Locke was the anatomist of the human mind, and in his *Philosophical Letters* he refers to Bacon as the father of experimental philosophy and Newton as the greatest man who has ever lived. "It is to him who holds sway over men's minds by force of truth...."[42] Newton explained what others disputed for centuries: gravity is responsible for all "the planets to revolve, and what keeps them in their orbits, and also over what causes all bodies here below to come down to the surface of the earth." Voltaire said the law of gravitation "alone explains all the apparent irregularities in the motion of the heavenly bodies. The inequalities of the moon's motion follow necessarily from these laws."[43] This law of gravitation also explains the rise and fall of the ocean, and the motion of comets.

These curiosities had been exceedingly mysterious to the Ancients and medieval philosophers. The law of attraction is the means by which all of nature is moved; "the certain and indisputable effect of an unknown principle, a quality inherent in matter."[44] Voltaire also praised Newton's study on color and light found in Newton's "Optics", his invention of a telescope "that works by reflection rather than refraction" and Newton's "method of submitting infinity everywhere to algebraic reckoning. This is referred to as differential calculus, or fluxions and integral calculus."[45] Voltaire also wrote one of the best popularizations of Newton's philosophy: *Elements of Newton's Philosophy Made Accessible to Everyone.*

Voltaire also revered John Locke, who "has unfolded to man the nature of human reason as a fine anatomist explains the powers of the body... instead of defining at once what we know nothing about, he examines, bit by bit, that which we want to understand..."[46] Voltaire applauds both Locke's argument against innate ideas and his claim that all our ideas come to us via our senses. Voltaire said, "He examines our ideas both simple and complex, follows the human mind in all his operations, and shows the imperfections of all the languages spoken by man, and our constant abuse of terms."[47]

In his *Preliminary Discourse to the Encyclopedia* of Diderot, D'Alembert says that the *Encyclopedia* has two aims. The first step is "the genealogy and the illation of the parts of our knowledge; the causes that brought the various branches of our knowledge into being. The second step is citing the characteristics that distinguish them."[48] As with Locke, D'Alembert argues that all our knowledge of the world comes to us through our senses. "We can divide all our knowledge," he says, "into direct and reflective knowledge. We receive direct knowledge immediately, without any operation of our will. It is the knowledge which finds all the doors of our souls open, so to speak, and enters without resistance and without effort. The mind acquires reflective knowledge by making use of direct knowledge, unifying and combining it."[49]

Restating Newton's reflections on hypothetical reasoning, D'Alembert says,

"any deduction which is based on facts or recognized truths is preferable to one which is supported only by hypotheses, however ingenious. Why suppose we have purely intellectual notions at the outset, innate ideas, if all we need to do in order to form them is to reflect upon our sensations?"[50]

D'Alembert extends Locke's empiricism to incorporate what was once conceived of as intellectual concepts; "vice and virtue, the principle of the necessity of laws, the spiritual nature of the soul, the existence of God and of our love and obligations toward him—in a word, the truths for which we have the most immediate and indispensable need—are the fruits of the first reflective ideas that our sensations occasion."[51]

Denis Diderot, in his essay on "Art" in the *Encyclopedia*, draws the same conclusions as Francis Bacon; whom he calls "one of the foremost genius of England."[52] He believed the mechanical arts were denigrated by intellectuals who believed it was beneath "the dignity of the human spirit to apply oneself diligently and continuously to specific and concrete experiments and objects, and our mind forfeits its dignity when it descends to the study, let alone the practice, of the mechanical arts."[53] "The result of this prejudice has "tended to fill the cities with useless spectators and with proud men engaged in idle speculation, and the countryside with petty tyrants who are ignorant, lazy, and disdainful."[54] If we compare the most honored arts with the advantages of the mechanical arts "you will discover that far more praise has been heaped on those men who spend their time making us believe that we are happy, than on those who actually bring us happiness." 55

Diderot also praised the empiricism of Locke and the experimental philosophy of Newton. The new science was not concerned with fanciful and imaginative syllogisms, mystical incantations or religious disquisitions. It was concerned with useful results that benefit the welfare of man. Science, in the age of the Enlightenment, had to be practical and utilitarian, not speculative and abstract. French science, just as the science in the American colonies, had its origins in the new science of Bacon, Newton and Locke.

Jefferson was familiar with the writings of the French Encyclopedists and purchased thirty-nine volumes of the *Encyclopedia*. He knew the *Encyclopedia* was the first effort in history to bring together the useful knowledge of his generation.

Jefferson's appreciation for the radical implications of Locke's theory was, in part, reflected in his departure from the more conservative leaders of American thought. Adams believed human nature, although capable of improvement, was not as impressionable or as capable of imprinting as the French materialists, Diderot, D'Alembert, Helvetius and La Mettrie or Jefferson suggested. Adams, Franklin, Hamilton and Madison also did not believe there was a law applicable to both man and nature. Human nature, according to them, was not as malleable as the materialists claimed. Jefferson, on the other hand, had more confidence in the application of the scientific method to human behavior. He saw in Locke's principle of the relation of ideas an epistemological demonstration of man's relationship to the external world.

Jefferson believed Locke, as did the French philosophes, laid the groundwork for the physical and moral sciences of man. Man, like all of nature, is a material being. The mind is the thinking faculty which has the power to receive and reflect different external and internal sensations, to compare and distinguish them from one another and to abstract to form general concepts. It is a property of the animal body, specifically of the material mechanism of the brain. In a letter to Thomas Cooper he expressed what he believed was the materialism of Locke's thought. He wrote, although spiritualism "is most prevalent with all these sects, yet with none of them, I presume, is materialism declared heretical, Mr. Locke, on whose authority they often plume themselves, openly maintained that materialism of the soul; and charged with blasphemy those who denied that it was in the power of an almighty creator to endow with the faculty of thought any composition of matter he might think fit..."[56]

Man was not only the measure of all things, he was also the mirror of nature. Everything man has learned through science testifies to the fact that the body and mind of man are not separate entities, as Descartes claimed, but one. Since God could endow matter with the faculty of thought, it is senseless to talk about the existence of a nonmaterial realm. God was the "Fabricator of all things from matter and motion."

Jefferson further expressed his materialistic credo to John Adams in reply to a letter Adams sent him on the subject of matter, spirit and motion. Jefferson wrote,

I was obliged to recur to my habitual anodynme, 'I feel therefore I exist.' I feel bodies which are not myself; there are other existences then. I call them matter. I feel them change places. This gives me motion. Where there is an absence of matter, I call void, or nothing, or immaterial space. On the basis of sensation, of matter and motion, we might erect the fabric of all the certainties we can have or need. I can conceive thought to be an action of a particular organization of matter, formed for that purpose by its Creator, as well as that attraction is an action of matter, or magnetism of loadstone... When once we quit the basis of sensation, all is in the wind.[57]

Jefferson thought it was preposterous heresy to deny "the Creator the power of endowing matter with the mode of action called thinking...To talk of immaterial existences, is to talk of nothing. To say that the human soul, angels, God are immaterial, is to say, they are nothings, or that there is no God, no angels, no soul. I cannot reason otherwise..."[58]

Jefferson, following the lead of the French philosophes, thought it "heresy" to deny the "Creator the power of endowing matter with thought, a belief he shared with the radical French materialists. The French materialists recognized that the mechanistic explanation of man and nature failed in physiology because it could not account for the reproduction of organisms and the regrowth of body parts.[59] Life was not a mechanical arrangement of bits of matter, but the result of organic matter's tendency to live. Physiologists, like Buffon, turned away "from the description of the body's organs as levers, pulleys, pumps, and sieves to an investigation of those characteristics such as growth, nutrition, and regeneration that make living things different from machines."[60] By endowing matter with life they explained natural phenomena by forces rather than by the organization of matter...The materialist philosophers of the eighteenth century made matter active by giving it the properties of life. In essence, they distributed the soul throughout matter in order to get rid of it.[61]

Jefferson told Adams that his materialist philosophy was supported "by Locke, Tracy and Stewart." Jefferson's reference to Locke and Stewart demonstrates the extent to which he had completely accepted and was apparently not aware of the French materialists' radical reinterpretation of Locke's epistemology. Locke had never reduced the two sources of our ideas, sensation and reflection, to sensations alone. He always retained man's inner state of reflection.

There was, in Locke's epistemology, the possibility of conflating two sources of our understanding of the world to one, but there was an unmistakable and unbridgeable gap between mind and body in the writings of Thomas Reid, the founder of the Scottish School of Common Sense, and Dugald Stewart, the last representative of that school. Jefferson met Stewart in Paris and considered "Stewart to be "a great man, and among the most honest living. I consider him and Tracy as the ablest metaphysicians living, by which I mean investigators of the thinking faculty of man. Stuart seems to have given its natural history from facts and observations, Tracy its mode of action and deduction."[62] The writings of Stewart, he wrote, are

an examination into the certainty of our knowledge, and the most complete demolition of the Sceptical doctrines which I have ever met with...I place him and Dugald Stewart so much in a line, that I can decide no more than that they are the two greatest men in that line at present known to the world.[63]

Stewart would have been surprised to learn that Jefferson placed him in the same school of materialism as Tracy. Scottish common sense philosophy began as a critical response to the philosophical skepticism of David Hume, the materialism and sensationalistic philosophy of David Hartley and Joseph Priestley, and the rationalism of Descartes, Malebranche and Leibniz. The starting point of the Scottish common sense school was the belief that the phenomena of mind and matter, "as far as they come under the cognizance of our faculties, are more completely dissimilar than any other class of facts, and the sources of our information concerning them are in every respect so radically different that we should be careful to avoid assimilating them."[64]

In the *Elements of the Philosophy of Mind*, and in his essay, "On the Influence of Locke's Authority in France," Stewart attributes Locke's reputation in France not to Voltaire, who claimed to be the first person to make Locke's name known to his countrymen, but to Fontenelle "whose mind was probably prepared for its reception, by similar discussions in the works of Gassendi. It has since been assumed, Stewart says, by "Condillac, Turgot, Helvetius, Diderot, D'Alembert, Destutt de Tracy, Degerando," by "the implicit confidence which they have reposed in Condillac as a faithful expounder of Locke's doctrines...."[65] Condillac, whom Destutt de Tracy distinguished by the title of the Father of Ideology, inferred from Locke's writings that all our knowledge is derived from the senses and that "our ideas are only sensations, or portions abstracted from some sensation, in order to be considered apart."[66] On another occasion, Stewart informs us that Condillac believed that all the operations of understanding "are only transformed sensations, and that the faculty of feeling comprehends all the other powers of the mind."[67]

The extravagant interpretation of the French materialists, he continues, fails to take into consideration the emphasis Locke places on reflection as an original source of our ideas. In his *Essay* Locke was aware that "the mind furnishes the understanding with another set of ideas, which could not be had from things without; and such are Perception, Thinking, Doubting, Believing, Reasoning, Knowing, Willing, and all the different activities of our minds."[68] "This source of our ideas, although having nothing to do with our senses or with external objects, yet is very like our senses and might properly be called 'internal sense.' As evidence against the materialist thesis, Stewart cites a celebrated passage from Locke's *Essay*: "external objects furnish the mind with the ideas of sensible qualities; and the mind furnishes the understanding with ideas of its own operations."[69] There was sufficient evidence in Locke's writings, as Stewart revealed in passage after passage from Locke's *Essay*, to clearly distinguish mind from matter and sensation from reflection.

Stewart argues the nature of the mind is different from the nature of the body. Bodies cannot change their state unless a force is impressed upon them, whereas the mind has the active power of perception in its constitution. The materialists confound the organs of perception with the being that perceives. "The eye is not [that] which sees; it is only the organ by which we see."[70] We know that in order to perceive an external object, an impression must be made upon the organs of sense and communicated through the nerves to the brain. However, we do not know how these impressions can produce an idea in our minds.

The materialists cannot prove that the impressions made upon our organs of sense resemble the objects they are made by. In fact, "we are so far from perceiving images in our brains, that we do not perceive our brain at all...."[71] We know only, for example, that "the eye forms a picture of visible objects upon the retina; but how this picture makes us see the object we know not... ."[72] When we perceive a thing to exist, it does really exist. The stone I kick must be something different from the sensation of pain I feel.

Stewart maintains, in contrast to the French materialists, it is only by the evidence of consciousness that we know of the existence of our various sensations, affections, passions, hopes, fears, desires and volitions, and not the other way around as Jefferson believed. Although the material world exists, therefore, it is only by the constitution of our minds that we can ever have knowledge of it. The mind of man has an innate structure and does not derive ideas from nature. Without an innate structure, knowledge of the external world or oneself is not possible.

Stewart proposes, against Locke's representative theory of perception, the doctrine of natural realism. According to this doctrine we do not start with ideas, but judgments. We do not have sensations first and refer them afterwards to a subject and an object; our first having of a sensation is, at the same time, the knowledge of it as both objective and as mine. Whether judgment ought to be called a necessary concomitant of perception or a part or ingredient of it, Stewart does not question. In perception we have both a conception of the object, and the belief of its present existence. There are no perceptions without a judgment.

It is difficult to understand how Jefferson could have confused the mind-body dualism in Stewart's philosophy, a founding principle in Scottish common sense philosophy, with the materialism of De Tracy, D'Holbach, Condillac, Diderot, La Mettrie and Grimm. The differences between them were, to use Descartes' language, "clear and distinct." It appears, on the surface at least, that Jefferson either completely misinterpreted Stewart's philosophy, or reinterpreted the meaning of the moral sense to accord with the materialism of the French school.

The Scots used the terms 'moral instinct' and 'moral faculty' interchangeably and Jefferson may not have understood Stewart's efforts to correct this false notion of the moral sense. Jefferson's materialism, con-sequently, was not owing to the Locke's and Stewart's, but principally to the writings of Desutt de Tracy and Cabanis.

The admiration which Jefferson held for De Tracy led him to translate and edit two of Tracy's books: *A Commentary and Review of Montesquieu's Spirit of Laws*, and *A Treatise on Political Economy*. Tracy's influence was so great that Jefferson persuaded the president of William and Mary College to adopt the Commentary as a basic text of study. Later, Jefferson sent a copy of the Commentary to his friend Du Pont de Nemours, and recommended it so enthusiastically that Du Pont accused him of having written it himself.

The ideology of De Tracy was a synthesis of the ideas of Bacon, Locke and Condillac. Ideology was a program designed to reduce general ideas to feelings, activities and sensations. "Knowledge of our environment is founded upon specific biological feelings, relating us as moving and demanding organisms to a partially obstructing environment: I am cold, I am hot, this is what informs me that I exist, that I am alive."[73] Ideology was also a philosophical method by which the barren tyranny of metaphysics could be distinguished from the proper study of nature. Tracy's contribution to the advancement of the sciences lay in his scientific analysis of ideas in the context of zoology. Unlike Descartes, Tracy's motto is not "I think therefore I am," but "I feel therefore I exist." Thought and feeling are unified under the principle of resistance. Through his experiences of resistance, man learns to know of himself and the existence of external objects. Man's understanding increases in proportion to his exposure It is through the experience of resistance and the relationship between man and his environment that man comes to know of himself and his surroundings.

Jefferson referred to his familiar anodyne "I feel therefore I exist," in a letter to John Adams. "Rejecting all organs of information, therefore, but my senses, I rid myself of the Pyrrhonisms with which an indulgence in speculations hyperphysical and antiphysical, so uselessly occupy and disquiet the mind...I am satisfied, and sufficiently occupied with the things which are, without tormenting myself about those which may indeed be, but of which I have no evidence."[74]

In the field of experimental psychology, the studies of Cabanis impressed Jefferson. He considered Cabanis's

Rapports du Physique et du moral de l'homme "the most profound of all human compositions...."[75] Cabanis was a member of the American Philosophical Society, and a notable physician and philosopher in France. Cabanis' work, as that of Locke's, was designed to reveal the unity between man and nature. However Cabanis provided an anatomical foundation for the study of the physical and moral sciences rather than an epistemological and psychological one, as did Locke.

When Jefferson received Cabanis' empirical demonstrations, he wrote to Adams describing his materialist heritage and the recent investigations of Cabanis. Jefferson said Cabanis investigated particular organs in the human structure to show "which are most likely to exercise the faculty of thought." Jefferson asked Adams "Why may not the mode of action called thought, have been given to a material organ of peculiar structure?"[76] Referring to his Lockean heritage, Jefferson said that he preferred "the single incomprehensibility of matter endowed with thought" rather than to swallow the incomprehensibility of matter and spirit.

Two months later, Adams replied to Jefferson's query by arguing, "matter is but matter... it is incapable of memory, judgment or feeling, or pleasure or pain, as far as I can conceive."[77] Adams was uncertain as to "how Spirit can think, feel or act, any more than matter."[78] As for Cabanis, Adams found his experiments and claims unconvincing. He wrote: "Cabanis Ignition can destroy nothing in the magnet. But motion, magnetism, Electricity, Galvanism, Attraction, Repulsion, are nothing but motion, and have no more relation to, Analogy or resemblance to, memory, Perception,

Conception or Volition, than black has to white, or falsehood to truth, or right to wrong."[79]

Jefferson continued to be persuaded by the logic of materialism, finding the "incomprehensibility of matter" to be preferable to the incomprehensibility of matter and spirit. Jefferson's view of materialism was further reinforced after reading Flouren's *Recherches sur le systeme nerveux dans les animaux vertebre*s. In 1825 he wrote Adams to say he had "lately been reading the most extraordinary of all books, and at the same time the most demonstrative by numerous and unequivocal facts. It is Flourend's experiments on the function of the nervous system, in vertebrated animals."[80] Jefferson claimed Flourens' experiments demonstrated that when the cerebrum is completely removed "leaving the cerebellum and other parts of the system uninjured the animal loses all its senses of hearing, smelling, feeling, seeing, tasting, it totally deprived of will, intelligence, memory, perception, etc., yet lives for months in perfect health, with all its powers of motion, but without moving but on external excitement..."[81]

Flourens also proved when the cerebellum is removed, "leaving the cerebrum untouched the animal retains all its senses, faculties, and understanding, but loses the power of regulated motion, and exhibits all the symptoms of drunkenness." Cabanis' research not only proved there were certain anatomical structures of the human frame that might be capable of receiving the faculty of thinking from the Creator, but Flourens proves that they have received it: that the cerebrum is the thinking organ; and that life and health may continue, and the animal be entirely without thought, if deprived of that organ." Jefferson then added "I wish to see what the spiritualists will say to this."[82]

That same month, Adams wrote: "Incision knives will never discover the distinction between matter and spirit...That there is an active principle of power in the universe is apparent, but in what substance that active principle resides, is past our investigation. The faculties of our understanding are not adequate to penetrate the Universe."[83]

Adams was not willing, as Jefferson was, to reduce human thought to matter in motion. It was incomprehensible to Adams that matter could give rise to thought, or that thought could move matter. He was certain that there were ideas and material entities, but the interaction between them, or the reduction of one to the other, was an eternal mystery to him. Jefferson had no such reservations. He believed that, by His Divine Will, God endowed matter with the faculty of thought.

Jefferson's materialism also raises serious questions about Jefferson's understanding of the universe of Newton, or, at the very least, God's role in the universe. In a letter of John Adams in 1823, Jefferson stated that he could not agree with the cosmological hypotheses of Spinoza, Diderot and D'Holbach who believed "that it is more simple to believe at once in the eternal pre-existence of the world, as it is now going on, and may forever go on by the principle of reproduction which we see and witness, than to believe in the eternal pre-existence of an ulterior cause, or Creator of the world, a being whom we see not, and know not...."[84]

Jefferson's cosmology, like his belief in God, was based on the argument by design, that is, the design of the universe, its beauty and laws was sufficient proof of God's existence. "The movement of the heavenly bodies," he wrote

So exactly held in their course by the balance of centrifugal and centripetal   forces, the structure of the earth itself...it is impossible...for the human mind not to believe...that there is...design, cause and effect...a fabricator of all things from matter and motion...evident proofs of the necessity of a superintending power to maintain the Universe in its course and order."[85]

The universe of Newton was not, however, as Jefferson stated in his letter to Adams, a universe of matter and motion; and God was not "a Fabricator of all things from matter and motion." In Newton's universe God "has nothing in common with the material world. He is a pure mind, an infinite mind whose very infinity is of a unique and incomparable non-quantitative and non-dimensional kind....."[86] In Descartes' universe, Alexandre Koyré reasons, there "is nothing else in the world but matter and motion; or, matter being identical with space or extension, there is nothing else but extension and motion. Descartes practically excludes spirits, souls, and even God from the universe; he simply leaves no place for them in it... ."[87]

Jefferson accepted the materialist interpretation of God in Descartes' universe while rejecting the deterministic implications of it. He continued to believe comets would "run foul of suns and planets," races of animals would become extinct and "all existences might extinguish successively, one by one, until all should be reduced to a shapeless chaos" if there were no Superintending power in the universe.[88]

Jefferson was aware, however, as he wrote in 1803, that "As many as two or three times during my seven years residence in France new discoveries were made which overset the whole Newtonian Philosophy."[89] He recognized as well that LaPlace demonstrated "that the excentricities of the planets of our system could oscillate only within narrow limits, and therefore could authorize no inference that the system must, by its own laws, come one day to an end."[90] Jefferson refused to accept, what he knew the French astronomer Pierre-Simon LaPlace proved, that the universe was a self-regulating and self-perpetuating mechanism.

Jefferson could also agree with D'Holbach's argument in *The System of Nature* that God is a material being and "the brain is the common center, where all the nerves, are distributed through every part of the body meet and blend themselves...." while rejecting the naturalist implications of the argument that man could appeal to no higher authority than his own animal nature.[91] Unlike D'Holbach, he did not believe the universe was utterly devoid of moral values or meaning, and there are no moral truths. He believed, as did the Scottish common sense philosophers, that moral truths are implanted in our minds by God, and through education man's goodness will naturally come to the surface. D'Holbach, Helvetius, and La Mettrie, on the other hand, believed that conscience is entirely the product of conditioning, a position more consistent with Jefferson's own materialism.

It appears that Jefferson believed that matter could produce thought, but that our thoughts were not subject to the same inexorable laws of physics as other physical objects in nature. God, and the moral instinct in man, had a different status from other physical objects in the universe.

Jefferson's materialism encompasses four general

characteristics: First: the laws of the physical sciences are the same for the moral sciences of man Second: Man derives his knowledge from sense experiences. Third: Thought is nothing but the interaction of material forces. Fourth: Man is subject to a variety of modifications depending upon his culture, climate, government and education.

Jefferson's philosophy of science was a marriage of English empiricism and French materialism. He derived from the empirical tradition of Bacon, Newton and Locke the aims and objectives of science, the methodological rules for the investigation of nature, and his faith in the uniformity of nature. He retained his scientific heritage from the English but enlarged its scope and extended its logic to accommodate the more radical theories of the French materialists. During and after his ministry to France, Jefferson became a convert to the scientific materialism of Destutt de Tracy, Flourens, and Cabanis.

The philosophers of the Enlightenment agreed that a science of man was possible, even though they disagreed about the founding principles of that science. They believed it was possible to build a rational society that conformed to man's nature. Jefferson's empiricism and materialism contributed, in no small measure, to his understanding of the relationship and interdependence of man, nature and society. It was an article of faith with Jefferson and the French philosophes that a republican form of government best served the interests of the people. The great suffering of the French people, he observed, had nothing to do with their manners, industry, culture, climate or soil; it was due exclusively to a bad government, a government that exploited the great mass of the French people for the benefit of the few. It was the role of science, not only "to render the elements subservient to the purposes of man," but to illuminate public opinion and liberate man from the oppressive institutional shackles of the past, from governments and religions that did not respect the inalienable rights of man.

CHAPTER 2

MINISTER TO FRANCE

In his first three years in France, Jefferson became acquainted with the city of Paris and its environs and France's leading scientists and writers. As America's minister to the Court of Louis XVI, he continued to work toward the recognition of America's commercial rights in foreign ports with the French government and other European nations, but he had not yet given any indication, with the exception of his letter to Reverend James Madison about his concept of private property, that his political philosophy had evolved and changed as a result of his experiences in England with the Adamses, and his observations and thoughts about the political, scientific, and cultural life of the French people.

In 1787 the political fortunes for both France and the United States had suddenly and unexpectedly changed. Jefferson was informed of a rebellion in Massachusetts, the adoption of the Federal Constitution of the United States, and the meeting of the Assembly of Notables in France. The opinions he expressed in his correspondence on these events provide early indications of the evolution of his political philosophy.

When Jefferson heard of Shay's Rebellion, an uprising of farmers and debtors in Massachusetts, which began in the late summer of 1786 and was put down by force early in 1787, he was at first embarrassed, "partly because the group on which he counted most, the independent farmers, was involved, partly because he had been correcting false reports of American disorders," and then became "fearful of its effects on opinion at home."[1] America's national leaders, like Washington, Madison and General Knox believed the uprising "was designed to bring about an abolition of debts, public and private, and to effect a new distribution of property."[2] Jefferson, although unaware of the actual danger posed by the uprising, "was practically alone among the national leaders in minimizing the peril of this disturbance."[3]

In a letter to Edward Carrington on January 16, 1787, Jefferson said:

The people are the only censors of their governors... and even in their errors will tend to keep these to the true principles of their instruction. To punish these errors too severely would be to suppress the only safeguard of public liberty.[4]

Commenting on the rebellion a few days later he wrote: I hold it that a little rebellion, now and then, is a good thing, and a necessary in the political world as storms in the physical. Unsuccessful rebellions, indeed, generally establish the encroachments on the rights of the people, which have produced them. An observation of this truth should render honest republican governors so mild in their punishment of rebellions, as not to discourage them too much. It is a medicine necessary for the sound health of good government.[5]

In yet another letter to James Madison he said:

[T]he late rebellion in Massachusetts has given more alarm than I think it should have done. Calculate that one rebellion in thirteen states in the course of eleven years, is but one for each state in a century and a half. No country should be so long without one.[6]

Even nations with a great degree of power, he continued, cannot prevent insurrections.

In England, where the hand of power [is heavier] than with us, there are seldom half a dozen years without an insurrection. In France, where it is still heavier, but less despotic, as Montesquieu supposes... there have been three in the course of the three years I have been here.[7]

In his letter to Madison, Jefferson cited the opinions of Montesquieu. Montesquieu argued that dissenters must be defended against harsh treatment by their governments. He believed the task of the government during an insurrection is not repression and punishment, but education. Dissenters must be educated to understand their true interests in preserving peace and order. Political leaders, Montesquieu feared, will use the excuse of defending the republic to augment their own power at the expense of the general interests of the people. "Sous pretexte de la vengeance de la republique," he wrote, "on etabliront la tyrannie des vengeurs. Il n'est pas question de detruire celui qui domine, mais la domination."[8]

"The tree of liberty," Jefferson wrote, "must be refreshed from time to time with the blood of patriots and tyrants. It is its natural manure...."[9] The rebellion would serve as a warning to the American leaders that the liberties of the people must be secured and their interests protected or rebellion would ensue. "Where wrongs are pressed," he wrote to Madame de Stael, "because it is believed they will be borne, resistance becomes morality."[10]

The U.S. Constitution

The news of Shay's Rebellion and his fears there would be even more storms ahead for the American republic were eased when Jefferson learned of the new Federal Constitution. In a letter to Madison on December 20, 1787, Jefferson discussed what he liked and what he disapproved of in the Constitution. He favored six features of the new Federal Constitution. He supported: First, the idea that the constitution could be peacefully changed without continual recurrence to the State legislatures; second, the organization of the government into legislative, judicial and executive bodies; third, the power that was given to the legislature to levy taxes and the direct popular election of the greater House; fourth; the "Compromise of the opposite claims of the great and little States, of the latter to equal, and the former to proportional influence;" fifth, the method of voting by person instead of voting by states; and sixth, the "negative given to the Executive conjointly with a third of either House...."[11]

There were also certain defects and weaknesses of the Federal Constitution which Jefferson mentioned in his letter to Madison. The most significant flaw was that the Constitution lacked a bill of rights which provided for "freedom of religion, freedom of the press, protection against standing armies, restriction of monopolies, the eternal and unremitting force of the habeas corpus laws, and trials by jury...."[12] The people were entitled, Jefferson said, to a bill of rights against every government on earth.

Jefferson also strongly disliked the abandonment of the principle of rotation in office for the President. The perpetual reelection of the President would be an open invitation to every foreign nation "to interfere with money and arms" to aid their own cause. Life-tenure would destroy the liberties of the people and embroil the state in foreign entanglements and domestic disorder. Jefferson feared and warned:

The natural progress of things is for liberty to yield and government to gain ground. As yet our spirits are free. Our [jealousy] is put to sleep by the unlimited confidence we all repose in the...president. After him inferior characters may perhaps succeed and awaken us to the danger which his merit has led us into.[13]

The perpetual reelection of the President must have reminded Jefferson of Locke's observations in his *Treatise on Government*. After a review of the history of England, Locke noticed that the largest prerogatives to the exercise of power were given to the wisest and best princes. The people trusted them to act always in the public interest.

The people, therefore, finding reason to be satisfied with those princes whenever they acted without or contrary to the letter of the law, acquiesced in what they did, and without the least complaint let them enlarge their prerogatives as they pleased....[14]

It was upon this foundation, Locke claims, that the saying

> the reigns of good princes have always been most dangerous to the liberties of their people; for when their successors, managing the government with different thoughts, would draw the actions of those good rulers into precedent...as if what had been done for the good, of the people was right in them to do, for the harm of the people if they so pleased....15

This practice occasionally caused public disorders before the people were able to recover their original rights.

Locke's description of the dangers inherent in the exercise of prerogatives by popular and well-intentioned leaders must have caused Jefferson to reflect on President Washington's political stature and popular appeal in the United States. Although Jefferson was confident President Washington was a good and honorable man whose intentions and actions were beyond suspicion, he feared other men after him would eventually take advantage of their tenure in office.

In a letter to John Adams in 1787, Jefferson expressed his opinions about the permanent eligibility of the President to hold office. "The President," he said:

> seems a bad edition of a Polish king. He may reelect from 4. years to 4. years for life. Reason and experience prove to us that a chief magistrate, so continuable, is an officer for life. When one or two generations shall have proved that this is an office for life, it becomes on every succession worthy of intrigue, of bribery, of force, and even of foreign interference. It will be of great consequence to France and England to have America governed by a Galloman or Angloman. Once in office, and possessing the military force of the union, without

either the aid or check of a council, he would not be easily dethroned, even if the people could be induced to withdraw their votes from him.[16]

Throughout his correspondence concerning the details, mechanics and principles of the Federal Constitution, Jefferson urged its ratification and approval by the various states and continued to hope remedies would be found for its defects. To Madison in 1788 he said, "I sincerely rejoice at the acceptance of our new Constitution by nine States. It is a good canvas, on which some strokes only want retouching."[17]

The French Revolution

While Jefferson was corresponding with American leaders about the rebellion in Massachusetts and the new Federal Constitution, he was also aware of a political movement for revolutionary change in France. It was evident to him on August 6, 1787 that, when the French Parlement refused to register new taxes, but was compelled by a *lit de justice* to do so by the King, "a spirit of this is advancing towards a revolution in their constitution."[18]

On Sept. 22, 1787, in writing to John Jay, Jefferson stated the struggle for liberty was not between the Crown and Parlement, but a confrontation between the Crown and the people. "In its initial contest with the Crown, the Parlement was the mouthpiece of the popular will. But the Parlement was now little esteemed, requiring the public voice to throw themselves into the same scale."[19]

When the contest began to shift from the Parlement to the people, Jefferson had serious misgivings about the success of the struggle. On July 18, 1788, he said that the struggle in France

is, as yet, of doubtful issue...The danger is that the people, deceived by a false cry of liberty, may be led to take side with one party, and thus give the other a pretext for crushing them still more. If they can avoid the appeal to arms, the nation will be sure to gain much by this controversy.[20]

On the other hand, he continued, if they resort to arms everything will depend on the "disposition of the army, whether it issue in liberty or...despotism. Those dispositions are not yet known."

The political unrest and conversations Jefferson had with Lafayette and other political leaders in Paris gave him an insight into the causes of the revolution. In a letter to Dr. Price, Jefferson expressed this opinion:

Though celebrated writers of this and other countries had already sketched good principles on the subject of government, yet the American war seems first to have awakened the thinking part of this nation in general from the sleep of despotism in which they were sunk.[21]

The French officers who served in the American Revolution were less shackled by habit and prejudice, "and more ready to assent to dictates of common sense and common right." The press began to disseminate liberal ideas. Conversations between men and women were centered on politics and the principles of good government. During this time "a very extensive and zealous party was formed... the Patriotic Party, who, sensible to the abusive government... longed for occasions of reforming it."[22]

According to Jefferson, this Patriotic Party was comprised of, "the men of letters, the easy bourgeoisie, [and] the young nobility." Jefferson realized, however, that good sentiments and the inward persuasion of the mind were not sufficient causes to reform the political system of France. It was the state's declaration of bankruptcy, and Charles Alexandra de Calonne's appeal to the nation which first began to set the wheels of reform in motion.

Jefferson observed that the Patriots were primarily responsible for goading the King toward reforms and keeping up "the public fermentation at the exact point which borders on resistance, without entering on it."[23] The Patriots allied themselves with the Parlements who, for the first time, espoused the rights of the nation and called for the convocation of the States General. The Notables, however, consisting mostly of the privileged order, proposed a method of composing the States "which would have rendered the voice of the people, or Tiers Etats, in the States General, inefficient for the purpose of the court."[24] The French people, he was sure, would send their deputies

expressly instructed to consent to no tax... unless the unprivileged part of the nation has a voice equal to that of the privileged... They will have the young noblesse in general on their side, and the King and court. Against them will be the ancient nobles and clergy.[25]

By March 14, 1789, Jefferson believed the general prospect for reform in the French state was good, although he feared that an excessively cold winter would suspend all outdoor labor, leaving the poor without wages, bread or fuel. Jefferson wrote, "All communications almost, were cut off. Dinners and suppers were suppressed, and the money laid out in feeding and warming the poor, whose labors were suspended by the rigors of the season."[26]

As the bread crisis became more acute, Jefferson said, "We are in danger of hourly insurrection for want of bread, and an insurrection once begun for that cause, may associate itself with those discontented for other causes and produce incalculable events."[27] Falling short of an insurrection for want of bread, Jefferson was confident the nation could establish a good constitution.

The food crisis was only the first danger to a successful and peaceful revolution. Jefferson identified a second danger, "the absconding of the King from Versailles." He feared the flight of the King, "would be the signal of a St. Barthelemi against the aristocrats in Paris and perhaps through the kingdom."[28] This was a prophetic judgment, considering the September Massacres of 1792 which followed in the wake of the King's flight to Varennes.

The third danger facing the revolutionaries, he believed, was the financial crisis of the French state. "The embarrassment of the government," he wrote on August 27, 1789, "for want are extreme. The loan of thirty millions, proposed by Necker, has not succeeded at all. No taxes are paid. A total stoppage of all payments to the creditors of the State is possible any moment...."[29] Jefferson saw people besieging the doors of the bakers, as they scrambled with one another for "bread, assembled in crowds all over the city and [needing] only a slight incident to lead them to excesses." The want of bread, the flight of the King from Versailles and the financial crisis of the state, therefore, were the chief dangers and obstacles to peaceful reform and a good constitution for the French people.

By March of 1789, Jefferson expressed his excitement over the events which had taken place in France. To Colonel Humphreys he wrote:

A complete revolution in this government has, within the space of two years (for it began with the Notables of 1787), been effected merely by the force of public opinion, aided, indeed, by the want of money, which the dissipations of the court had brought on. And this revolution has not cost a single life....[30]

Like so many of his Parisian friends, Jefferson thought the revolution could succeed without violence and civil war. The King, he writes:

stands engaged to pretend no more to the power of laying, continuing or appropriating taxes, to call the States General periodically; to submit lettres de cachet to legal restrictions, to consent to freedom of the press; and that all this shall be fixed by a fundamental constitution, which shall bind his successors.[31]

At this stage of the revolution, Jefferson had two chief concerns about the political leadership in France. First, he doubted the revolutionaries were sufficiently aware of the need for trial by jury; and second, and most importantly, he was concerned that France's political leaders might be demanding too many concessions from the King, causing possibly a violent reaction from the monarchy, the nobles, and the people and jeopardizing the successes they had already achieved. In time, he wrote to Rabaut de St. Etienne on June 3, 1789,

the public mind will continue to ripen and to be informed, a basis of support may be prepared with the people themselves, and expedients occur for gaining still something further at your next meeting, and for stopping again at the point of force.[32]

On June 29, 1789, Jefferson wrote to John Jay informing him that the triumph of the Tiers was now complete, and that this great crisis was over. And to Thomas Paine, on June 11, he said that the National Assembly was in "complete and undisputed possession of the sovereignty... the executive and aristocracy are at their feet; the mass of the nation, the mass of the clergy, and the army are with them...."[33]

Almost three months after the Fall of the Bastille, on September 13, Jefferson told Thomas Paine that the French Revolution was over and

Tranquility is well established in Paris, and tolerably so thro' the whole kingdom; and I think there is no possibility now of any things' hindering their final establishment of a good constitution, which will in it's principles and merit be about a middle term between that of England and the United States.[34]

Jefferson's attitude toward the French Revolution, his hopes and fears, changed with each passing stage of the revolution. In its early stages, he was willing to have the revolutionaries settle for modest constitutional reforms. He questioned whether the people and their leaders were prepared to receive a full measure of their freedoms, as the revolutionaries were demanding from their King.

He was disappointed with the frivolity and "the number of puns and bon mots" the convention generated. "I think were they all collected," he wrote to Abigail Adams in February, 1787, "it would make a more voluminous work than the Encyclopedie."35 The behavior of the French political leaders at the convention convinced Jefferson

that this nation is incapable of any serious effort but under the word of command....When a measure so capable of doing good as the calling of the Notables is treated with so much ridicule, we may conclude the nation desperate, and in charity pray that heaven may send them good kings.36

By late summer of 1787, after expressing his frustration to Abigail Adams about the meeting of the Notables, Jefferson was encouraged by the disposition of the French nation toward change. He observed, in a letter to John Adams in 1787,

I think that in the course of three months the royal authority has lost, and the rights of the nation gained, as much ground, by a revolution of public opinion only, as England gained in all her civil wars under the Stuarts. I rather believe too they will retain the ground gained, because it is defended by the young and the middle aged, in opposition to the old only. The first party increases, and the latter diminishes daily from the course of nature.37

By July 13, 1789, Jefferson reported jubilantly to Thomas Paine:

The National Assembly, "having shewn thro' every stage of these transactions a coolness, wisdom, and resolution to set fire to the four corners of the kingdom and to perish with it themselves rather than to relinquish an iota from their plan of a total change of government, are now in complete and undisputed possession of the sovereignty.38

On July 22, 1789, Jefferson described in detail to James Madison the events leading to the storming of the Bastille and the establishment of the National Guard. "In the rest of Europe," he wrote, "nothing remarkable has happened; but in France such events [have occurred] as will [be] for ever memorable in history."[39] The King, he observed, "took on himself to decide the great question of voting by persons or by orders, by declaration made at a *Séance royale* on the 23rd of June. In the same declaration he inserted many other things, some good, some bad. The Tiers undismayed resolved that the whole were a mere nullity, and proceeded as if nothing had happened. The majority of the clergy joined them, and a small part of the Nobles."[40] After witnessing the French guards mixing in with the people, the King "wrote to the clergy and Nobles who had not yet joined the Tiers, recommending to them to go and join them."[41]

"It was soon observed," he continues,

that troops, and those the foreign troops, were marching towards Paris from different quarters. The States addressed the King to forbid their approach. He declared it was only to preserve the tranquility of Paris and Versailles; and I believe he thought so...On the 11th. There being now 30,000 foreign troops in and between Paris and Versailles Mr. Necker was dismissed...The next day the whole ministry was changed...A body of cavalry were advanced into Paris to awe them. The people attacked and routed them, killing one of the cavalry and losing a French guard. The corps of French guards gathered stronger, followed the cavalry, attacked them in the street...and killed four. The insurrection became universal.42

On the 14th a committee was named by the city," he observes,

with powers corresponding to our committees of safety. They resolve to raise a city militia of 48,000 men. The people attack the invalids and get a great store of arms. They then attack and carry the Bastille, cut off the Governor's and Lieutenant governors heads, and that also of the prevost des marchands...43

Once the King heard of the decapitations and that there were 50,000 or 60,000 men in arms, the king went to the States, referred everything to them, and ordered away the troops. The city committee named the Marquis de Lafayette commander in chief...a noise spread about Versailles that they were coming there to massacre the court, the ministry, etc. Every minister hereupon resigned and fled....44

The king then recalled Necker, "reappointed Monmorin and St. Preist, friends of Necker, and came with the States general to satisfy the city of his dispositions."45 On July 29, 1789, Jefferson gave Madison another detailed report of the progress of the Revolution. "No plan," he wrote, "is yet reported; but the leading members (with some small differences of opinion) have in contemplation of the following:

The Executive power in hereditary king, with a negative on laws and power to dissolve the legislature, to be considerably restrained in the making of treaties, and limited in his expences. The legislative in a house of representatives. They propose a senate also, chosen on the plan of our federal senate by the provincial assemblies, but to be for life…but to have no other power as to laws but to remonstrate against them to the representatives, who will then determine their fate by a simple majority…The representatives to be chosen every two or three years. The judiciary system is less prepared than any other part of their plan… The provinces will have assemblies for their provincial government, and the cities a municipal government, all founded on the basis of popular election. These subordinate governments, tho completely dependent on the general one, will be entrusted with almost the whole of the details which our state governments exercise…In short ours has been professedly their model, in which such changes are made as a difference of circumstance rendered necessary and some others neither necessary nor advantageous, but into which men will ever run when versed in theory and new in the practice of government, when acquainted with man only as they see him in their books and not in the world.[46]

Jefferson feared that the Duke of Orleans

is caballing with the populace and intriguing at London, the Hague and Berlin and have evidently in view the transfer of the crown to the D. of Orleans. He is a man of moderate understanding, of no principle, absorbed in low vice, and incapable of abstracting himself from the filth of that to direct anything else. His name and his money therefore are mere tools in the hands of those who are duping him. Mirabeau is their chief.[47]

Although concerned about the cabal, he insisted the

King, the mass of the substantial people of the whole country, the army, and the influential part of the clergy, form a firm phalanx which must prevail…a constitution the principle of which are pretty well settled in the minds of the assembly, will be proposed by the national militia…urged by the individual members of the assembly, signed by the king, and supported by the nation, to prevail till circumstance shall permit it's revision and more regular sanction.[48]

The proceedings in the United States, he continues, "have been viewed as a model for them on every occasion; and tho in the heat of debate men are generally disposed to contradict every authority urged by their opponents, ours has been treated like that of the bible, open to explanation but not to question."[49] He thought it was wrong

in the moment of such a disposition any thing should come from us to check it. The placing them on a mere footing with the English will have this effect. When of two nations, the one has engaged herself in a ruinous war for us, has spent her blood and money to save us, has opened her bosom to us in peace, and receive us almost on the footing of her own citizens, while the other has moved heaven, earth and hell to exterminate us in war, has insulted us in all her councils in peace, shut the doors to us in every part where her interests would admit it, libeled us in foreign nations, endeavored to poison them against the reception of our most precious commodities, to place these two nations on a footing, is to give a great deal more to one than to the other….[50]

The French and American Revolutions Compared

Jefferson was aware that the political, social and economic conditions in France were significantly different from those the American people encountered during their Revolution.

"For the American colonists" Jurgen Habermas observes,

Locke's conclusions had been commonplaces; in the place of learned arguments, their own experiences of government were sufficiently convincing...The American people were already schooled in democratic town meetings in New England and representative assemblies in the other colonies before their revolution.[51]

"With their recourse to the *Rights of Man*," Habermas continues:

the American colonists want to legitimize their independence from the British Empire; the French to legitimize the overthrow of the ancient regime...the French declaration, in contrast, is intended to assert positively for the first time a fundamentally new system of rights. In France the revolutionary meaning of the declaration is to lay the foundation for a new constitution. In America, however, it is to justify independence, as a consequence of which, to be sure, a new constitution becomes necessary.[52]

Malouet, a delegate to the National Assembly, also recognized another fundamental difference between the two revolutions:

the Americans had been able to declare their Natural Rights without any hesitation because their society consisted in a majority of proprietors who were already accustomed to equality and who hardly knew the yoke of taxes and prejudice. Such people were without question ready for freedom, unlike the people in France at that time....The majority of the Assembly considered a declaration to be necessary, because the public required effectively publicized enlightenment. This meaning is unmistakably set forth in the preamble: a declaration is desired, because 'the ignorance, forgetting and neglect of the rights of man are the universal causes of public misfortune and the corruption of the regime." In America the Declaration was itself the expression of 'common sense'; in France it had first to form the opinion publique.[53]

"In the presence of this gap between individual insight and majority opinion," Habermas continues:

the practical task falls to the philosophe to secure political recognition for reason itself by means of his influence on the power of public opinion. The philosophers must propagate the truth, must disseminate their unabridged insights publicly, for only when reason 'hits the mark everywhere,' does it hit it properly, for only then will it form that power of public opinion

In his letter to Adams in 1787, as we have already seen, Jefferson was ecstatic about the gains made by the French by the "revolution of public opinion only." In America the "positivization of Natural Law did not demand a revolutionary role of philosophy...."[54] The American colonists

were concerned with the prudent application of already given norms to a concrete situation. The philosophical minds of the National Assembly, on the other hand, had realized the break of modern Natural Law with the classical in a more rigorous fashion they discussed the organizational means for the construction of a total order of society.[55]

There was also a critical difference between France and the American colonies "that turned the French Revolution into something radically different than its American counterpart: class relations."[56] The American Revolution was a widespread social movement that represented all sectors of society and focused primarily on economic issues, while the French Revolution received the most support from the lower class."[57] "American society, which already had extremely limited stratification, became even less stratified, as, in general, free white men considered themselves to be equals... .There was little to no shifting of economic or political power."[58] "A mainly middle-class society with some degree of social equality, one can clearly see the desire by many of the Patriots to 'maintain the status quo'...."[59] The "existing political, economic, and social circumstances of the citizenry...were scarcely changed by independence"[60]

"In contrast to the lack of social change in the American Revolution, there was an abundance of social changes in the French Revolution." (6) The "gains in social equality experienced by many in France can be attributed to the lower class revolution that was taking place, as it greatly increased the position of the lower classes in society. This stands in contrast to the American Revolutions' relative lack of major social change because of the middle class nature of the revolution."[61]

It was clear to Jefferson that the French monarchy had more direct and coercive control over the population than English monarchs could ever hope to exert over the American people. The authoritarianism of an absolute monarchy, the privileged and hereditary status of the aristocracy, and the orthodoxy of the Catholic Church militated against even the most modest political and social reforms in France.

Jefferson was also aware of similarities between the American, English and French Revolutions. Like the Country politicians in England, the French Parlements in 1775 took the lead in asserting its traditional right to act on behalf of the nation. "The quarrel with the monarchy involved the very topics which in England had led to revolution—the political domination of Rome and the right of the King to tax without consent."[62] The French Parlements, like the English Parliament and the American revolutionaries, supported their case by an appeal to ancient rights and natural law. "Although there was 'no right of rebellion' against the King, his sovereignty was checked both by his duty to God and his obligation to recognize the ancient usages of the French monarchy. Among these usages [was] the constitutional right to register his edicts."[63]

Like the English and the American revolutionaries, moreover, the French "were able to find justification in their own most famous legal writers; they had no need to borrow from Coke."[64] "Montesquieu

revived the ancient French Constitution and transformed the struggle of the Parlements with the King from being a mere struggle to retain inherited privilege into a broader and more objective attempt to restore [to] the nation the ancient safeguards of its rights on which the seventeenth century monarchy had trampled. It was this conception that inspired early leaders of the Revolution...in their efforts to make France a constitutional monarchy....[65]

By 1718 the Parlements

declared themselves to be the 'true depositary of the fundamental laws of the State,' the only body in the State which met without royal permission, 'continually assembled to give justice to your subjects in the name and at the instruction of Your Majesty; the only channel through which the voice of the people has been able to reach you, since there has been no Assembly of the States-General.'[66]

When the King finally called the States-General, it was an admission that he needed popular support and an "acknowledgement of the people's right to give or withhold."[67]

Jefferson recognized that the Parlements were initially "the mouthpiece of the popular will," but had since lost their influence with the people. The contest was now between the people and the King, as it was for the American revolutionaries.

The French revolutionaries, like the American revolutionaries, abandoned any hope of wrestling constitutional reforms from an intransigent King and his corrupt ministers and instead based their claims for liberty and justice, not on the ancient rights of the French people, but on the natural rights of man, as the Americans had done.

French writers, and to a large extent many American political leaders,

delighted in using abstract terms, such as liberty and equality, reason, nature and humanity...The philosophes...relied on reason to produce valid conclusions from given premises... They all believed that just as examination of physical phenomena showed the existence of certain general laws or principles, so a full understanding of economics and politics would discover natural laws of society.[68]

The political demands the *philosophes* made of the French monarchy were also similar to the rights Americans demanded from the British—free trade and free markets, freedom of speech, a free press, the right of assembly, a government by the consent of the governed, religious toleration and a constitution guaranteeing the fundamental rights of man.

Jefferson was sympathetic to the philosophy and reform agenda of the philosophes. He did not yet believe that the French people were ready to receive their full measure of freedom, but he was prepared, if they decided to go further, to support them and the revolution.

John Adams did not share Jefferson's enthusiasm for the French Revolution or the philosophy of the French philosophes. He expressed instead his utter disdain for their philosophy.

No man is more Sensible than I am of the Service to Science and Letters, Humanity, Fraternity, and Liberty, that would have been rendered by the Encyclopedists and Economists, By Voltaire, D'Alembert, Buffon, Diderot, Rousseau, La Lande, Frederick the Great and Catharine, if they had possessed Common Sense. But they were all totally destitute of it...They seemed to believe, that whole Nations and Continents had been changed in their Principles Opinions Habits and Feelings by the Sovereign Grace of their Almighty Philosophy, almost as suddenly as Catholicks and Calving believe in instantaneous Conversion. They had not considered the force of early Education on the Millions of Minds who had never heard of their Philosophy.[69]

French revolutionary ideas, he believed, were likely to destroy both the revolutionaries and the French nation.

Jefferson was shocked to hear of John Adams' proposal to give the President of the United States a title other than his personal name, such as "His Highness the President of the United States and Protector of their

Liberties." Jefferson said he agreed wholeheartedly with Benjamin Franklin's assessment of him: "Always an honest man, often a great one, but sometimes absolutely mad."[70] Jefferson wished "he could have been here during the latest scenes. If he could then have had one fibre of aristocracy left in his frame he would have been a proper subject for bedlam."[71]

Jefferson believed, as Adams did not, that the radicalism of the French revolutionaries was justified by the extraordinary political, cultural, religious and socio-economic conditions the French people faced under the Ancient Regime. A hierarchical system ensured by authority and life firmly based on dogmatic principles. The Ancient Regime and its supporters were upholders of Christianity and the Catholic Church and were quite content to live in a world composed of unequal social orders and economic classes. It was a political culture founded on duty to God and the sovereign, and not to the equal rights of the individual or freedoms of speech, or of assembly and the press. The French revolutionaries had no choice but to remake French society on the foundation of reason and natural law.

Jefferson was, for the most part, cautiously optimistic about the success of the French Revolution before the storming of the Bastille. He had some doubts about the experience of its leaders and the receptivity of the French people to a liberal reform agenda. He thought it best for the French revolutionary leaders to move steadily, cautiously and slowly toward social and constitutional reforms.

As the French Revolution became more violent, however, and its revolutionary leaders proved to be more unified and steadfast in their struggle against the military and political maneuverings of the King, he found it easier, not only to support the revolution, but to encourage the French revolutionaries toward their goal of a total reformation of the French government and society.

Jefferson hated monarchies and the mysticism and power of the Church, both of which had cruel effects on the people. He knew that the nobility in France was exempt, not only from the military service, but also from regular taxation while the clergy drew their principal revenue from tithes "In the first half of the century," Henry Higgs noted, "large territories lay waste and over great tracts of country the poor were reduced to live on grass and water, like the beasts of the field. Beggars abounded, bread riots were frequent, and so desperate that they were only quelled by lead and cold steel."[72]

After personally observing these gross inequities in France, Jefferson reacted to it, not only theoretically, but viscerally. Kings were "wasteful in his habits, covetous of power, and unrestrained, thoroughly unhealthy, and as much a sore on the body politic as the urban squalor Jefferson found symptomatic of the worst kind of social inequality."[73] "The sickly, weakly, timid man," Jefferson wrote, "fears the people." "The lunacy of the King of England," he said, "is a decided fact...The truth is that the lunacy declared itself almost at once, and with as few concomitant complaints as usually attend the first development of that disorder...."[74]

"The King of Sardinia was a fool," he said, "The Queen of Portugal, a Braganza, was an idiot by nature... The King of Prussia, successor to the great Fredrick, was a mere hog in body as well as in mind. Gustavus of Sweden, and Joseph of Austria, were really crazy, and

George of England, you know, was in a straight waistcoat."75

The French revolutionaries, in this sense, were surgeons, removing the malignancy in the body politic of French society. They prescribed a modest regime at first to deal with this malady, but when it failed to cure the patient (the French people), they were prepared, if necessary, to remove the head (the King's), to save the republic.

There could be no "pursuit of happiness" if men were denied the right to appropriate nature for their personal needs, if the lands they once held in common were taken away from them and they were forced to live in squalor. In the United States, the wealthy did not have the financial resources or the political influence, as did the aristocrats in England and France, to buy and to enclose the vast and unchartered territories of the United States, keeping the lands for themselves while locking out the laboring classes from ownership.

Jefferson's radical egalitarianism was a theoretical and emotional reaction to these social and economic injustices in England and France. It was not enough to proclaim man's equality, as he did in the Declaration of Independence; it was now necessary to make equality a living reality. Jefferson had become, as Adams wrote sarcastically of the French philosophes, a man who believed "that whole Nations and Continents had been changed in their Principles Opinions Habits and Feelings by the Sovereign Grace of their Almighty Philosophy."

On September 5, 1789, Jefferson placed in Lafayette's hands a document he had written, "The Earth Belongs in Usufruct to the Living and not the Dead," a document that dealt specifically with the issue being debated in the

National Assembly on "whether the fundamental law of the French constitution could be revised and if so how." Jefferson's document, if accepted by the Assembly, would have completely undermined the foundations of the French monarchy. This doctrine, the most radical doctrine produced by any philosopher during the French Revolution, signified Jefferson's radical transformation during the French Revolution and his own revolution of the mind.

The Earth Belongs in Usufruct to the Living

Jefferson expressed his radical egalitarian philosophy in his new revolutionary doctrine "The Earth Belongs In Usufruct to the Living, and not the Dead." In a letter to Madison on September 6, 1789, Jefferson asked:

whether one generation of men has a right to bind another, seems never, to have been started on this or our side of the water. Yet it is a question of such consequences as not only to merit decision, but place also among the fundamental principles of every government. The course of reflection in which we are immersed here, on the elementary principles of society, has presented this question to my mind; and that no such obligation can be so transmitted I think very capable of proof. I set out on this ground, which I suppose to be self-evident, 'that the earth belongs in usufruct to the living.'[76]

Jefferson believed he had seized upon a new concept of revolutionary significance concerning the liberties of all people. His personal involvement in the French Revolution is indicated by his reference to the course of reflection in which "we are immersed here."

This doctrine had three applications for Jefferson. In

the first application of this principle, discussed in Chapter 3, Jefferson unequivocally claimed property to be a civil right, not a natural right. "The portion (of land) occupied by any individual ceases to be his when he himself ceases to be, and reverts to the society."[77] If the society has no rules for the appropriation of a person's land then it will be taken by the first occupants. These are generally the wife and children of the deceased. If, on the other hand, the society does have rules of appropriation

the child, the legatee, or creditor takes it, not by any natural right, but by a law of the society of which they are members, and to which they are subject. Then no man can, by natural right, oblige the lands he occupied, or the persons who succeed him in that occupation, to the payment of debts contracted by him. For if he could, he might, during his own life, eat up the usufruct of the lands for several generations to come, and then the lands would belong to the dead, and not the living, which would be the reverse of our principle.[78]

Every generation, consequently, have "the same rights over the soil on which they were produced, as the preceding generations had. They drive these rights not from their predecessors, but from nature. They then and their soil are by nature clear of the debts of their predecessors."[79]

The second application of this principle is "no generation can contract debts greater than may be paid during the course of its own existence."[80] Because Jefferson wanted to limit debts to a generation, it was necessary for him to define the birth and death of a generation. He calculated that at 21 years of age an individual reaches maturity, and has another 34 years in which to live. Accordingly, a generation at 21 years of age "may bind themselves and their lands for 34 years to come, at 22 for 33... and so on."[81] What is true of a generation, Jefferson wrote, will vary somewhat with generations. Generations arrive at the same day and die at the same day whereas generations "changing daily by daily deaths and births have one constant term, beginning at the date of their contract, and ending when a majority of those of full age at that date shall be dead."[82] Applying Buffon's mortality tables Jefferson concluded "19 years is the term beyond which neither the representatives of a nation, nor even the whole nation 48 assembled, can validly extend a debt."[83]

By applying Buffon's mortality tables to the contraction of debts, Jefferson believed a nation could reduce the faculty of borrowing within natural limits. If this principle were applied "it would put the lenders, and the borrowers also, on their guard...[and] would bridle the spirit of war, to which too free a course has been procured by the inattention of money-lenders to this law of nature...."[84]

The third application of this principle, and in many respects the most radical, was Jefferson's new constitutional argument that a society has no right to bind future generations to a perpetual constitution. "Every constitution and every law, naturally expires at the end of 19 years. If it be enforced longer it is an act of force, and not of right."[85] Jefferson was even opposed to admitting the alternative procedure of repeal rather than expressly specifying the natural limits of expiration. He reasoned it to be too difficult and cumbersome for one generation to repeal the laws of its predecessors, and therefore it was necessary that every law have a limited duration. There are, he says, "no municipal obligation no umpire but the law of nature. We seem not to have perceived that, by the law of nature, one generation is to another as one independent nation to another."[86]

Jefferson had now embraced what Adams characterized sarcastically as "the Sovereign Grace of their Almighty Philosophy." He abandoned his earlier, more cautious advice to the French revolutionaries to advance no further than the people were prepared to go and was prepared instead to join them in reinventing a nation on the grounds of abstract reason. Adams understood what Jefferson had now forgotten, that the French revolutionaries lacked experience, "patience, moderation, reflection, perseverance, firmness...necessary qualities of republicans."[87]

Jefferson, it appears, recognized the radical nature of his doctrine may draw the ridicule and scorn, and not the admiration and respect of his friends. "At first blush," he wrote, "it may be laughed at, as the dreams of a theorist; but examination will prove it to be solid and salutary."[88] Madison, however, was immersed in the practical affairs of the American government and was critical of the radical implications of this doctrine in the United States

Replying to Jefferson's letter on Feb. 4, 1790, after Jefferson's return to the United States, Madison said his first thoughts led him "to view the doctrine as not in all respects compatible with the course of human affairs."[89] He restated the fundamental principles of Jefferson's doctrine, and divided them into three classes.

In the first class, Madison argued that an automatic limitation of 19 years on the constitution and laws of a society would have three distinct disadvantages: First: a government so often revised would become too mutable, resulting in a failure to inspire a sense of patriotism and loyalty. Second: periodic revisions of the laws would invite "pernicious factions." [and]Third: governments limited to a fixed term would be subject to the dangers of an interregnum."[90]

Madison's second objection was aimed at Jefferson's insistence that one generation does not have the right to bind its successors in debts. Debts, Madison claimed, "may be incurred for purposes which interest the unborn...[or] incurred principally for the benefit of posterity...."[91] One generation had the right to impose obligations on its successor because the benefits and gains of their labors and industry redounds to the next generation.

Madison's last criticism was directed at Jefferson's theory of property. Madison foresaw, "the most violent struggles...between those interested in reviving and those interested in new—modelling the former state of property."[92] In the eyes of Madison, Jefferson failed to distinguish between tacit assent in the constitution and laws of society, and express consent. Here Madison's reasoning, and not Jefferson's, followed the reasoning of John Locke.

Locke distinguished between tacit and express consent in his chapter "Of the Beginning of Political Societies" in the *Treatise on Government*. He asked "what shall be understood to be a sufficient declaration of a man's consent to make himself subject to the laws of any government?"[93] On entering civil society from the state of nature, man exercises his express consent to abide by the rule of the majority and to accept the inequalities of wealth. Locke believed when succeeding generations come of age and have not given their express consent to the laws and constitution of society, consent is imparted when they have "possession or enjoyment of any part of the dominions of any government...."[94] There is, however, an alternative to tacit consent, Locke says:

whenever the owner who has given nothing but such a tacit consent to the government, will, by donation, sale, or otherwise, quit the said possession, he is at liberty to go and incorporate himself into any other commonwealth or to agree with others to begin a new one....[95]

Madison's critique of Jefferson's doctrine on practical and theoretical grounds, demonstrates Jefferson's departure, not only from the thinking of America's national leaders, like James Madison, but also from the English Whig and republican writers.

It is true, as scholars have noted, that the principle the earth belongs to the living, his remarks on public debt and his analysis of private property were a commonplace in the eighteenth century. Algernon Sydney, a martyr to the cause of republicanism in England, also said 'the laws of one generation are not binding on succeeding generations, and the explicit approbation of a people is required before a right (law) is created. If the laws are enforced against the will of the people they cease to be just and "ought not to be obeyed."[96]

Jefferson's doctrine "the earth belongs to the living and not the dead," although similar in many respects to Sidney's, was different from his in form, style and application. Jefferson extended the meaning of the concept while broadening specific areas of its application. It was Jefferson's "definition of a generation as nineteen years," Herbert W. Sloan recognizes, "and the addition of in usufruct-that made the difference...."[97] It was Jefferson's transformation, "of otherwise commonplace ideas of uncertain extent and application into a law of nature, a law that, for Jefferson, has all the rigor of a scientific fact."[98]

By "adding the qualifying "in usufruct" to the widely accepted notion that the earth belongs to the living and substituting "generation" for the dominant Anglo-American and French term "the people," Jefferson alerts us that he is transforming familiar ideas...to arrive at something new."[99]

By substituting people for generation, Jefferson establishes "exactly who can exercise rights. With "the people," the rights are inchoate; with a "generation" we now know whom and what we are dealing with...Now, at last, it would be possible to specify the "distant but fixed period" when constitutional revision was to take place."[100] It was Jefferson's transformation, "of otherwise commonplace ideas of uncertain extent and application into a law of nature, a law that, for Jefferson, has all the rigor of a scientific fact."[101]

These were certainly original innovations made by Jefferson to the commonplace notion of the earth belongs to the living, but the originality of his document was not limited to these revisions alone. Jefferson expressed his ideas in a style and form more in the rationalist spirit of Descartes' *Meditations* than in the constitutional tradition of the English, Scottish and Americans. His doctrine starts with a self-evident truth and deduces elementary truths from it; it is deductive and not inductive, abstract and not historical. The self-evident truths of his doctrine, like the self-evident truths of the Declaration of Independence, demands one's immediate consent. His principle has the full weight of a law of nature, applicable to all states and societies, just as the law of gravitation applies to all physical bodies, terrestrial and celestial.

Jefferson's doctrine regarding man's ownership of the earth was more radical than the meaning ascribed to it by the English and Scottish writers, and even by his contemporaries, Condorcet, Thomas Paine, Lafayette, Destutt de Tracy, J.B. Say, and Dr. Gem. This was most evident in his analysis of private property.

CHAPTER 3

JEFFERSON'S CONCEPT OF PRIVATE PROPERTY

Every natural law philosopher in the eighteenth century believed that our civil rights are those which secure our command over our natural rights. The issue is not between rights, or what rights are acquired or surrendered by individuals when they agree to the terms of the social compact, but which rights are truly inalienable and which rights are civil.

Liberal, or Lockean scholars have argued that our right to private property is coextensive with our rights to life and happiness. The right of property is grounded in the right to life, the right to satisfy our natural wants and needs, while the pursuit of happiness in Jefferson's Declaration comprehends the right to acquire and dispose of property as an individual saw fit. "Human beings cannot do without some sort of property in that they must appropriate, make entirely their own, parts of the external world in order to live...From the natural right to life arises a natural right to property."[1]

Locke's concept of property is stated clearly in his *Second Treatise on Government.* In his chapter on "Property," he claims property is the chief aim for men entering civil society from the state of nature. "God, who has given the world to man in common has also given them reason to make use of it to the best advantage of life and convenience."2

In his original state of nature, no man had exclusive dominion over any other man. The land was owned in common. The earth is given in common to all men, "yet every man has a property in his own person...the labor of his body and the work of his hands are properly his."3 It is understood once man has invested his labor into nature he excludes the common right of other men and appropriates it to himself. Whatever man removes from nature, or whatever he mixes his labor with, now becomes his own possession.

However, there is a law of nature which stipulates that a man does not have a right to property unless he can make use of it 'before it spoils...Whatever is beyond this is more than his share and belongs to others. Nothing was made by God for man to spoil or destroy."4 God gave the world in common to man, but did not mean it to remain common and uncultivated. He gave it to the use of the "industrious and rational" to add their personality and labors to it.

Locke maintained inequalities arose in society, not only because some men were more industrious than others, but, more importantly, because men tacitly agreed to accept gold and silver as exchangeable values for perishable goods. "No man's labor," Locke wrote,

could subdue or appropriate all, or could his enjoyment consume more than a small part, so that it was impossible for any man, this way, to entrench upon the right of another, or acquire to himself a property to the prejudice of his neighbor, who would still have room for as good and as large a possession—after the other had taken out his—as before it was appropriated.[5]

It was the invention of money, Locke says, and the tacit agreement of men to put a value on it that created inequalities in the state of nature. Once men "agreed that a little piece of yellow Metal, which would keep without wasting or decay, should be worth a great piece of flesh," mankind had the power to circumvent nature's spoilage limitation on acquisition.[6] Locke further acknowledges that

men have agreed to disproportionate and unequal Possession of the earth, they having, by a tacit and voluntary consent, found out a way how a man may fairly possess more land than he himself can use the product of, by receiving in exchange for the overplus gold and silver....[7]

"One might well wonder why," Thomas Pangle argues,

it should be the case that mixing one's labor with a thing that was previously common makes it wholly and exclusively belong to oneself. Yet Locke at first bends... all his considerable skills to mute the revolutionary character of his teaching. Locke breaks new ground in asserting [as] unqualifiedly as he does that property rights antedate government; but he does not explicitly base his discussion on the state of nature... Nonetheless,...Locke seems to retain an umbilical cord to the tradition, insofar as he contends that labor can give a man title in which was originally common only where there is enough, and as good left in common or others.[8]

Scholars who disagree with the liberal, or Lockean analysis of the Declaration and Jefferson's political philosophy argue that "the roots of Jefferson's political ideas are to be located in the Scottish Enlightenment, and not in the English republican or English liberal tradition. In contrast with Locke's depiction of man in the state of nature as isolated and independent, fearful for his life and liberty, and insecure in his possessions, the Scottish moral sense philosophers believed that man was made for society, that man was by nature a social animal with an inner, moral sense of duty to others.

The Scottish philosophers believed that we have compassionate, generous and benevolent affections for others which has nothing at all to do with the calculations of one's self-interest. We have a natural desire for the happiness of others.

"It would be strange," Lord Kames wrote, "If we be fitted by our nature for society, if pity, benevolence, friendship, love, dislike of solitude and desire of company, be natural affections, all of the conducive to society, it would be strange if there should be no natural affection, no preparation of faculties, to direct us to do justice, which is so essential to society. But nature has not failed us here, more than in the other parts of our constitution."[9]

The Scottish philosophers recognized man's interdependence, and the natural affections, duties and obligations each man felt, by his very nature, for other members of the society, before the advent of civil society. They were also very critical of moral theories, like Mandeville's, which extolled the virtues of selfishness. They believed man's sense of duty and benevolence toward others was the foundation of morality, and not man's passion for profit and gain.

Jefferson shared these moral beliefs and social values with the Scottish moral sense philosophers, a set of beliefs that were clearly distinguishable from the "possessive individualism" attributed to Locke's political philosophy and the English liberal tradition. Because Jefferson had the same concept of human nature as the Scottish philosophers, some historians have suggested and, at least, one has asserted, that Jefferson's concept of private property was influenced by them.

In Francis Hutcheson's *An Inquiry into the Original of Our Ideas of Beauty and Virtue* and Lord Kames' *Essays on the Principles of Morality and Natural Religion*, the Scottish philosophers stated, clearly and unambiguously, their positon on private property. "It is well now," Hutcheson wrote,

that general Benevolence alone, is not a Motive strong enough to Industry, to bear Labour and Toil...Self-love is really as necessary to the Good of the Whole, as Benevolence...Depriving any Person of the Fruits of his own innocent Labour, takes away all Motive to Industry from Self-love, or the near Ties; and leaves us no other Motive than general Benevolence: nay, it exposes the Industrious as a constant Prey to the Slothful, and sets Self-love against Industry. This is the Ground of our Rights of Dominion and Property in the Fruits of our Labours; without which Right, we could scarce hope for any Industry, or any thing beyond the Product of uncultivated Nature.[10]

Lord Kames was even more emphatic than Hutcheson that property was a natural, and not a civil right. Kames was opposed to the idea that, "in a state of nature, there can be no such thing as property...and that the idea of property arises, after justice, is established by convention, securing every one in their possessions."[11] Property is founded, on the contrary, "on a natural sense independent altogether of agreement or convention; and that violation of property is attended with remorse, and a perception of breach of duty."[12]

Although man's natural beneficence and moral sense of duty to others tames his appetites and passions,

self-preservation is of too great moment to be left entirely to the conduct of reason. To secure against neglect or indolence, man is provided with a principle that operates instinctively without reflection; and that is the hoarding appetite...The hoarding appetite, while moderate, is so natural and so common as not to be graced with a proper name. When it exceeds just bounds, it is known by the name of avarice.[13]

There is in society, Kames continues, a relation that is formed between

every man and the fruits of his own labour, the very thing we all call property, which he himself is sensible of, and of which every other is equally sensible. Yours and mine are terms in al languages, familiar among savages, and understood even by children ...Thus it is clear, that the sense of property owes not its existence to society... society owes its existence to the sense of property....[14]

There can be no doubt, and this is also true for English republicans, like Algernon Sydney, that private property is a natural right, an unalienable right. The Scottish disagreed with Locke's theory of human nature, but they wholeheartedly agreed with his concept of private property as a natural right. If Jefferson questioned, as he did, man's inalienable right to private property, it had nothing to do with his reading of the Scottish philosophers.

This apparent impasse, resolving the conflicting statements Jefferson made about private property as a natural and a civil right, Morton White claims, is to be found in the writings of Jean Jacques Burlamaqui.

Burlamaqui on Private Property

In Jean Jacques Burlamaqui's book, *The Principles of Natural and Politic Law*, Burlamaqui distinguishes between three states: the state of nature, a state of secondary or natural rights, and civil rights. Property is not an inalienable right, but it is a natural right. Jefferson's concept of private property was derived from the writings of Jean Jacques Burlamaqui, and not from Locke, the Scots or the French.

Burlamaqui was a Swiss-born legal scholar who wrote the most complete study on natural law in the eighteenth century. His major work, *The Principles of Natural and Politic Law*, published in 1747 and found in Jefferson's library, "accounts for a well-balanced system that describes the different states of men and their relations through different social contracts, all different in nature, content and parties from the others."[15] There are three different stages in man's evolution: the state of nature, a state of society and "a set of relations between political communities through the law of nations. Each set with its own and particular rules."[16]

Like the Scottish moral sense philosophers, Burlamaqui

believed that men associate with each other for love, convenience and protection from a hostile environment. Man's sociability "is seen as something translating [into] a common advantage that will procure men...the tools for pursuing their own happiness."17

For Burlamaqui, man's liberty in the state of nature does not imply that man is at war with every other man, as Hobbes wrote in the *Leviathan*. Man's liberty is limited by the law of nature which, Burlamaqui believes, can be attained by the simple use of his reason. "Natural law is then self-evident and known to all mankind; they are so clear and manifest that no one can claim ignorance over its principles."18 Burlamaqui theorizes men abandoned the state of nature because it "was in their nature to perfect the social body by giving themselves a certain legal framework and a ruler in order to achieve in a more efficient way the goals set by the whole community, rather than by trying to achieve them on their own."19 Unlike Locke, Rousseau and other natural law theorists who believed in one compact, Burlamaqui believed that when man abandoned the state of nature he engaged his fellow man in three compacts: The first establishes a civil society or political community; the second creates a constitution; and the third selects those who will be entrusted with the exercise of sovereign power.

The state and the sovereign, both of which are the creation of the association of its members, are bound by the law of nature to assure the happiness of their members. The rights bequeathed to man by God cannot be alienated since they are constitutive of man's nature, but those rights which man has created by his own act, do not have the status of alienability.

The rights man creates for himself in compact with other individuals are adventitious rights. Some adventitious rights, according to Burlamaqui, such as the right to private property, are also natural rights, derived from what he defines as a secondary state of natural law. Consequently, natural rights are derived from, and are a result of, man's primary rights; they are not primary or inalienable; God-given and original. They are the result of a social compact between members of a society.

The right of property for Burlamaqui was not an inalienable right, as Locke assumed, nor a right established by civil society, as Rousseau believed; it was a natural right established before the formation of states. The differences between the natural and adventitious states, therefore, "is that the former being annexed, as it were, to the nature and constitution of man, such as he has received them from God are, for this very reason, common to all mankind. The same cannot be said of the adventitious states...."[20] Adventitious rights require an act of agreement between men.

All the principal adventitious states, Burlamaqui says, are produced by human consent. When man enters civil society, he agrees to restrain and limit his liberty, property and authority in exchange for peace and tranquility. He may not surrender entirely his original rights but he may consent to modify and limit them.

Property rights are adventitious because man must relinquish his "right to all earthly goods" in his original state. Man's right in his original state to "all earthly goods" is quite different from his right in civil society. An individual's right to private property in the original state is not recognized as a private right. It is only with the institution of civil society or, by virtue of man's desire to establish a civil society, that man's right to private property is recognized as such. If an accord was reached between individuals and families in the original state regarding their private possessions, it would constitute a separate state, distinct from the original state and civil society; a state of natural rights. The distinction, then, between man's original or primitive rights, and his natural rights, presumably accounts for Jefferson's references to private property as both as a right of compact and a natural right.

The claim, then, that Burlamaqui's analysis of private property is the source of Jefferson's concept of private property is based entirely on two assumptions: First, that there is a state between man's original state and the establishment of civil society; and second, that Jefferson was aware of this distinction in Burlamaqui's philosophy.

It is doubtful that Burlamaqui's natural rights state, a state on the margins of man's original state and civil society, a transitional state that is implied, but not clearly defined in Burlamaqui's analysis was recognized by Jefferson or influenced his thinking about the private property. There is certainly no mention of it in his writings. It is far more likely that Jefferson would have understood Burlamaqui to say, as he did, that private property is an adventitious right, a right of compact.

Private Property's Role in Inequality

Jefferson's earliest and most complete statement about private property was expressed in a letter he wrote to Rev. James Madison in 1785. This letter not only answers many of the questions and objections made by liberal historians, but it reveals, at the same time, his agreements and disagreements with Locke's account of man in the state of nature.

During a visit to England, at the request of John Adams in 1786, Jefferson witnessed a population expropriated from the land for the benefit of the industrialists, nobility, priesthood, and offices of government. He feared that the inequalities in wealth and property he saw in England and in France would accompany industrial growth in the new republic.

In his letter to Rev. Madison on October 28, 1785, Jefferson shared his thoughts about the causes of the misery and wretchedness of the people he observed in the French countryside.

The property of this country is absolutely concentrated in very few hands, having revenues of from half a million of guineas a year downwards. These employ the flower of the country as servants ...They employ also a great number of manufacturers and tradesmen, and lastly the class of laboring husbandmen. But after all these comes the most numerous classes, that is, the poor who cannot find work.[21]

He puzzled why "so many should be permitted to beg who are willing to work, in a country where there is a very considerable proportion of uncultivated lands?"[22] To his dismay he realized "these lands are undisturbed only for the sake of game. It should seem then, it must be because of the enormous wealth of the proprietors which places them above attention to the increase of their revenues by permitting these lands to be labored."[23]

Jefferson recognized

an equal division of property is impractical, but the consequences of this enormous inequality producing so much misery to the bulk of mankind, legislators cannot invent too many devices for subdividing property, only taking care to let their subdivisions go hand in hand with the natural affections of the human mind. The descent of property of every kind therefore to all the children, or to all the brothers and sisters, of other relations in equal degree, is a politic measure and a practicable one.[24]

Another means of addressing this problem, he suggests,

is to exempt all from taxation below a certain point, and to tax the higher portions or property in geometrical progression as they rise. Whenever there are in any country uncultivated lands and unemployed poor it is clear that the laws of property have been so far extended as to violate natural right. The earth is given as a common stock for man to labor and live on. If for the encouragement of industry we allow it to be appropriated, we must take care that other employment be provided to those excluded from the appropriation. If we do not, the fundamental right to labor the earth returns to the unemployed.[25]

Locke and Jefferson on Private Property

Jefferson agrees with Locke that the earth was given in common to all men, that every "man has a property in his own person," in "the labor of his body and the work of his hands," and that man has a natural right to the fruits of his labors. Jefferson, however, did not accept man's natural right to the use of one's property beyond its advantages to his own life. "Whatever is beyond this," as previously noted, is more than his share and belongs to others." It is this last point made by Locke, and accepted by Jefferson, that has proven so perplexing to liberal scholars.

Jefferson did consider one's possessions a natural right, but it was a right with an expiration date, a right which ceases with the death of the property owner. Jefferson recognizes that man is entitled to the fruits of his labor but he did not believe that human beings have a right to property in perpetuity.

Jefferson's letter to Rev. James Madison also makes it very clear that, contrary to Locke and the liberal interpretations of Jefferson's concept of private property, he regarded the gross inequalities in ownership and wealth he witnessed in England a violation of man's natural rights, and not an expression of it. It was not, as Locke argued, the invention of money in the state of nature that created the inequalities between men but, "the encouragement of industry we allow...to be appropriated." The appropriation of nature "we allow" beyond an individual's personal needs, consequently, is not an individual act of appropriation sanctioned by natural law but a social agreement between members in civil society.

Individuals in any given society, Jefferson believed, agree collectively to allow certain individuals among them to appropriate the earth to encourage industry. These individuals may be, as Locke believed, more "industrious and provident" but their appropriation of nature beyond their personal needs is not a natural right, that is, an inalienable right because there is a corresponding responsibility and duty associated with it; the duty to release "uncultivated lands" in their possession and to employ the unemployed poor. These rights are civil rights, requiring the mutual recognition of others.

What distinguishes Jefferson's analysis of the state of nature from Locke's is the principle of "perishability," or in Locke's language, "spoilage." Jefferson agrees with Locke that man is born equal, free and independent in the state of nature and possesses, with every other man, the inalienable right to appropriate nature for his use and enjoyment.

Man's appropriation of nature, in the state of nature, is limited, first, to his use and enjoyment of it. If his appropriations extend beyond what a man and his family can properly make use of, it becomes the common property of every man. Second, the natural right a man has to the fruits of his labor is limited to his use of it while he is alive. After he dies the property reverts to society.

The principle of "perishability" also applies to property in civil society. First, all men have a natural right to appropriate nature for their use and enjoyment but, if their appropriations prevent, hinder, or otherwise deny that same right to other men, they forfeit their right to it. Second, every man's estate becomes the common property of society upon his death. The inequalities in ownership and wealth in civil society, Jefferson recognized, because they are protected by the laws of civil society, however unjustly, are not easily expropriated. Jefferson counsels governments to act in, at least, two ways to deal with this very serious problem.

First, governments should tax, at geometrically higher

rates, the surplus wealth of this class of citizens; and secondly, governments should enact laws that partition the estates and the wealth of these individuals and families. It may be impolitic, Jefferson recognizes, to act aggressively toward the redistribution of their estates while these individuals are still alive, although he still believes it is prudent and necessary for the society to do so. Upon their death, however, the government has the right and obligation, founded in the natural rights of man, to partition these estates more equally among the members of the family or to creditors, and return, if possible, the bulk of their estates to society.

Jefferson simply refused to accept inequality in the state of nature, as did Locke, as a natural right. Throughout his life he expressed hostility to what he called Patrician Orders, those individuals and families who have accumulated, by unjust laws, extraordinary surpluses in property and wealth. The partitioning or redistribution of the wealth of this class, moreover, was not limited to their grand and luxurious estates; it also included the surplus wealth derived from their financial speculations. Jefferson was an enemy to aristocratic orders in land, commerce, manufactures and finance.

It is very clear that Jefferson did not derive his concept of private property from Locke, Hutcheson, Kames, Burlamaqui or any of the other English liberals or English republican and Scottish republican writers. The English and the Scottish philosophers believed that private property was an inalienable right of man, and not a right of compact. Only the French philosophers, Rousseau and Montesquieu, defined private property as Jefferson understood it, a civil right.

In all of the treatises on government, political

economy, morality and society Jefferson read or likely read, Rousseau was one of the few who distinctly and clearly defined the right of property as a civil right, and not as an inalienable right of man.

Rousseau's *Second Discourse*

In his *Second Discourse*, Rousseau says sarcastically that "the first person who, having fenced off a plot of ground, took it into his head to say this is mine and found people simple enough to believe him, was the true founder of civil society."[26] "The right of property," he claims, "is only conventional and of human institution, every man can dispose at will of what he possesses. But it is not the same for the essential gift of nature, such as life and freedom, which everyone is permitted to enjoy and of which it is at least doubtful that one has the right to divest himself...."[27]

Similarly, Jefferson wrote:

It is agreed, by those who have seriously considered the subject that no individual has, of natural right, a separate property in an acre of land, for instance. By an universal law... whether fixed or movable, belongs to all men equally and in common, is the property for the moment of him who occupies it, but when he relinquishes the occupation, the property goes with it. Stable ownership is the gift of social law, and is given late in the progress of society.[28]

In both statements about private property, Rousseau and Jefferson use the language of the "gift," one referring to the gift of life and freedom and the other referring to the gift of ownership, or private property.

The resemblance between these two formulations about the status of private property and the state of nature, and the influence Rousseau may have exercised over Jefferson, however, has been either completely ignored or denied by scholars. They claim that Jefferson never referred to or read any of Rousseau's writings.

There does exist, in fact, at least one letter to John Adams in 1816, where Jefferson refers specifically to Rousseau. John Adams, on March, 2, 1816, asked Jefferson if he knew Grimm in Paris. In his reply, on April 8, 1816, Jefferson said he did know Grimm while in Paris. "Yes, most intimately," he wrote:

He was the pleasantest, and most conversable member of the diplomatic corps while I was there: a man of good fancy, acuteness, irony, cunning and egoism: no heart, not much of any science, yet enough of every one to speak it's language. His fort was Belles-lettres, painting and sculpture. In these he was the oracle of the society, and as such was the empress Catherine's private correspondent....[29]

"It was in D'Holbach's conventicles," he continues, "that Rousseau imagined all the machinations against him were contrived, and he left, in his *Confessions* the most biting anecdotes of Grimm. These appeared after I left France; but I have heard that poor Grimm was so much afflicted by them, that he kept his bed several weeks. I have never seen these Memoirs of Grimm."[30]

Adams later replied that he read "fifteen Volumes of more than five hundred pages each."[31] In Grimm's writings, Adams wrote, "he spares no Characters, but Necker and Diderot. Voltaire, Buffon, D'Alembert, Helvetius, Rousseau, Marmontel, Condorcet, La Harpe,

Beaumarchais and all others are lashed without Ceremony."[32]

As an intimate friend of Grimm's, Jefferson knew about Grimm's intimate relationship with Rousseau and the celebrated rupture in Rousseau and Grimm's friendship when Rousseau discovered Grimm had a romantic affair with his lover, Madame d'Epignay. It also seems unlikely that Jefferson, one of the most erudite and widely read among the Founding Fathers, was aware of the intimate details of Grimm and Rousseau's stormy relationship, spent five years as minister to France on the eve of the French Revolution, befriending the leading French intellectuals in Paris, and had a presence in the most celebrated salons in Paris, including Madame d'Houdetot's, Rousseau's lover, forever memorialized in Rousseau's Sophie of the *Confessions*, but had no knowledge of Rousseau's philosophy. It is far more likely he read more than just Rousseau's *Confessions*.

It is also possible that Jefferson was inspired by Rousseau's *A Discourse* upon the Origin and the Foundation of the Inequality among Mankind in his *Notes on the State of Virginia*. In his Query XI, Jefferson described the life of the native aborigines in his State.

They never submitted themselves to any laws, any coercive power, any shadow of government. Their only controls are their manners, and that moral sense of right and wrong, which, like the sense of tasting and feeling, in every man makes a part of his nature. An offence against these is punished by contempt, by exclusion from society... Imperfect as this species of coercion may seem, crimes are very rare among them: insomuch that were it made a question, whether no law, as among the savage Americans, or too much law, as among the civilized Europeans, submits man to the greatest evil, one who has seen both conditions of existence would pronounce it to be the last: and that the sheep are happier of themselves, than under care of the wolves. It will be said, that great societies cannot exist without government. The Savages therefore break them into small ones.[33]

Jefferson's description of the political and social life of aborigines is interesting for two important reasons. First, he regards them to be equal to Americans and Europeans; they, too, have a moral sense of right and wrong; and secondly, that their existence without government and laws is preferable to the civilized life of Europeans. Of all the political theorists in the eighteenth century Jefferson read, or likely read, Rousseau was the only political philosopher who raised this question and answered it affirmatively. Again, Jefferson does not refer specifically to Rousseau in these passages, but his analysis is very similar to Rousseau's.

Rousseau and Jefferson believed property was an alienable right, and democracies the most perfect form of government. They believed that in a republic man is closer to the "hypothetical and conditional" state of nature; a state in which men were free, equal and independent. The advantage of a republic, they believed, lay in its greater ability to promote man's virtue and happiness. Locke and the Scottish philosophers, on the other hand, considered property to be an inalienable right of man, and the model of the British monarchy to be the perfect form of government. Jefferson and Rousseau also believed that monarchies and aristocracies were more likely to pursue war and profits and that sovereignty must be vested in the people and not in legislative bodies, as the English Whigs believed.

Rousseau's vision of an ideal state in the *Discourse* also mirrors Jefferson's democratic vision of the American republic. Rousseau envisioned a republic where the citizens, long accustomed to prudent independence, were not only free but worthy of being so.[34]

A republic safeguarded by an even more fortunate location from the fear of becoming itself the conquest of another State; a free city, situated among several peoples none of whom had an interest in invading it, while each had an interest in preventing the others from invading themselves...a country where the right of legislation was common to all citizens...where the individuals, being content to give sanction to the laws and to decide in a body and upon the report of their chiefs the most important public affairs, would establish respected tribunals, distinguish with care their various departments, elect from year to year the most capable and most upright of their fellow citizens to administer justice and govern the State....[35]

A people fortunate to live in such a republic would be both happy and virtuous.

It should be apparent, at the very least, Jefferson and Rousseau had similar thoughts about the state of nature, private property, and the virtues required of citizens living in a democratic republic.

Jean Jacques Rousseau, however, was not the only French philosopher with these views. Montesquieu also believed that property is a civil and not a natural right.

Montesquieu's Theory of Private Property

"It is a paralogism to say," Montesquieu wrote:

that the good of the individual should give way to that of the public; this can never take place, except when the government of the community, or, in other words, the liberty of the subject is concerned; this does not affect such cases as relate to private property, because the public good consists in everyone's having his property, which was given him by the civil laws, invariably preserved.[36]

Montesquieu believed it does not serve the best interests of society to deprive an individual of his property and possessions, yet he does not deny the civil magistrate the authority to do so. It may be unwise and impolitic to do so, but an individual's right to property, unlike his liberty, is not a natural right. Montesquieu encouraged the citizens' representatives in a republic to enact specific legislation for the distribution of property.

It is absolutely necessary there should be some regulations in respect to women's dowries, donations, successions, testamentary settlements, and all other forms of contracting. For were we once allowed to dispose of our property to whom and how we pleased, the will of each individual would disturb the order of the fundamental law.

Montesquieu was aware of the difficulties which would arise with regulation of private property. He proposed, therefore, "to establish a census, which shall reduce or fix the differences to a certain point: it is afterwards the business of particular laws to level, as it were, the inequalities, by the duties laid upon the rich, and by the ease afforded to the poor."[37]

During Jefferson's time as a member of the House of Delegates in 1776, he introduced legislation abolishing the laws of entail and primogeniture in Virginia. The law of entail, Jefferson later wrote in his *Autobiography*: raised up a distinct set of families, who, being privileged by law in the perpetuation of their wealth formed into a Patrician Order, distinguished by the splendor and luxury of their establishments...

Jefferson later said to the Rev. James Madison on Oct. 28, 1785:

I am conscious that an equal division of property is impracticable, but the consequences of this enormous inequality producing so much misery to the bulk of mankind, legislators cannot invent too many devices for subdividing property, only taking care to let their subdivisions go hand in hand with the natural affections of the human mind. The descent of property of every kind therefore, to all the children or to all the brothers and sisters, or other relations in equal degree, is a politic measure and a practicable one.[38]

Jefferson believed the laws of civil society should protect the property rights of its citizens, but he agreed with Montesquieu that a republican government has the authority and the right, not only to tax the wealthiest estates at a geometrically higher rate than small landholders, but to partition, if necessary, for the general welfare of the society, those great landed estates.

According to Jefferson:

Man can exercise no rights in opposition to his social duties, and he can retain only those rights which he has power to exercise fully. These I conceive to be civil rights or rights of compact, and are distinguishable from natural rights, because in the one we act wholly in our own person, and in the other we agree not to do so, but act under the guarantee of society.[39]

Natural rights, Jefferson writes, "are the rights of thinking, speaking, forming and giving opinions, and perhaps all of those which can be fully exercised by the individual without the aid of exterior assistance..."[40] Our civil rights "are those of person protection of acquiring and possessing property, in the exercise of which the individual natural power is less than the natural right."[41]

It may be true, as Andrew Burstein and Nancy Isenberg claim that Jefferson's doctrine is "an extension of his earlier attempts to reform the laws of Virginia by ridding society of entail and primogeniture. "Entail," they write, "had allowed the dead to control the destiny of future generations by circumscribing how land could be distributed; primogeniture in effect disinherited younger offspring by automatically bequeathing the main estate to the elder son."[42] Jefferson's doctrine, however, was more than just an extension of his earlier efforts to reform property laws in his native state of Virginia; it was a radical redefinition of man's right to private property.

Jefferson's use of the concept 'usufruct' in this doctrine underscores the difference between his earlier efforts at property reform and his new position on property rights. Usufruct comes from Roman civil law,

under which it is a subordinate real right...of limited duration, usually for a person's lifetime. The holder of the usufruct, known as a usufructuary, has the right to use the property and enjoy its fruits... The usufructuary never had possession of this property...but he did have an interest in the property... Unlike the owner, the usufructuary did not have a right of alienation, but he could sell or lease his usufructory interest. Even though a usufructuary did not have possessory title, he could sue for relief in the form of a modified possessory interdict (prohibiting order).[43]

Jefferson considered the entail and primogeniture, as Burstein and Isenberg wrote, a dangerous practice, making "it impossible for the heirs of a wealthy landowner to sell or bequeath his land." An heir could farm the land and build on it, but he did not own the property outright and could not freely dispose of it. The earth belonged to the heirs, in succession, which usually meant each firstborn son.[44] As "distribution of property became more and more inequitable over time... larger chunks of land were concentrated in fewer and fewer hands."[45]

Jefferson's earlier reforms were intended to "democratize the distribution of property for future generations," empowering individual landowners to sell or dispose of their properties as they saw fit. Jefferson's doctrine of 'the earth belongs to the living,' however, also empowered the state to partition large estates to allow for a more equitable distribution of property. The state was granted the authority to determine the future use made of these lands. This radical turn in Jefferson's thinking, even more than his legislation to reform the laws of entail and primogeniture in Virginia, as Burstein and Isenberg wrote, was evidence of Jefferson's conviction "for moral restraints to be imposed by law—he continued to believe in social engineering."[46]

Among Jefferson's inner circle of friends, Brissot de Warville also expressed similar views to Jefferson's in his *Philosophic Researches on the Right of Property and on Theft in their Relations to Nature and Society*, which appeared in 1780. His main argument is that, since property is a social not a natural institution, theft is not a crime against natural law, and should not be punished by death. Property is justified by nature only in so far as it fulfils essential needs.

We do not know if Jefferson had a conversation about private property with de Warville before he wrote his document "the earth belongs to the living," but they were close friends and shared similar ideas about the subject.

Jefferson's letters and writings before his departure to France, namely, the Declaration of Independence, his drafts for the Virginia state constitution and *Notes on the State of Virginia* reveal only his deep concern over the issue of the inequality of wealth in the American colonies and, as he put it later, a "distinct set of families" with wealth and power, "privileged by law." It was not until his ministry to France that Jefferson began to define and articulate his philosophy of private property.

Jefferson's concept of private property was not a momentary lapse of judgment or a radical interlude in an otherwise unblemished record of support for private property as a natural right, as the liberal historians claim, but a statement of his mature political thinking on the subject of property. Jefferson repeated his reasoning in the document he sent to James Madison in 1789, and to John Eppes on June 24, 1813; to John Eppes again in September 11, 1813; to William Plumer on July 21, 1816; and to Thomas Earle on September

24, 1823, a few years before his death. All men have the right to appropriate nature for their use and enjoyment, but this right does not confer ownership to them over nature itself. Nature remains the common property of every man.

Jefferson's doctrine of the earth belongs to the living, his concept of the inalienability of labor in his letter to Rev. James Madison, and his materialism, place him not in the English liberal or the Scottish communitarian traditions, but in the French liberal tradition. Jefferson did not consider the inequalities of wealth and ownership, as did the English Whigs, a natural right of man. He agreed instead with Rousseau, Montesquieu and de Warville that private property was a civil right.

Jefferson was an enemy of inequality and an uncompromising advocate for democratic egalitarianism. He wanted to remove all legal barriers that prevented individuals from acquiring and transferring properties necessary for the full enjoyment of their lives, properties held by an aristocratic class in England, France and, in a far more limited way, in the United States. He also desperately wanted to limit the political power and influence conferred by such possessions and wealth by the few, the Patrician Orders.

CHAPTER 4

THE ECONOMIC THOUGHT OF
THOMAS JEFFERSON

In his document The Earth Belongs In Usufruct to the Living, and not the Dead Jefferson specified that "no generation can contract debts greater than may be paid during the course of its own existence." Debt, inherited debt especially, and the financing of it, he believed, was a burdensome tax paid by future generations for the improvident and wasteful spending of past generations. Inherited debt, not unlike the inherited ranks, titles, and the wealth and power of the aristocratic class he observed in England and France, was a cancer in the body politic of a democratic society.

Jefferson's economic theory reflects his concern that institutions which shape, to a large extent, the social interactions between people must be designed to serve two overlapping functions: they must provide general principles and practices that promote economic growth while promoting civic virtues that are vital to the health and well-being of a democratic society, principally, the virtue of sacrificing one's private interests for the sake of the public good.

The wealth of a nation, for Jefferson, cannot be

measured solely by the growth of its Gross Domestic Product, important as that is; it must be measured as well by the wealth it produces for the great bulk of its people, a shared wealth, distributed more equally among all classes of society. Jefferson's understanding of debt, finance, taxes, and banking, and the theories, policies, and programs he favored or opposed, must be measured, then, not only by their ability to foster economic growth, but also by their conformity to the demands of his political and economic egalitarianism. Economic theory for Jefferson was, as it was for the classical economists, the Physiocrats and Adam Smith, a branch of morality.

Jefferson's early economic thought was shaped by the French economists or, as they were also called, the Physiocrats. In his library, Jefferson collected the economic works of Francois Quesnay, Nicolas Baudeau's *Explanation du Tableau économique* (1776), Francois Le Trosne's *De l'Order social* (1779), Rivière's *L'ordre naturel et essential des société's politique* (1768), Victor Mirabeau's *Théorie de l'impôt* (1761), numerous works by Du Pont de Nemours, and later when he was in Paris, he purchased four of six volumes of *Les Oeuvre de Turgot*. Jefferson's economic philosophy was a comprehensive, theoretical and practical analysis of the economic forces and classes in American society, eventually informed by his time in Europe.

We first learn of Jefferson's understanding of economic conditions in the American colonies and the economic theories he favored in the only book he wrote, *Notes on the State of Virginia*. In this volume Jefferson provides detailed accounts of the climate, rivers, seaports, minerals, vegetables, animals, commerce, manufactures, mountains, buildings, roads, population, weights, measures and money, and public revenues and expenses in his native state of Virginia and other bordering states.

In Query VIII, Jefferson recognized that Virginia and the other states were rich in resources with an abundance of land. They lacked only workers to cultivate and mine the lands for its riches. Based on his own calculations taken from census figures between 1700, 1748, and 1759, Jefferson reasoned that there was demonstrable proof of a uniform rate of growth in the population.

Should this rate of growth continue we shall have between six and seven millions of inhabitants within 95 years. If we suppose our country to be bounded...by the meridian of the mouth of the Great Kanhaway...there will then be 100 inhabitants for every square mile, which is nearly the state of population in the British islands.[1]

However, we could "at once double our numbers" by the importations of foreigners. We should "Spare no expence in obtaining them."

They will after a while go to the plough and the hoe; but, in the mean time, they will teach us something we do not know. It is not so in agriculture. The indifferent state of that among us does not proceed from a want of knowledge merely; it is from our having such quantities of land to waste as we please.[2]

In Query XIX, "the present state of manufactures, commerce, interior and exterior trade," Jefferson recognized

The political economists of Europe have established it as a principle that every state should endeavor to manufacture for itself; and this principle, like many others, we transfer to

America, without calculating the differences of circumstances which should often produce a difference of result.3

The different circumstances Jefferson referred to were the confluence and interplay of land, labor and manufactures. "In Europe the lands are either cultivated or locked up against the cultivator. Manufactures must therefore be resorted to of necessity not of choice, to support the surplus of their people."4 Here Jefferson clearly, if theoretically, sees the importance of free land and economic freedom. In America, on the other hand, we have "an immensity of land courting the industry of the husbandman...It is best then that all our citizens should be employed in its improvements, or that one half should be called off from that to exercise manufactures and handicraft arts for the other."5

As long as there was an abundance of land, Jefferson wished never to "see our citizens occupied at a work-bench, or twirling a distaff. Carpenters, masons, smiths, are wanting in husbandry; but, for the general operations of manufacture, let our work-shops remain in Europe."6

Because land was so plentiful and cheap, and labor so scarce, Jefferson observed, landlords were only able to produce one-tenth of what they would otherwise be capable of producing from the land. Cheap land and high wages also allowed the laborers, in a relatively short period of time, to accumulate sufficient capital to buy their own land. The cycle of expansion and growth continued to raise the wages of laborers, bringing more lands into cultivation while contributing to the wealth of the nation. The availability and cheapness of land was one of the greatest inducements to immigration, productivity, and a high birthrate in the new nation.

Implied in Jefferson's analysis of farming and industry was the notion that workers in the manufacturing sector of the economy are, if not wage slaves, certainly not free actors. This became even more apparent to Jefferson after his travels through England where he witnessed the abject poverty and misery of England's industrial working class.

Agricultural labor was preferable, as he stated it to John Adams in 1813, because the worker was able to extract from the land "such compensation...for a cessation of labour in old age."7 Their labor, coupled with the self-generative powers of the earth, as the physiocrats understood it, provided the agriculturalist with a surplus beyond the wages of the industrial worker, thereby allowing him to provide for himself and his family in his retirement, a retirement denied the industrial worker. Moreover, if a citizen wanted to labor in manufacturing, the fact that he had a viable choice for alternative employment meant that those who owned the business were not at a negotiating advantage and would have to pay workers a real wage. The abundance of cheap land and the scarcity of labor also shielded America against the inequality and the class divisions of Europe. Jefferson envisioned a middle-class society composed primarily of agricultural workers and proprietors.

"Those who labour in the earth," Jefferson wrote:

are the chosen people of God, if ever he had a chosen people, whose breasts he has made his peculiar deposit for substantial and genuine virtue....Corruption of morals in the mass of cultivators is a phenomenon of which no age nor nation has furnished an example…generally speaking, the proportion which the aggregate of the other classes of citizens bears in any state to that of its husbandmen, is the proportion of its unsound to its healthy parts, and is a good-enough barometer whereby to measure its degree of corruption.[8]

Jefferson was not alone in his recognition of the role of agriculture and the agriculturalist in America's economic and social life. "The Founding Fathers shared the belief that "agriculture and the small independent farmer were the building blocks of the new nation. Ploughing, planting and vegetable gardening" were, not only "more profitable and enjoyable occupations: they were political acts, bringing freedom and independence."[9]

George Washington, Benjamin Franklin, John Adams and James Madison all regarded the farmer as the backbone of the country and agriculture as the source of the nation's wealth. "George Washington…the man who defeated the British army idealized not the military tactician or he political revolutionary, but the farmer. 'The life of a Husbandman of all others,' Washington wrote, 'is the most delectable,' both 'honorable' and 'amusing.'"[10] Washington also believed the United States would become 'a storehouse and granary for the world.'"[11]

Benjamin Franklin made similar observations in his essay "Observations Concerning the Increase of Mankind, Peopling of Countries, etc." Franklin recognized three important facts: First: Marriages are delayed because the cost of living is high, and individuals are less likely to have the financial means to support a family, tending instead to remain servants and journeyman. Second: Where lands are fully settled and labor is plentiful, as in Europe, wages are low and families endure much hardship. Third: When lands are plentiful and cheap, as in America, a man can "in a short time save Money enough to purchase a Piece of new Land sufficient for a Plantation, whereon he may subsist a Family...."[12] Franklin also observed the vast territory of the Northwest will "require many Ages to settle it fully; and till it is fully settled, Labour will never be cheap here, where no Man continues long a Labourer for others, but gets a Plantation of his own, no man continues long a journeyman to a Trade, but goes among those new Settlers, and sets up for himself...."[13]

In his "Positions to be examined concerning National Wealth," Franklin listed in 1769 the "three ways by which a nation might acquire wealth... The first is by War...This is robbery: The second by Commerce which is generally Cheating. The third by agriculture the only honest Way."[14] Franklin believed that the colonists' reliance on agriculture for their main income, combined with the seemingly endless resources of land, could be turned to their advantage" against the British. "Americans could be self-sufficient."[15]

John Adams chiseled the promotion of useful arts into the constitution of Massachusetts in 1779," and Madison declared that the greater the proportion of husbandmen, 'the more free, the more independent, and the more happy must be the society itself. The well-tended fields of small farms became a symbol for America's future as an agrarian republic."[16]

Even Hamilton, who believed an "entrepreneurial urban elite... should be the backbone of American society, because the wealth of the country depended on commerce and, crucially, on close trading relationships with Britain,"[17] recognized that land was a far greater source of America's wealth than was commerce or manufactures. England was an example of this. Agricultural lands therefore had to be the primary source of the nation's revenue. A tax, not too burdensome or heavy, yet must be imposed on the agriculturalists or

the quantity of unimproved land will invite the husbandmen to abandon old settlements for new, and the disproportion of our population for some time to come, will necessarily make labor dear, to reduce which, and not to increase it, ought to be a capital object of our policy.[18]

The Economics of Physiocracy

In his analysis of the American economy, Jefferson recognized the scientific insights of the French economists, particularly its founder Francois Quesnay. The Economists, he later wrote,

made it a branch only of a comprehensive system on the natural order of societies. Quesnai first, Gournay, Le Frosne, Turgot, and Du Pont de Nemours...led the way in these developments, and gave to our inquiries the direction they have since observed. Many sound and valuable principles established by them, have receive the sanction of general approbation....[19]

The Economists or physiocrats were the first group to make political economy into a science. It was in 1757 that Francois Quesnay, then doctor to Madame de

Pompadour and first doctor-in-ordinary to the King, had begun his writings on economics.[20] After a brief interview with Mirabeau, the co-founder of this new economic sect, physiocracy became a popular and widespread subject of interest to the French literati.

The French school of Economists arose principally as an ethical protest against the evils which plagued the corrupt feudal French society, as well as a reaction against mercantilism; specifically, its discriminating tariffs, promotion of manufactures and its balance of trade policy. Their fundamental assumption evolved from the notion that agriculture was the only true source of a nation's wealth, and therefore the only productive occupation for the citizenry. The mercantile class, on the other hand, was unproductive of riches and consequently a sterile group.

In his *Extracts from Rural Philosophy*, Francois Quesnay, the founder of this economic sect, wrote:

If the moralists and politicians do not base their science on the economic order, on agriculture, their speculations will be useless and illusory; the[y] will be doctors who perceive only the symptoms and ignore the disease. Those who depict for us the morals of their age without going back to causes are only speculators and not philosophers.[21]

The cause of all social misery was blamed on the failure of governments to implement economic programs and policies that favored the agricultural class.

The physiocrats believed in free trade but regarded foreign trade a necessary evil. Numerous examples of commercial warfare, as well as the jealousies and animosities which accompany foreign trade convinced

the physiocrats that a nation should provide manufactures and produce for its own inhabitants. Recourse
to the raw materials and manufactures of other nations
should arise only if there were no other means to satisfy
the needs of the people. This same idea was expressed
by Jefferson in his Query about manufactures in his
Notes where he refers to the Economists of Europe.

Because agriculture was the only occupation which
could produce wealth, the physiocrats thought it best to
reduce the number of artisans from the towns and cities
and transfer them to the countryside "where sufficient
land should be given to them for subsistence. The
holding should be moderate in size, and there should
not be a landless family in the country."[22] Generally, the
prosperity and happiness of a society is directly
proportional to the number of its agriculturalists.

In a society predicated upon the truths of physiocracy,
the burden of taxation imposed on the cultivator is
eased. Quesnay believed, "The wealth employed in
meeting the costs of cultivation ought to be set apart for
the cultivators and exempted from all taxation: for if it
is appropriated, agriculture is destroyed..."[23] Again,
Jefferson expressed, in almost the same language as
Quesnay, the proportional analysis of the strengths of
different economic classes and economic interests in
agricultural societies. He also voiced Quesnay's belief
that the agriculturalists were God's chosen people.

Among the articles of faith which militated against
the adoption of physiocracy was the mercantile belief in
a favorable balance of payments, or stock of specie and
precious metals held by the Crown. The mercantilists
measured the strength of a nation by the amount of its
exports. According to the Economists, it is not what a

nation exports but what it consumes at home that indicates its real condition.

A country may have large exports while its people live in poverty, and conversely, the exports may be inconsiderable, not because the people are poor, but by reason of their large effective demand. A country is most prosperous when inland production and consumption are of such dimension that there is little need for foreign trade...[24]

The accumulation of pecuniary wealth by means of foreign trade only enriches the traffickers and financiers, while the nation, as a whole, far from benefiting by it, must bear all the useless charges which traffic incurs.[25] The man who is engaged in foreign trade, the merchant, is portrayed by the physiocrats as one who only thinks of his gains, his bargains, his profits on the exchange of coins in different markets. The merchant is a stranger in his own country. His name is unknown, and he cannot be counted upon to share the burdens and responsibilities required of a nation's inhabitants. Foreign trade is useful and necessary only if left completely free, allowing parties to negotiate on equal terms.

The general reasoning of the physiocrats was most favorable to the cultivators of the soil while adverse to the interests of the mercantile and industrial classes. The physiocrats assumed that the system of market exchange was subject to certain objective laws which operated independently of human will and was discoverable by reason.

Physiocratic theory played an important role in Jefferson's political economy. He agreed with the physiocrats that the prosperity of a nation was dependent upon increased expenditures to the agricultural sector of society, on the productive capacity of agriculture to yield a surplus profit greater than that of manufacturing, and their belief that labor should be diverted from commerce and manufactures to agriculture He also believed with them that cultivators of the earth were God's chosen people.

Jefferson expressed his physiocratic faith in a letter to Hogendorp in 1785.

"You ask

what I think on the expedience of encouraging our states to be commercial? Were I to indulge my own theory, I should wish them to practice neither commerce nor navigation, but to stand with respect to Europe, precisely on the footing of China. We should thus avoid wars, and all our citizens would be husbandmen...26

Jefferson's understanding of economic theory was relatively unsophisticated before his departure to France. Under the tutelage of J.B. Say and Destutt de Tracy, however, he learned, as he later wrote:

Adam Smith, first in England, published a rational and systematic work on Political Economy, adopting the ground of the Economists, but differing on the subjects before specified. The system being novel, much argument and detail seemed then necessary to establish principles which now are assented to as soon as proposed....27

In France, he observed:

John Baptist Say, has the merit of producing a very superior work on the subject of Political Economy. His arrangement is luminous, ideas clear, style perspicuous, and the whole subject brought within half the volume of Smith's work. Add to this considerable advances in correctness and extension of principles.[28]

The work of his friend, Destutt de Tracy, he continues

comes forward with all the lights of his predecessors in the science, and with the advantages of further experience, more discussion, and greater maturity of subjects. It is certainly distinguished by important traits; a cogency of logic which has never been exceeded in any work....[29]

In *The Wealth of Nations*, Smith argued that there were evolutionary, developmental stages in a nation's economy, and that it was not necessarily wise or prudent for a nation to invest its financial resources equally in agriculture, commerce and manufactures. In less developed economies, like the American colonies, where capital reserves were low, investing the financial resources of a nation in agriculture was not only preferable, but offered the greatest return on investment. It was only in more advanced economies like England, where there were sufficient capital reserves for investment in all three branches of the economy, that it made economic sense for a nation to invest its financial resources in agriculture, commerce and manufactures. Like the physiocrats, however, Smith remained sentimentally attached to the agricultural class and the superiority of country life over that of the merchants and traders in the towns.

Similarly, Jefferson expressed his preference for the agricultural class over the merchants and traders until his second presidential term. The growth in manufacturing, he realized, due, in large measure, and unexpectedly from his Non-Intercourse and Embargo Acts, not only contributed to the wealth of the United States, but had become an economic occupation favored by the American people. The language of physiocracy, so apparent in Smith's writings, was supplanted by the language of J.B. Say and Destutt de Tracy, a language that was analytical, not preferential or sentimental.

The Political Economy of Adam Smith

Jefferson's conversion to the economic theories of Adam Smith during his ministry to France had a major impact, not only on his own understanding of economic theory, but ultimately on the economic philosophy and policies of the Republic Party. Jefferson's chief objections to Hamilton's economic programs, and the policies he pursued during his presidency relied, almost exclusively, on his understanding of Smith's arguments and reasoning in *the Wealth of Nations*, an economic analysis championed by the French economists, Desutt de Tracy and J.B. Say. It was also in the salons of Paris that Jefferson was first alerted to the dangers of a national bank, the perpetual funding of debts and bounties or subsidies to manufacturing. The French economists laid the groundwork for, what was to become, Jefferson's theoretical assault on the economic theories and arguments of Hamilton and the Federalists.

Jefferson's knowledge of Smith's economic theories and arguments were put to the test only months after his return from Paris when, on January 9, 1790, Alexander Hamilton introduced his Report on Public Credit to the House of Representatives, the first in a series of three Reports by the Secretary of the Treasury to address the urgent financial and economic needs of the new nation.

Alexander Hamilton's "Report on Public Credit"

Alexander Hamilton's "Report on Public Credit recognized, as did most of America's leaders, that measures were required to solve the growing problem of the nation's public and domestic debt. The Continental Congress and each of the states, independent of one another, issued public securities to pay for the goods and services and salaries of its armies in pursuing the War of Independence against England. The war, lasting much longer and costing far more than originally expected, resulted in a growing and unmanageable public and domestic debt. There was little disagreement among America's elite that the public debt, the debt incurred from loans issued by foreign countries, had to be paid in full, but there was a bitter and rancorous debate over the methods of payment for the domestic debt; it was a debate that was soon to create a political divide among the leaders of the American Revolution.

The issue, as Hamilton well understood, was between the original holders of the public securities, often debts owed to those who fought and risked their lives for America's independence, and the present possessors of those securities. Because of the protracted nature of the war and the financial instability of the states to make good on the securities they issued, a disproportionate number of the original holders of public securities were forced to sell their securities to speculators for a fraction of their original value in order to avoid bankruptcy and starvation. The question before the House, Hamilton said, was

> whether a discrimination ought not to be made between the original holders of the public securities, and present possessors, by purchase. Those who advocate a discrimination are for making a foil provision for the securities of the former, at their nominal value; but contend, that the latter ought to receive no more than the cost to them, and the interest. And the idea is sometimes suggested of making good the difference to the primitive possessor.[30]

Hamilton realized that it may seem unreasonable to expect the first owner of the securities, who by misfortune and necessity, "parted with his property at so great a loss...to contribute to the profit of the person, who had speculated on his distress."[31] Hamilton contended, nevertheless, that any sort of discrimination would be a breach of contract. The government issuing the securities, and not the buyer, was solely responsible for the present inequities. The buyer simply paid the market value "and took the risks of reimbursement upon himself."[32] The risk in this case, he reminds those opposing this measure, was nothing short of a revolution. It would, of course, be difficult to imagine a greater risk or hazard of fortune.

After a careful review, Hamilton argues that the assumption of the debts of each of the individual states by the union is also required. When each state creates distinct provisions for itself, there arise distinct interests and jealousies which will, in turn, play into the hands of foreign countries. Foreign nations, seeking an advantage, will favor one state at the expense of another, weakening the bonds of union. If all public credit is received from one source, on the other hand, all will unite in support of the government and its fiscal arrangement. Foreign and domestic creditors will have more confidence and trust in the government, sensing their investments are more secure. Future government borrowing will be made easier and interest rates, by virtue of this arrangement, will be lower, thereby benefiting the citizens of every state.

Hamilton presented a number of ways the government could honor its debts, including, but not limited to, the sale of western lands to European nations. He also suggested that the debt be maintained as a perpetual debt with interest paid annually to the creditors, thereby alleviating part of the financial obligations of the government. Jefferson and Madison found it unconscionable that Hamilton's measures would underwrite depreciated public securities at face value instead of on a basis of discrimination between the original subscribers to the debt and the speculators in securities while assuring, at the same time, payment of the interest and principal by the federal government.

Although feigning ignorance of the issues at the time, he later wrote in *The Anas*, that when investors knew the Assumption Bill would pass a scramble began.

Couriers and relay horses by land, and swift sailing pilot boats by sea, were flying in all directions. Active partners and agents were associated and employed in every State, town, and country neighborhood, and this paper was bought up a five shillings, and even as low as two shilling in the pound, before the holder knew that Congress had already provided for its redemption at par. Immense sums were thus filched from the poor and ignorant, and fortunes accumulated by those who had themselves been poor enough before. Men thus enriched by the dexterity of a leader, would follow of course the chief who was leading them to fortune, and become the zealous instruments of all his enterprises.[33]

As a student of Adam Smith, Jefferson realized that nations tend to borrow without making the necessary provisions for repayment of the debt. The state, as Smith knew, becomes like "an improvident spendthrift, whose pressing occasions will not allow him to wait for the regular payment of his revenue, the state is in constant practice of borrowing of its own factors and agents, and of paying interest for the use of its own money."[34] When the state fails to anticipate repayment of the loan, however,

it will be forced to borrow and the greater part of the taxes which before had been anticipated only for a short term of years... [are] rendered perpetual as a fund for paying, not the capital, but the interest only, of the money which has been borrowed upon them by different successive anticipation... such improvident anticipation necessarily gave birth to a more ruinous practice of perpetual funding.[35]

Of course, what a public administrator can accomplish in this manner, Smith tells us, is to relieve "the present exigency" rather than the "future liberation of the public revenue [which] they leave to the care of posterity.[36]

The system of perpetual funding, furthermore, contributes to the impoverishment of the state. Because land and capital stock are two sources of all revenue both private and public, it follows that the different land taxes will diminish the revenue of the landlord, thereby preventing him from maintaining or improving his land. As the distress of the landlord increases, the agriculture of the country must necessarily decline.

Jefferson was opposed to perpetual funding of debts on both moral and economic grounds. Morally speaking, perpetual funding saddles posterity with the burdens and obligations which should rightfully be paid by the generation which justly or unjustly, profitably or ruinously, contracted them. "The will and the power of man expire with his life," Jefferson wrote, "by nature's law... We may consider each generation as a distinct nation, with a right, by the will of its majority to bind themselves, but none to bind the succeeding generation, more than the inhabitants of another country.[37] A nation that contracts debts must pay them off without recourse to perpetual funding.

The funding of a perpetual debt makes it easier for nations to engage in war. Adam Smith observed that

the ordinary expenses of governments in time of peace, are equal to their ordinary revenue, [but] when war comes, they are both unwilling and unable to increase their revenue in proportion to the increase of their expence. They are unwilling, for fear of offending the people, who by so great Sand so sudden an increase in taxes, would soon be disgusted with the war.[38]

The system of perpetual funding delivers the government from this embarrassment. By means of borrowing they are enabled, with a very moderate increase of taxes, to raise, from year to year, money sufficient for carrying on the war, and by the practice of perpetual funding they are enabled, with the smallest possible increase of taxes, to raise annually the largest possible sum of money.[39]

Similarly, Jefferson wrote, that "We must raise, then, ourselves the money for this war, either by taxes within the year, or by loans; and if by loans, we must repay then ourselves, proscribing forever the English practice of perpetual funding; the ruinous consequences of which...should be a sufficient warning to a considerate nation to avoid."[40]

Economically, a public debt is a tax on productive labor. "To preserve our independence we must not let our rulers load us with the perpetual debt. We must make our election between economy and liberty, or profusion and servitude."[41] When he was accused of not wanting to pay the public debt, Jefferson wrote to George Washington saying "no man is more ardently intent to see the public debt soon and sacredly paid off than I am. This exactly marks the difference between Colonel Hamilton's views and mine, that I would wish the debts paid tomorrow; he wishes it never to be paid, but to be a thing wherewith to corrupt and manage the Legislature."[42]

The effect of the Funding System, and of the Assumption, he wrote,

would be temporary. It would be lost with the loss of the individual members whom it had enriched, and some engine of influence more permanent must be contrived while these myrmidons were yet in place to carry it through all opposition. The engine was the Bank of the United States.[43]

Alexander Hamilton's Report on a National Bank

Once the issue of public and private debt was successfully resolved, and the confidence and trust of future investors secured, it became imperative, Hamilton believed, to establish a National Bank for the future growth of the American economy. In his "Report on a National Bank," introduced to the House of Representatives on December 13, 1790, Hamilton argued that a National Bank augments "the active or productive capital of a country."[44] Banks augment the active capital of a country by becoming the basis of the circulation of a paper currency, bank notes, which "as the signs or representations of value they then acquire life... an active and productive quality."[45] When money is deposited in a bank, money which otherwise would be kept out of circulation, yields a profit to the depositor. The money deposited may be withdrawn at any time by the depositor but, in the interval, when the depositor is drawing only interest from his deposit and not the whole of the principal, the money he deposited in the bank is circulating throughout the economy in the form of loans.

A second advantage to the bank, Hamilton said, is the "Greater facility to the Government in obtaining pecuniary aids, especially in sudden emergencies."[46] A mass of capital, composed of many individual investors, located in one place, "magnified by the credit attached to it," and "placed under one direction," allows the government to act quickly and expeditiously in the advent of an emergency, as in the more dramatic instance of war or revolution.[47]

Lastly, banks facilitate the payment of taxes. Bank notes, serving as substitutes for gold and silver, are easier to transfer from distant locations, and less cumbersome for payment of taxes than precious metals. It is also evident, he said, "that whatever enhances the quantity of circulating money adds to the ease, with which every industrious member of the community may acquire that portion of it, of which he stands in need; and enables him the better to pay his taxes, as well as to supply his other wants."48

Hamilton recognized that the chief objection to his proposal was "that Banks tend to banish gold and silver of the Country." Hamilton argued that the substitution of a paper credit for precious metals is, in its truest application, leveled, not only against banks, but against "all species of paper credit." The wealth of a nation should not be measured by the abundance of its precious metals, Hamilton said, but rather by the quantity of the productions of its labor and industry. One need only consider those nations which have no mines of their own and must, of necessity, derive precious metals from others in exchange for their products and labor. The quantity of metals possessed, consequently, will depend on a favorable or unfavorable balance of trade. It is the general state of a nation's economy, therefore, that determines the increase or decrease in the quantity of gold and silver, and any mechanism which augments the activity of capital of a country, such as a bank, will increase the flow of precious metals to its borders.49

In *The Wealth of Nations*, Adam Smith argued in favor of small banks competing with one another and against the establishment of a national bank. Smith wrote:

The late multiplication of banking companies, instead of diminishing increases the security of the public. It obliges all of them to be more circumspect in their conduct, and by not extending their currency beyond its due proportion to their cash, to guard themselves against... malicious runs...[50]

In general, Smith concluded that competition in the system of banking, as in all companies serving the public, is more advantageous when free of monopolistic practices. A national bank, then, as Jefferson argued, would constitute an unnatural restraint on public credit and saddle the farmer with additional and unnecessary costs, benefiting the few at the expense of the many. A system of small banks, on the other hand, each competing with one another for the highest interest on investment and the lowest interest rates for borrowers, would produce a more equitable banking system which was beneficial for the general public, and not just for the speculators in government securities.

Although it was not Hamilton's intent to build an aristocracy in the United States, Jefferson was convinced, after his experiences in France and England, and his studies with the French economists, that Hamilton favored a financial aristocracy in America, a class of people whose loyalty was won by opening the vaults to the nation's treasury.

The "monied phalanx," "bank-mongers" and "stock-jobbers," as Jefferson commonly referred to them, Hamilton was creating through the good offices of the national bank were determined take the earnings of the most depressed interests of the country and give them to the most flourishing. In short, the agricultural interests of the country would be at the mercy of Hamilton's bank and the phalanx of investors and creditors he had in his pocket. Since agriculture was America's greatest source of wealth, an observation shared by the physiocrats, Smith, Tracy, J.B. Say, the profits of the Bank would be at the expense of agriculture and the agriculturalists.

In his answer to Hamilton's *Report* on December 5, 1790, Jefferson pointed out that the Bank "intended to break down the most ancient and fundamental laws of several States, such as those of Mortmain, the laws of alienage, the rules of descent, the laws of escheat and forfeiture, the laws of monopoly."[51] But, even more important than these fundamental laws of the several states was Jefferson's conviction that the system developed by Hamilton would deluge the states with paper money, chasing away gold and silver. The extensive use of paper money, he believed, resulted in many abuses, abuses, in fact, recognized by Hamilton, whereas the use of specie protected its holders against loss through depreciation.

"Specie," Jefferson wrote, "is the most perfect medium because it will preserve its own level: because having intrinsic and universal value, it can never die in our hands, and it is the surest resource of reliance in time of war..."[52] He indicated that the members of Congress had been gambling in stocks and, consequently, could no longer be depended upon to vote in a disinterested way; for they "feathered their nests with paper." Jefferson, quite obviously, was not convinced by Hamilton's argument that it was the quantity of the active capital of a country and a favorable balance of trade which guaranteed the accumulation of specie. Nor was he as confident as Hamilton that the Bank would manage its affairs sufficiently well to prevent the abuses Hamilton considered only occasional and temporary.

Because Hamilton and his "tribe of stock-jobbers" were to profit through the creation of a national bank, the belief emerged, Jefferson wrote, that

a public debt was a public blessing; that the stock representing it was a creation of active capital for the aliment of commerce, manufactures and agriculture... Here are a set of people," Jefferson wrote, "who have bestowed on us the great blessing of running in our debt about two hundred million dollars, without our knowing who they are, where they are, or what property they have to pay this debt when called on....[53]

There was, in fact, according to Jefferson, no creation of active capital, no additional money employed, nor even a change in the employment of a single dollar. "Capital may be produced by Industry, and accumulated by economy, but jugglers only will propose to create it by legerdemain tricks with paper."[54]

that being of universal value, it will keep itself at a general level, flowing out from where it is too high into parts where it is lower. Whereas, if the medium be of local value only, as paper money, if too little, indeed, gold and silver will flow in to supply the deficiency; but if too much, it accumulates, banishes the gold and silver not locked up in vaults, and hoards, and depreciates itself; that is to say, its proportion to the annual produce of industry being raised, more of it is required to represent any particular article of produce than in the other countries. This is agreed by Adam Smith, the principle advocate for a paper circulation; but advocating it on the sole condition that it be strictly regulated. He admits, nevertheless, that 'the commerce and industry of a country cannot be so secure when suspended on the Daedalian wings of paper money, as on the solid ground of gold and silver; and that in time of war, the insecurity is greatly increased, and great confusion possible where the circulation is for the greater part in paper. But in a country where loans are uncertain, and a specie circulation the only sure resource for them, the preference of that circulation assumes a far different degree of importance.55

Jefferson said the only real advantage

which Smith proposes by substituting paper in the room of gold and silver money is 'to replace an expensive instrument with one much less costly, and sometimes equally convenient;' that is say... 'to allow the gold and silver to be sent abroad and converted into foreign goods,' and to substitute paper as being a cheaper measure.56

banks...seem to have thought [they] could extend their credits to whatever sum might be wanted, without incurring any other expense besides that of a few reams of paper...It was the duty of the banks, [the traders] seemed to think, to lend for as long a time, and to as great an extent, as they might wish to borrow.57

As a student of the physiocrats and Adam Smith, Jefferson found it useful to distinguish between the employment of capital in useful industry rather than "in a species of gambling," by which he was referring to "stock-jobbers" and public creditors. He feared that the establishment of a national bank would have a pernicious effect on agriculture and was, in effect, an immoral and illegal expedient for public financing. He deplored the creation of a large monied interest in an agricultural society and spoke of the prostration of agriculture at the feet of commerce.

It is also historically important to point out that Jefferson also considered the establishment of the National Bank, as he stated it to President Washington, to have no legal basis in the Constitution. Hamilton's "ultimate object" was clear to Jefferson: Hamilton wanted "to prepare the way for a change from the present republican form of government to that of a monarchy, of which the English constitution is to be the model: that this was contemplated by the convention is no secret, because its partisans have made more of it."[58] It was clear to Jefferson, as he later wrote in his Anas, that "Hamilton was not only a monarchist, but for a monarchy bottomed on corruption."[59]

Alexander Hamilton's Report on Manufactures

Hamilton, however, was not finished with the final touches on his economic system. On the fifteenth of January, 1790, Hamilton submitted to the House of Representatives his "Report on the Subject of Manufactures." Hamilton felt it was crucial that a more extensive demand be created at home for the surplus of America's agricultural produce which, he believed, could be accomplished only by the promotion and encouragement of manufacturing in the United States.

Instead of shipping our raw materials to Europe for their factories and then buying finished goods from them, Hamilton reasoned, we could more profitably stimulate industry in America to produce the same manufactured goods for the home market. Commercial restrictions, subsidies and monopolies in manufacturing in foreign countries, however, conspired against the growth of manufacturing in the United States. American manufacturing, to compete fairly and vigorously with foreign manufactures, therefore, required protective tariffs, bounties and tax inducements for the encouragement and promotion of manufacturing. A strong manufacturing capability in the home market, so essential to the financial security and stability of the country, required protection from foreign companies. Americans would certainly be paying higher prices for manufactured goods in the early development of these industries, but, in the long run, manufactured goods in the United States would be cheaper than they were at the present time.

A nation with an extensive domestic market of manufactures is beneficial to an agricultural society by creating a larger demand for its produce. The need for raw materials in manufacturing, the increasing number of workers from abroad and at home, especially women and children of a tender age who were previously unemployable, conspire to foster the growth of the agriculturalist. With a greater demand for the produce from agriculture and greater wealth for the agriculturalist, Hamilton argues, agricultural lands will be improved and more productive.

Hamilton recognized that men are reluctant to make even the simplest of changes, owing to habitual forms of thinking, and are reluctant to consider new and different possibilities. The transition to manufactures, owing to the scarcity of labor and capital, the natural reluctance of investors to engage in new enterprises and the fear of financial losses, required, therefore, the expedient of government patronage. Hamilton believed it was imperative for the government to offer protection in the manufacture of iron, copper, lead, fossil coal, wood, skins, grain, flax and hemp, cotton, wool, silk, glass, gunpowder, and paper.

Jefferson opposed Hamilton's plan for the encouragement of manufacturing in the United States for reasons very similar to those he expressed against Hamilton's reports on public credit and the national bank. The greatest source of America's wealth was agriculture, and any diversion of capital assets from agriculture to manufacturing placed an unnecessary burden on the agricultural class, not only in the form of tax subsidies, but in higher costs for manufactured goods.

Jefferson agreed with Adam Smith that the wealth of the American colonies, as Smith expressed it, was because

their whole capitals have been hitherto been employed in agriculture...Were the American either by combination or by any other sort of violence, to stop the importation of European manufactures, and, by thus giving a monopoly to such of their own countrymen as could manufacture the like goods, divert any considerable part of their capital into this employment, they would retard instead of accelerating the further increase in the value of their annual produce, and would obstruct instead of promoting the progress of their country towards wealth and greatness.[60]

Jefferson's criticism of Hamilton's Report on Manufactures was not limited to the economic consequences of Hamilton's policies; it also had to do with what he perceived were the moral and social dislocations caused by his policies.

Adam Smith, Benjamin Franklin, Adam Ferguson, Lord Kames, and other eighteenth century political economists were fearful, as Franklin expressed it, that "Manufactures are founded in poverty, for it is the multitude of poor without land in the country, and who must work for others at low wages or starve, that enables undertakers to carry on a manufacture."[61]

This was a belief predicated on the common assumption in the eighteenth century "that society was composed of two broad and distinct groups. The property and the respectable classes on the one hand, and the great mass of unpropertied laborers, who were condemned to lives of grinding poverty, on the other."[62] A "man's character was formed to an overwhelming extent by his profession...(and) as the division of labor became more specialized in commercial society, so too did the activities of individual working men and the result, Smith argued, was a frightening dehumanization of the laboring classes."[63] Adam Smith "could never conceive of entrusting this great body of the people with political power since (they) feared that their condition would permit them to be nothing other than the tools of their employers...unable to participate responsibly in the political process...."[64] Personal ownership of property, then, conferred on individuals, unlike the property-less laboring class, an independence that allowed them "to pursue spontaneously the common or public good, rather than the narrow interest of the men-or the government on whom (they) dependent for support."[65]

By 1805 however, Jefferson had a change of heart, placing manufacturing on an equal footing with agriculture as an economic activity essential to the nation's wealth and independence. This change was not so much an abandonment of his earlier economic thinking, as assumed by many historians, but instead a recognition, and acceptance of Adam Smith's evolutionary model of economic growth.

In less developed economies, Smith wrote, like the American colonies in the eighteenth century, where capital reserves were low, investing the financial resources of a nation in agriculture was not only preferable, but offered the greatest return on investment. It was only in more advanced economies like England, where there were sufficient capital reserves for investment in all three branches of the economy, that it made economic sense for a nation to invest its financial resources in agriculture, commerce and manufactures.

Jefferson could agree with Smith, as he did in 1790 after returning from Paris, that manufactures played a vital economic role in the national economy while disagreeing with Hamilton's preference for manufactures in that same year. There were developmental stages in a nation's economy, just as there were, Jefferson believed with the French philosopher, Condorcet, evolutionary stages in cultures and civilization, from the most primitive to the most advanced. The United States, by 1805, was a more advanced economy than it was in 1790, allowing, by Smith's economic calculus, for the transfer of capital reserves from agriculture to manufacturing. There were not two or more economic systems reflecting different periods in his public life, but one theory, Adam Smith's economic theory, a theory Jefferson learned in his studies with J.B. Say and Tracy in Paris.

Jefferson's Protectionism and the Embargo Acts

Jefferson's protectionist policies during his second presidential administration do, in fact, represent a departure from his free trade policy in the years before 1790, but they do not represent a new stage in his economic thought.

Confronted with hostilities from England and France on the high seas, Jefferson believed the embargo acts were necessary to punish England and France for their transgressions against American shipping and commerce. The Embargo Acts were intended, as Jefferson said, to be only temporary expedients, acts of economic coercion to avoid war with England and France.

As minister to France, Secretary of State, and then later as Vice President of the United States, Jefferson sought to use France as a counterbalance to British power. Jefferson regarded England as a genuine threat to America's security, prosperity and independence. France was the only country, Jefferson believed, that "could perform the twofold function of replacing Britain in the economic life of the United States and of protecting America from British military designs."[66]

The failures Jefferson encountered when he was Secretary of State and the "Quasi-War" between the United States and France while he was Vice-President, however, did not deter him from aligning the United States with France when he became President. Even in his second presidential administration, Jefferson continued to believe that trade agreements with France would provide an excellent market for America's goods and an economic weapon against England's commercial hostilities. Nevertheless, the passage of Napoleon's

Continental System forced Jefferson to abandon any hope of stronger ties with France.

During his second Presidential administration, consequently, Jefferson passed the Embargo Act of 1807 and the Non-Intercourse Act to coerce the British and the French governments into recognizing the commercial rights of the United States. These "retaliatory policies," quite surprisingly, Jefferson wrote to Dupont De Nemours on June 28, 1809, were instrumental in furnishing assistance to American manufacturing. "The interruption of our commerce with England, produced by our embargo and non-intercourse law," Jefferson reasoned,

have generated in this country an universal spirit for manufacturing for ourselves, and of reducing to a minimum the number of articles for which we are dependent on her... The spirit of manufacture has taken deep root among us, and its foundation[s] are laid in too great expence to be abandoned.[67]

Jefferson was not completely aware of

the extent and perfection of the works produced here by the late state of things...in the cities I can add my own as to the country, where the principal articles wanted in every family are now fabricated within itself. This mass of household manufacture, unseen by the public eye, and so much greater than what is seen, is such at present, that let our intercourse with England be opened when it may, not one half the amount of what we have heretofore taken from her will ever again be demanded.[68]

There has been, he notes, "Great progress among us" in the art of printing. "Henceforth we imported our books, and with them much political principle from England. We now print a great deal, and shall soon supply ourselves with most of the books of considerable demand."[69]

Jefferson now believed, as he expressed it to Governor James Jay on April 7, 1809

An equilibrium of agriculture, manufactures, and commerce, is certainly become essential to our independence. Manufactures, sufficient for our own consumption, of what we raise the raw materials of agriculture, beyond our consumption, to a market for exchanging it for articles we cannot raise... These are the true limits of manufactures and commerce. To go beyond them is to increase our dependence on foreign nations, and our liability to war.[70]

Jefferson recognized, with Adam Smith, that manufactures and commerce were on a more equal footing with agriculture. The United States would remain largely an agrarian republic, but, as an unintended consequence of the embargo and non-importation laws, the national economy evolved more rapidly toward a manufacturing economy with "the capital sufficient both to improve [and] cultivate its lands to transport the surplus part either of the rude or manufactured produce to those distant markets where it can be exchanged for something for which there is a demand at home."[71]

Jefferson also recognized, as importantly, that home-spun manufacturing in the United States contributed to the political sovereignty of the nation. The embargo and non-importation laws may have failed to bring the powers of Europe" to a sense of justice...Yet they have had the important effects of saving our seaman and property, of giving time to prepare for defense..."[72] Homespun manufactures has the advantage, too, he wrote, "of lessening the occasions of risking our peace on the ocean, and of planting the consumer in our own soil by the side of the grower of produce...."[73] Jefferson now considered it a patriotic duty "of every good citizen to use no foreign article which can be made within ourselves, without regard to difference of price...."[74]

"The Republican Revolution in political economy," McCoy believes, "was based on the assumption that America would remain at a middle stage of development' between an agricultural and a commercial society. "Their republic was thus to be more advanced, commercialized society than many of the primitive, even barbarous, republics of the past, but it was to stop short of a perilous descent into Mandevillian decadence... Above all, this republican America was to be characterized by an unprecedented degree of social equality, whereby even the poorest man would at least be secure, economically competent, and independent."[75] The United States "would not have the permanent classes of privileged rich and dependent poor that Americans associated with the 'old world' societies of mercantilist Europe...The evils of densely populated society...particularly an economy based on manufacturing for export, could be forestalled in America as long as its citizens were able to expand across space rather than through time."[76]

Jefferson now abandoned the teachings of the physiocrats, especially, the notion that manufactures add nothing to the wealth of a nation, and accepted without reservation Adam Smith's economic analysis that placed agriculture and manufactures on an equal footing.

Jefferson did not reject free trade and free markets in favor of protectionism and mercantilism, as he accused Hamilton of doing, but considered his free trade policies impractical in the face of England's and France's hostilities toward the United States. Barred from trade and commerce by warring nations, the United States would return to its free trade practices when peace was restored.

The Economics of J.B. Say and Destutt de Tracy

After his departure from public office, Jefferson continued to express his views about perpetual funding and the banking system in the United States to two men who likely introduced him to the writings of Adam Smith when he was minister to France. He recalled, in a letter to Destutt de Tracy on July 12, 1803, the "sanguine" days he spent with Tracy "at the house of our late excellent friend, Mme. Helvetius and how soon the virtuous hopes and confidence of every good man [were] blasted."[77] The correspondence between Tracy and J.B. Say reveals Jefferson's mature reflections on economic theory and policy, and the ideas he continued to favor in his retirement.

The economist who received Jefferson's greatest praise was Destutt de Tracy. De Tracy had already made a conspicuous contribution to Jefferson's philosophy of science and now appears to have been influential on Jefferson's economic thought as well. The admiration which Jefferson held for de Tracy led him to translate and edit two of his books. *A Commentary and Review of Montesquieu's Spirit of the Laws and A Treatise on Political Economy.* In the preface of de Tracy's *Treatise* Jefferson said:

It goes forth therefore with my hearty prayers that while the Review of Montesquieu, by the same author, is made with us the elementary book of instruction in the principles of civil government, so the present work may be in the particular branch of Political Economy.[78]

Tracy's work has "all the advantages," Jefferson wrote, "of further experience, more discussion and greater maturity of subject. It is certainly distinguished by important traits; a cogency of logic which has never been exceeded in any work...not a word can be changed but for the worse...."[79]

In economic writings of Say and Tracy we learn once again about the economic advantages of free trade and free markets, the contribution of manufactures and commerce, and not just agriculture, to the wealth of a nation, the hidden costs to consumers of bounties, or privileges, to a particular class of merchants on a certain branch of trade, and the dangers inherent in the establishment of a national bank and the perpetual funding of a nation's debts. Both agree that speculators in public debt are "natural enemies to the true interests of society," and that banks do not have the right "to burden men not yet in existence, and to compel them to pay in future times their present expenses."[80] There is nothing more "grievous," Tracy argues, than the "effects of loans on the social organization, of the enormous power they give to the governors of the facility. They afford them of doing whatsoever they please, of drawing everything to themselves, of enriching their creatures, of dispensing with the assembling and consulting the citizens; which operates rapidly the overthrow of every constitution."[81]

The system of perpetual funding was more than just an economic concern for Smith, Say, Tracy and Jefferson; it was a political one as well. Investors in these funds, they believed, exercised an inordinate influence over the political decision making of executives and legislators in every government. Profiting from the indebtedness of a nation, amassing great fortunes from the interest paid to them from their loans to the government, and working through a national bank, investors in public securities were able to persuade and corrupt, by financially supporting political candidates at every level of government, to borrow ever increasing sums of money. As governments borrowed more and more, in times of peace and war, investors' stranglehold over the government and its people was strengthened while the national economy was weakened. The profits of investors in public securities were a hidden tax on the people and on generations yet unborn.

Say's and Tracy's *Treatises*, however, added little to Jefferson's understanding of economic theory; they simply stated more succinctly and clearly the arguments Jefferson was now fond of using against those who favored Hamilton's programs and ideas. Jefferson's overriding interest, his not so hidden agenda, in publishing Tracy's *Treatise* was stated clearly in the Preface to Tracy's *Treatise on Political Economy*. "By diffusing sound principles of Political Economy, it will protect the public industry from the parasite institutions now consuming it, and lead us to that just and regular distribution of the public burthens from which we have sometimes strayed."[82]

Jefferson's preference for a policy of free trade and laissez-faire economics remained an essential part of his economic outlook and was only interrupted by the hostilities of other nations. His protectionism, therefore, was only a practical calculation to coerce England and France to recognize America's commercial rights, and not indicative of any significant changes in Jefferson's economic thought.

Although Jefferson's adoption of the teachings of Smith, Say and de Tracy during his ministry to France represents an intellectual transformation in his thinking, it did not signify a paradigmatic shift in his reasoning about the science of economics. It was instead a transformative synthesis of the doctrines of physiocracy with the economic theories of Smith, Say and Tracy.

Adam Smith, as we have seen, shared the physiocrats' preference for agriculture, the labor theory of value, and their arguments in favor of free markets and free trade. He recognized, as the physiocrats did not, however, that manufactures and commerce were also sources of a nation's wealth. As importantly for Jefferson, Smith underscored the dangers of a national banking system and the perpetual funding of debts in any society, republican or monarchist.

If not for his studies with the French economists in Paris, it is difficult to know what Jefferson's response to Hamilton's economic policies would have been. He would have certainly opposed Hamilton's program of bounties for manufacturing, based on his understanding of physiocratic doctrine, but it is not clear if he would have had a cogent analysis, or even recognized the threat posed by Hamilton's system of public credit and banking in a democratic republic, two features of Smith's and the French economists analysis that was the basis for Jefferson's economic thought and policies in his years of political opposition and during his presidential administrations. Jefferson's economic vision for the new republic was shaped and molded in revolutionary France.

Jefferson's adoption of the teachings of Smith, Say and Tracy also puts to rest the charges by many historians that Jefferson's economic thinking was reactionary, a "flight from history," a "dread of modernity," a pastoral vision of some distant past. Jefferson conversed with, and studied with, the leading economists of the eighteenth century. His critique of Hamilton's economic programs was based on the economic reasoning of the leading thinkers of his day. If Jefferson's economic thinking was reactionary, traditional and unrealistic, then the founders of classical economic theory, Smith and Say must also be reactionaries and traditionalists rather than, as they are generally regarded, the founders of the science of economics.

The battle between Jefferson and Hamilton, was not "a conflict between the patrons of agrarian self-sufficiency and the proponents of modern commerce," Joyce Appleby noted, "but rather as a struggle between two different elaborations of capitalistic development in America."[83] Hamilton and the Federalists were committed to a mercantilist theory of economic growth, growth through foreign trade with England, supervised and administered by a financial elite, whereas Jefferson and the Republicans were committed "to growth through the unimpeded exertions of individuals whose access to economic opportunity was both protected and facilitated by government."[84] Jefferson's vision "was democratic and capitalistic, agrarian and commercial."[85] Jefferson was "not the heroic loser in a battle against modernity, but the conspicuous winner in a contest over how the government should serve its citizens in the first generation of the nation's territorial expansion."[86]

Jefferson's View of Political Economy

Jefferson accepted Smith's, Tracy's and Say's analysis of economic growth and development in free markets. He embraced Smith's labor theory of value, understood the benefits of the division of labor in society, and recognized the contribution household manufacturing made, not only to the wealth of the United States, but to its political sovereignty. He also understood that there are natural differences between individuals, some individuals are more frugal, industrious and energetic while others are more slothful, improvident and wasteful. There would inevitably be, consequently, a degree of social and economic inequality in society. The profits from the labors of the more industrious will be greater than those who were less provident.

He did not share the socialist utopian views of Charles Owen, who visited him at Monticello in 1825, that there should be complete equality and community of goods, although he wrote approvingly to William Ludlow, an Owenite, of his "experiment in creating a socialist commune. "A society of seventy families," he said, "may very possibly be governed as a single family, subsisting on their common industry, and holding all things in common..." but he was somewhat doubtful "at what period of your increasing population your simple regulations will cease to be sufficient to preserve order, peace, and justice."[87] "The advance of civilization" from "the earliest stage of association living under no law but that of nature...[to the] most improved state in our seaport towns," suggested to him that we can only step back so far.[88]

Jefferson understood there would likely be class differences in the United States, but he did not believe the differences between the classes would be nearly as great as they were in Europe. He believed that the abundance of uncultivated and fertile lands and a shortage of labor in the United States guaranteed a future with only modest class differences and social inequalities. Even workers in manufacturing sector of the economy, because of the high wages afforded them in the United States, would eventually have sufficient capital to buy their own farms.

The independence and freedom afforded the agriculturalist, he believed, was in sharp contrast to the dependency and venality of the industrial workers in Europe. He disagreed with Thomas Malthus' dire predictions in his Essay on the Principle of Population that the projected rate of growth in the population will eventually outstrip any nation's ability to feed its own people. Starvation is inevitable as the growth in population exceeds the rate of increase in the food supply.

In Europe, Jefferson wrote to J.B. Say, after acknowledging the "sound logic" of Malthus' theory, the quantity of food is fixed, or increasing in a slow and only arithmetical ratio, and the proportion is limited by the same ratio. Supernumerary births consequently add only to your mortality. Here the immense extent of uncultivated and fertile lands enables everyone who will labor to marry young, and to raise a family of any size. Our food, then, may increase geometrically with our laborers, and our births, however multiplied, become effective.[89]

The American worker was also shielded from David Ricardo's prediction that competition among laborers for employment will drive wages down to a minimal level. Ricardo's theory of the iron law of wages follows Malthus' population theory, according to which population increases when wages are above the 'subsistence wage' and falls when wage are below subsistence. Industrial workers, according to this theory, could never hope to earn or save enough money to free themselves from a subsistence level of existence. The American worker was spared this dependency, servility and degradation, Jefferson believed, because the wages of American workers, contrary to Ricardo's prediction, were rising, and not falling because the demand for their labor remained so high. Jefferson wanted to avoid at all costs the industrialization of the United States.

Jefferson was favorably disposed to manufacturing in his second presidential term, but he still thought of it in terms of household manufacturing, and not large-scale, industrial manufacturing as he experienced it in London. "We are going greatly into manufactures," he wrote to Dupont de Nemour in 1811, "but the mass of them are household manufactures of the coarse articles worn by the laborers and farmers of the family. These I verily believe we shall succeed in making to the whole extent of our necessities."90 By 1812, Jefferson believed

Our manufactures are now very nearly on a footing with those of England. She has not a single improvement which we do not possess, and many of them better adapted by ourselves to our ordinary use. We have reduced the large and expensive machinery for most things to the compass of a private family, and every family of any size is now getting machines on a small scale for their household purposes.91

Jefferson was proud to say that he had once "depended entirely on foreign manufactures; but I have now thirty-five spindles agoing, a hand carding machine, and looms with the flying shuttle, for the supply of my own farms...."92

Capitalist development in the United States was moving at a different pace and in a different direction than it did in Europe. Europe was closing in on itself, requiring major capital investments in equipment and machinery and armies of industrial workers to labor in their factories while the United States was spreading westward, requiring only minimal investments in machinery. American workers were able, after a few years of work, Jefferson said, to purchase the land and equipment necessary to become proprietors, masters of their own destiny rather than cogs in the wheels of industry.

The labor of the agricultural worker was also more ennobling and diversified than the overly specialized and monotonous labor of the industrial worker. A farmer had to master the skills of the carpenter, gardener, shoemaker, blacksmith and shepherd. It is clear, although he did not say it as such, that the dehumanization of the worker and, as importantly, the degradation of labor itself in the factories of Europe alienated man from himself, nature and society.

Capitalist development in Europe also required large banking institutions to finance capital investments in equipment and factories, and for the salaries of an army of industrial workers needed for large-scale manufacturing. In the United States proprietors required only modest loans from state banks for household manufactures. The United States, consequently, did not need a National Bank.

Agriculture, household manufacturing and commerce, Jefferson recognized, were productive of wealth, and the profits generated through these enterprises fueled economic growth in the United States. Jefferson did not believe, however, that traders in public securities, or "stock-jobbers", as he called them, with their "legerdemain tricks with paper" contributed to the wealth of the nation. They created no real value, and no real profits from their ruinous practices. They were, instead, parasites living off the earnings of the agriculturalist and manufacturer. Finance capitalism, consequently, had a very limited role to play in Jefferson's economic theory as compared to the economic theory of Alexander Hamilton.

Jefferson was aware that, when compared with laborers in England and France, American laborers, mainly agriculturalists, were most fortunate to have "an immensity of land courting the industry of the husbandman. Cheap land and high wages allowed laborers, in a relatively short period of time, to accumulate sufficient capital to buy their own land. He also knew that Americans had much more equal incomes than did West Europeans at that time. The American colonists, Thomas Piketty estimated, "had a higher income than his or her English of the same rank... Even American slaves were above the bottom of the Anglo-American income ladder."[93] In the United States" total wealth amounted to barely three years of national income...(as) compared with more than seven in Europe, "signifying, "in a very concrete way that the influence of landlords, and accumulated wealth was less important in the New World."[94] In 1774 the top 1% income share of American households was 7.6% and the top 10% had 30.8. In Britain the top 10% of household incomes was estimated at 49% and, in Western Europe the share of income to the top 1 percent was 17.5. In France, it is estimated that the top 10% had approximately 51-53% of the nation's wealth. The United States, in the late eighteenth and early nineteenth century, was the most egalitarian country in the world, and Jefferson was determined to keep it that way.[95]

Jefferson did not know, nor did Smith, Tracy and J.B. Say, the fundamental laws of inequality, but they did understand that inherited wealth, and the class possessing it, have a powerful and destabilizing effect on the structure and dynamics of social equality. They did not know that "the rate of return on capital was always at least 10 to 20 times greater than the rate of growth of output and income," and that when "the of return on capital (profits, dividends, interest, rents, and other income from capital) significantly exceeds the growth of the economy, then it logically follows that inherited wealth grows faster than output and income."[96] "Under such conditions, Piketty reasons, "it is almost inevitable that inherited wealth will dominate wealth amassed from a lifetime's labor by a wide margin, and the concentration of capital will attain extremely high levels—levels potentially incompatible with the meritocratic values and the principles of social justice fundamental to modern democratic societies."[97]

Jefferson was not knowledgeable of this law, but from his studies and observations of the labor markets, class stratification, and financial programs and economic policies in England and France, he did understand that wealth concentrated in the hands of the few, the class of individuals in the United States investing in Hamilton's financial schemes, receiving interest payments from the perpetual funding of debts, posed a clear and present danger to the economic equality he deemed necessary and essential in a democratic republic. He knew "the rate at which interest accumulated...might equal or exceed principal."[98] And he was worried, Sloan recognizes, "that debt may overwhelm the new Republic, just as it has already overwhelmed so much of Europe., that 'contagious and ruinous errors of this quarter of the globe' will find a second home in the New World."[99]

Jefferson's fear of debt was rooted in his under-standing, one he shared with Tracy and Say, that the perpetual funding of debts and the establishment of a national bank would create a class of individuals who, not only contributed little or nothing to the wealth of the nation, but who, because of their wealth and influence peddling (which he observed first in England in the 1770's, and later in France) would be in a position to undermine the egalitarian foundations of the American Republic. Jefferson associated debt, inherited debt, with the hierarchical class structure of European monarchies, the malfeasance of its aristocratic councilors, and its ruinous economic and financial policies and practices that bankrupted the French monarchy and drove the English monarchy to endless wars of conquest.

The dangers of a public debt were so great, he believed, that only its complete eradication, codified in law, a law of nature he articulated in his doctrine The Earth Belongs In Usufruct to the Living, and not the Dead, would prevent the Machiavellian machinations and rapacious appetites of a sterile class of investors, whose interests were decidedly against the values and virtues required of citizens living in a democratic republic. He did not agree with Adams and Hamilton, that only men of property, the wealthiest families, ought to have a seat, because of their wealth and class alone, in the Senate of the United States. He did not share Adams' belief "that the people, unrestrained, were 'as unjust, tyrannical, brutal, barbarous, and cruel as any king or senate possessed of uncontrollable power.'"[100] Jefferson believed "the people themselves could never be oppressive; only their elected agents were capable of tyranny."[101] Debt, he believed, was a major contributing cause of social and economic inequality in every society and, debt and inequality were for Jefferson synonymous with the hierarchical class structures of monarchies. Jefferson's liberal and egalitarian economic philosophy was one of the pillars of his republicanism.

CHAPTER 5

THE CONSTITUTIONAL THOUGHT OF JEFFERSON

The problem of inherited debt and the classes and social inequalities arising from it, plagued every society in Europe and Jefferson was determined to prevent it from taking root in the United States. Radical measure were required to ensure that future leaders were not able to return to the corrupt practice of the perpetual funding of debts.

In the third application of Jefferson's doctrine The Earth Belongs In Usufruct to the Living, and not the Dead, he claims that a society has no right to bind future generations to a perpetual constitution. "Every constitution and every law, naturally expires at the end of 19 years. If it be enforced longer it is an act of force, and not of right." Jefferson was even opposed to admitting the alternative procedure of repeal rather than expressly specifying the natural limits of expiration.

Before his departure to France, Jefferson's constitutional thought was largely contained in his writing in his *Notes on the State of Virginia* and draft Constitution for the state of Virginia. His thinking did not appear to be very different from the constitutional thought of Hamilton, Madison and Adams or other revolutionary leaders of his generation. Like Jefferson, they were educated in the political philosophy of Locke and Sydney, Puffendorf and Burlamaqui, Rousseau, Shaftesbury and Lord Bolingbroke, Voltaire and Montesquieu, many of the Scottish moral sense philosophers from Thomas Reid to Dugald Stewart, historians such as Gibbons, Robertson and Hume, and the legal scholars, Blackstone and Coke, whom they studied in law school. Jefferson's constitutional argument in the earth belongs to the living, however, demonstrates his radical departure from the constitutionalism of Montesquieu and Sir Edward Coke and the constitutional reasoning of Madison, Hamilton and Adams.

Like so many philosophers in the eighteenth century, Jefferson was influenced by the writings of Baron de Montesquieu. Jefferson was so impressed with Montesquieu's *Spirit of Laws* that he copied twenty-seven articles from it in his *Commonplace Book*, more than any other writer. Jefferson agreed with the Scottish philosopher, Adam Ferguson, widely read among the Founding Fathers, who regarded Montesquieu as the most profound writer on the nature and forms of government in the eighteenth century. Montesquieu, he also believed, although not a moral sense philosopher, was one of the first to understand that man is made for society.[1] Montesquieu's *Spirit of Laws* was for Jefferson, as it was for the political philosophers in the eighteenth century, a "political bible."[2]

In his studies of political philosophers in England, Scotland and France, Jefferson was interested in the reasoning of many of them, persuaded by the logic of some of them, and impressed and influenced by just a few of them. Among the few writers who profoundly influenced Jefferson's political philosophy was the Baron de Montesquieu. Montesquieu educated a generation of political philosophers in Scotland, England, France and the American colonies on the relationships between varying forms of government, and the social organization and laws conformable to each of them.

In Book One of *The Spirit of the Laws*, Montesquieu describes laws to be: "in their most general signification, are the necessary relations arising from the nature of things."[3] All beings have laws particular to their nature: "the Deity his laws, the material world its laws, the intelligences superior to man their laws, the beasts their laws, man his laws."[4] The laws of nature are fixed and invariable according to the "relations of the quantity of matter and velocity." However, the laws governing man's behavior in society "are far from being so well governed as the physical."[5] This is because: First, man is by nature finite, and liable to error. Second, man's nature requires him to be free and consequently, man does not always conform to his own nature or even those of his own constituting.[6]

The laws of civil society must consider man's weakness and timidity. Although the laws are a reflection of man's reason, they are not fixed and invariable like the laws of nature. The laws of civil society must be conformable to that which

best agrees with the humor and disposition of the people in whose favor it is established...They should be in relation to the nature and principle of each government...they should be in relation to the climate, of each country, to the quality of its soil, to its situation and extent, to the principal occupation of the natives, whether husbandmen, huntsmen, or shepherds; they should have a relation to the degree of liberty which a constitution will bear; to the religion of the inhabitants, to their inclinations, riches, numbers, commerce, manners and customs. In fine, they have relations to each other, as also to their origin, to the intent of the legislator, and to the order of things on which they are established.7

According to Montesquieu, each type of government has both a principle and a nature by which it functions. The nature of government is determined by its particular structure, and by the number of people possessing sovereign power. In a republican government, the people have possession of sovereign power. In a monarchy, only a single person governs by fixed and established laws. Despotic governments are governed by a single person who "directs everything by his own will and caprice."8

There are, Montesquieu claims, four fundamental laws in republican governments. In a republican government "there can be no exercise of sovereignty but by their suffrages, which are their own will." Thus, the first law of a republican government declares republics must, "fix the number of citizens who are to form the public assemblies." The people, with whom supreme power resides, must also be able to nominate ministers to help them manage the affairs of state.

A second fundamental maxim in republican governments is, "the people should choose their ministers, that is their magistrates."9 The people in democratic states, Montesquieu said, "are extremely well qualified for choosing those whom they are to intrust with part of their authority."10

A third fundamental maxim "determines the manner of giving suffrage"; whether suffrage ought to be secret or public. Montesquieu observes that by rendering suffrage secret in the Roman republic, "all was lost." In a republic "the people's suffrage ought doubtless to be public...."[11] The fundamental law in democracies is, "the people should have the sole power to enact laws."[12] The legislature, the representative body of the people, may enact laws, but the people must retain the right to ratify them.

The principle of government is determined by "the human passions which set it in motion." A republican government depends upon the love of virtue and equality, whereas a monarchy depends upon the principle of honor and inequality. The principle which animates a republic and monarchy expresses the passions and sentiments of its people.

The virtue of a republic, according to Montesquieu, was not a moral virtue but a political virtue; one which inspired its citizens to make sacrifices for the welfare of the entire community.

The love of equality in a democracy is likewise that of frugality. Since every individual ought here to enjoy the same happiness and the same advantages, they should consequently taste the same pleasures and form the same hopes, which cannot be expected but from a general frugality...The love of equality in a democracy limits ambition to the sole desire, to the sole happiness, of doing greater services to our country than the rest of our fellow citizens.[13]

Since the love of equality was essential to the preservation of a republican form of government,

Montesquieu believed that the ownership of property, a civil and not a natural right, should be regulated, and property even redistributed, if necessary, for the general welfare of society. Jefferson, as we have seen, wholeheartedly agreed with Montesquieu. He believed, as did Montesquieu, that equality was one of the principles of a republic.

Jefferson's love of equality was also reflected in his draft of the Constitution for Virginia, written in June 1776. In the section on "Rights Private and Public," Jefferson proposed: "Every person of full age neither owning nor having owned fifty acres of land shall be entitled to an appropriation of fifty acres...and no other person shall be capable of taking an appropriation...."[14] When we consider that Jefferson proposed, in the same document, that the only property qualification for voting be "one fourth of an acre of land in any town or...25 acres of land in the country," it is obvious that he favored universal white manhood suffrage.[15]

Jefferson was so impressed with Montesquieu he copied twenty-seven articles from Montesquieu's *Spirit of the Laws* in his *Commonplace Book*, more than any other writer. Jefferson, however, did not agree with all of Montesquieu's ideas, taking particular exception to what he believed was Montesquieu's love of the English constitution, and his notion that republics can exist only in small territories. He had "deemed Montesquieu's work of much merit," he wrote to Destutt de Tracy in 1811, but saw in it... so much false principles and misplaced fact as to render its value equivocal on the whole."[16]

Jefferson originally ordered the *Oeuvres de Montesquieu*

in 1769, and called attention to its weaknesses in 1790, during his ministry to France. In France, Jefferson became acquainted with many French philosophes, in particular Destutt de Tracy, Condorcet and Du Pont de Nemours. These men studied Montesquieu's *Spirit of the Laws*, and were critical of Montesquieu's praise of the English Constitution and his understanding that republics can exist only in small territories.

Like de Tracy, Jefferson thought Montesquieu's admiration for the English Constitution, and his belief that a republic must be small to succeed, was inaccurate and dangerous. If Jefferson read *The Spirit of the Laws* more carefully, however, he may have had a more favorable view of Montesquieu's reasoning. Montesquieu did believe a republic could succeed in a large territory if it was founded on a confederation of independent and republican states, and not by conquest. Montesquieu believed a confederate republic has

all the advantages of a republican, together with the external force of a monarchical government... This form of government is a convention by which several petty states agree to become members of a larger one...it is a kind of assemblage of societies, that constitute a new one, capable of increasing by means of further associations, till they arrive at such a degree of power as to be able to provide for the security of the whole body.[17]

Montesquieu's argument for a Confederate Republic was recognized and analyzed by Alexander Hamilton in the *Federalist Papers* No. 9. In this article, Hamilton cited Montesquieu's idea that a Confederate Republic extended "the sphere of popular government" while reconciling the advantages of monarchy with those of republicanism. It is very probable that mankind would be obliged at length to live constantly under the government of a single person, had they not contrived a kind of constitution that has all the internal advantages of a republican...together with the external force of a monarchical, government.18

Hamilton quoted Montesquieu's *Spirit of the Laws* at some length to "remove the false impressions which a misapplication of other parts of the work was calculated to make."19 Jefferson seems to have ignored this defense of Montesquieu when he read the *Federalist Papers*, just as he had neglected Montesquieu's statements regarding the nature and extent of a republican form of government. He instinctively revolted against any mention of the geographic morphology of a republic, and recalled only Montesquieu's assertion: "If a republic be small, it is destroyed by a foreign force; if it be large, it is ruined by an internal imperfection."20 Consequently, Jefferson considered Montesquieu an enemy of republican ideology. As a result, this judgment has misled historians to falsely assume that Montesquieu had little influence upon Jefferson.

Jefferson's instinctive revulsion and criticism of Montesquieu was based largely on Montesquieu's Anglomania; it was not based on other political and sociological truths he found in *The Spirit of the Laws*. Montesquieu's analysis of the influence of different physical or material causes—climate, manners and customs, laws and institutions of a nation—was readily assimilated and applied by Jefferson on innumerable occasions. In the recorded studies of Jefferson's writings and ideas, Montesquieu was the only author who stressed the influence of climate on government and laws. "It is our cloudless sky," Jefferson wrote to Volney in 1805, "which has eradicated from, our Constitution all dispositions to hang ourselves, which we might otherwise have inherited from our English ancestors...."[21] Jefferson was doubtlessly exaggerating the effect of the climate on the habits, manners and liberties of the American people, but this statement does suggest the weight of Montesquieu's influence on him.

Jefferson adopted from Montesquieu a relativist perspective of other nations and their laws. In a letter to Du Pont de Nemours in 1801, Jefferson expressed the opinion that what is good for the United States may be harmful for other nations. Even within the United States, Jefferson did not believe it was wise to enforce all the provisions of the Constitution. "The same original principles," he wrote, "modified in practice to the different habits of different nations, present governments of very different aspects."[22]

Separation of Powers

Uncertain of the success of America's experiment in a republic form of government, Jefferson was determined to find the principles and measures necessary to safeguard America's newly won freedoms. Montesquieu's analysis in *The Spirit of the Laws* again supported Jefferson's objectives and purposes. In *The Spirit of the Laws*, Montesquieu referred to the English Constitution as one in which "the safety of the whole depends on the balance of its parts." This contrasted with Locke's idea that the judiciary was a branch of executive power;

power was divided only between the legislative and executive branches of government.

Montesquieu stressed the separation of the powers of government into three branches: the legislative, executive and judiciary. Montesquieu wrote that if any of the three were joined, the life and liberty of the subject would be exposed to arbitrary control, violence and oppression.

There would be an end of everything, were the same man or the same body, whether of the nobles or of the people, to exercise those three powers, that of enacting laws, that of executing the public resolutions, and of trying the causes of individuals.[23]

In Jefferson's *Notes on the State of Virginia*, written before his ministry to France, Jefferson exposed three basic defects in Virginia's constitution, each of them restatements of Montesquieu's thoughts on representation, the separation of powers and the division of members in each house of Congress.

A major defect of the state constitution was the lack of separation of the three branches of government. The concentration of these powers in the same hands, Jefferson wrote, "is precisely the definition of despotic government."[24] Americans did not fight for an "elective despotism" but for one "in which the powers of government should be so divided and balanced among several bodies of magistracy, as that no one could transcend their legal limits, without being effectually checked and restrained by the others."[25] In his own draft of the Constitution for Virginia in 1776, Jefferson insisted, "The Legislative, Executive, and Judiciary offices shall be kept forever separate and no person exercising the one shall be capable of appointment to either of them."[26] His reference to "elective despotism" demonstrates not only his understanding of Montesquieu's *Spirit of the Laws*, but his use of Montesquieu's language and concepts. Democracy, monarchy and despotism were the three forms of government Montesquieu outlines in *The Spirit of the Laws*.

Jefferson first considered life appointments for senators, David Mayer notes, but "he finally decided on election of the senators by the popular body for staggered terms of nine years, with one-third removed every three years and incapable of reelection."[27] Jefferson also rejected the practice adopted by many of the other states; "of composing the upper house of men of distinguished property."[28] He always believed in the aristocracy of talent; the wisest, and not the wealthiest of men, should lead the nation. There was no correlation between wealth and integrity, or riches and character. "To insure that truly wise men would be chosen, he would have the senators chosen by the lower house...the House of Representatives...."[29]

David Mayer and Merrill Peterson insist that Jefferson was influenced by his study of English constitutional history and law, and more precisely, the legal principles and precedents of Sir Edward Coke's *Institutes*, which he studied in law school at William and Mary College under George Wythe. Mayer and Peterson, however, do not take into account Jefferson's interest in Montesquieu's *Spirit of the Laws*. Jefferson cited Montesquieu in his *Commonplace Book*, referred to him in his correspondence and translated and edited Destutt de Tracy's critical analysis of it in his Commentary and Review of Montesquieu's *Spirit of Laws*.

Before the American Revolution, Benjamin Wright notes, there was a marked separation between executive and legislative bodies in eleven of the thirteen colonies, and a growing demand for a separate judiciary.[30] Lord Bolingbroke and Algernon Sidney also wrote of the separation of powers; one of three defects of the Constitution which Jefferson considered. He was familiar with Lord Bolingbroke, and quoted him at length in his Literary *Commonplace Book*. However, it can be determined from Jefferson's writing, his interest in Bolingbroke did not rest in constitutional law. He focused on Bolingbroke's critical remarks on religion and the separation of church and state. And Jefferson does not refer to Sidney on the separation of powers.

Bolingbroke, who may have been an influence on Montesquieu, wrote, "the safety of the whole depends on the balance of its parts." The English philosophers expressed only a very general idea of the separation of powers, but none of them examined it with the breadth and clarity of Montesquieu. Jefferson may not have specifically referred to Montesquieu's separation of powers in his *Commonplace Book*, but he certainly seemed familiar with it when he wrote his draft of the Virginia state constitution.

A second defect in the state constitution was the inequality of representation of the citizens of different counties. In his Notes on State of Virginia, Jefferson cited the county of Warwick, with a population of merely one hundred fighting men. Even so, Warwick had equal representation with the county of Loudon, which had a population of 1,746. "In effect, every individual in Warwick had as much power as seventeen in Loudon."[31] Jefferson considered this to be an intolerable situation. The separation of powers in a government could preserve the liberties of a people only if there were a fair and equitable system of representation and apportionment. Jefferson's ideas on representation were also expressed by Montesquieu. This issue, however, was broadly discussed by philosophers and historians in England, France and in the American colonies.

The third defect in the state constitution for Virginia was its inability to properly divide the members of the Senate from the members of the House of Delegates. "The Senate is," Jefferson wrote, "by its constitution, too homogeneous with the house of delegates being chosen by the same electors, at the same time, and out of the same subjects, the choice falls of course on men of the same description. The purpose of establishing different houses of legislation is to introduce the influence of different interests or different principles."[32] Montesquieu also warned against the dangers of combining both houses of the legislature. He believed each body should have "their assemblies and deliberations apart, each their separate views and interests."[33]

While there were many examples of a separation between upper and lower houses in the state legislatures in each of the American colonies, Jefferson's language and analysis of the separation of powers, the method of representation and the division of the legislature into an upper and lower house, suggests a conscious understanding and deliberate application of Montesquieu's analysis in his *Spirit of the Laws*.

It should be noticed, first, that all three defects cited

by Jefferson in the state constitution for Virginia were succinctly stated in Montesquieu's chapter on the "English Constitution," in Book XI of *The Spirit of the Laws*. Second, Jefferson's reasoning and language were similar to Montesquieu's. Third, Jefferson presented his constitutional arguments in the same logical order as Montesquieu. Jefferson may not have referred specifically to this section in *The Spirit of the Laws*, but the similarities between Montesquieu's text and Jefferson's writings are too striking to ignore.

Slavery

Jefferson's *Commonplace Book* further illustrates his indebtedness to Montesquieu. He copied parts of *The Spirit of the Laws* which tackled the problem of slavery in a republic. The state of slavery, Montesquieu wrote, is in its own nature bad.

It is neither useful to the master nor to the slave; not to the slave, because he can do nothing through a motive of virtue; nor to the master, because by having an unlimited authority over his slaves he insensibly accustoms himself to the want of all moral virtues, and thence becomes fierce, hasty, severe, choleric, voluptuous, and cruel.[34]

Similarly, Jefferson condemned the institution of slavery and spoke of the unhappy influence slavery had on both the master and the slave. Jefferson wrote in his *Notes on Virginia*:

There must doubtless be an unhappy influence by the existence of slavery... The whole commerce between master and slave is a perpetual exercise of the most boisterous passions, the most unremitting despotism on the one part, and degrading submission on the other.[35]

Both Montesquieu and Jefferson addressed the dialectic of the master-slave relationship. They spoke of the vile effects slavery had on both parties, and the inherent cruelty of the institution of slavery.

The slave, Montesquieu wrote:

sees the happiness of a society, of which he is not so much as a member; he sees the security of others fenced by laws, himself without any protection. He perceives that his master has a soul, capable of enlarging itself; while his own labors under a continual depression. Nothing more assimilates a man to a beast than living among freedmen, himself a slave. Such people as these are natural enemies of society; and their number must be dangerous.[36]

In his *Notes on Virginia*, Jefferson also expressed his painful awareness of this ever-present danger. "There must doubtless be an unhappy influence by the existence of slavery...The whole commerce between master and slave is a perpetual exercise of the most boisterous passions, the most unremitting despotism on the one part, and degrading submission on the other."[37] "I tremble for my country," he wrote, "when I reflect that God is just; that his justice cannot sleep forever."[38]

Montesquieu believed the institution of slavery was morally grotesque, and a political liability in a republic. "The evil is, if they have too great a number of slaves they cannot keep them in due bounds; if they have too many freedmen, they cannot live, and must become a burden to the republic."39 To resolve this problem, Montesquieu proposed "to enfranchise every year a certain number of those slaves who, by their age, health, or industry, are capable of getting a subsistence."40

Montesquieu cautioned against freeing all the slaves at the same time because they did not possess the means of supporting themselves. The slave population would pose a threat to the state and society. The enfranchisement method was designed to reduce the general alarm of releasing too many slaves into society at once, thereby relaxing the tensions and dangers inherent in the institution of slavery. A second method suggested by Montesquieu was colonization.

Jefferson culled these sentences from Montesquieu's *Spirit of the Laws* and included an act in his draft of the constitution of the State of Virginia which, if passed, would have abolished slavery in Virginia and emancipated the slaves on a gradual and periodic basis. Elaborating on his purpose in his draft constitution, Jefferson wrote:

an amendment containing it was prepared to the legislature whenever the bill should be taken up, and further directed that they (slaves) should continue with their parents to a certain age, then be brought up, at the public expense, to tillage, arts or sciences, according to their geniuses, till the females should be eighteen, and the males twenty-one years of age, when they should be colonized to such a place as the circumstances of the time should render proper.41

Jefferson's bill proposed the same methods prescribed by Montesquieu for the manumission of slaves. Jefferson argued that if the slaves did not enjoy the same rights and privileges afforded other citizens, Americans could not expect them to obey the laws of the society. When laws are unjust, obedience to them is a matter of coercion and not respect. The similarities between Jefferson's and Montesquieu's analysis of the institution of slavery, and the methods of manumission they chose to peacefully eradicate the problem of slavery are too similar to dismiss as a mere coincidence. Jefferson was aware of these passages in *The Spirit of the Laws* and proposed the same methods.

Church and State

Jefferson was troubled by another danger in a democratic republic; the power of the church to undermine the political stability of a free, democratic society. In a republic, Montesquieu warned, laws should provide for religious toleration among all sects and the laws pertaining to one's religious observances must be distinguished from the laws regulating man's behavior in society. "The laws of perfection drawn from religion," Jefferson copied into his *Commonplace Book* from Montesquieu's *Spirit of the Laws*,

have more in view the goodness of the person that observes them than of the society in which they are observed; the civil laws, on the contrary, have more in view the moral goodness of men in general than that of individuals. Thus, venerable as those ideas are which immediately spring from religion, they ought not always to serve as a first principle to the civil laws; because these have another, the general welfare of society.[42]

Jefferson wanted to find, as did Bolingbroke, Montesquieu and Locke, the proper boundaries between church and state. The path of progress in a republic was through reason and free inquiry. Every man in a republic has the right to conceive of God as he pleases. "But it does me no injury," Jefferson wrote, "for my neighbor to say there are twenty gods or no god...Constraint may make him worse by making him a hypocrite, but it will never make him a truer man."

Jefferson proposed to eliminate religious instruction from primary schools and he believed it was necessary to build "a wall of separation between Church and State...." Only a mature and enlightened mind, disciplined by the virtue of a good government, could properly make such a religious decision.

Jefferson's attack on legally established state religions culminated in 1779 with the introduction of his "Act for Establishing Religious Freedom." Jefferson—and his European friends—found the best way to silence religious disputes was to avoid them altogether. When he heard of the Act's passage, Jefferson reflected on his achievement and the Act's reception in Europe.

In a letter to James Madison in 1786, Jefferson wrote: "The Virginia act for religious freedom has been received, with infinite approbation in Europe, and enthusiasm...It has been translated into French and Italian..., sent to the courts of Europe...[and] inserted in the new Encyclopedic...."[45]

After so many years in which "the human mind has been held in vassalage by kings, priests, and nobles," he continued, "it was honorable for us to have produced the first legislature who had the courage to declare, that reason of man may be trusted with the formation of his own opinions."[46]

Jefferson's constitutional argument in his drafts of the Virginia State Constitution reveals both the influence of

Montesquieu, and his understanding of the elementary principles of a constitution. A constitution is, as Mayer defines it, is a fundamental law which defines and limits the powers of the ordinary legislature and which cannot be altered or affected by ordinary legislation. Hence, a true constitution must be established by the people themselves, acting through special agents appointed for that purpose, in a constitutional convention or the equivalent.

Jefferson's understanding of a constitution, David Mayer believes, was fundamentally different "from the concept that prevailed in eighteenth-century England; descriptive rather than prescriptive, evolved out of the concept established by American Whigs in the 1760's and 1770's."[47] Mayer does know where Jefferson "came to hold this peculiarly American concept of constitution," but he assumes it was "merely a reflection of the broader Whig principle that government must derive its legitimacy from the consent of the governed."[48]

The Whig constitutional historians were, as Mayer said, descriptive rather than prescriptive. Montesquieu's constitutional philosophy, on the other hand, was prescriptive and not descriptive. Montesquieu traveled through England observing the political and social life of the English people and its monarchy. He studied the English political philosophers and historians, and he was aware that his analysis of English political institutions was not an historical description of the English monarchy. Instead it was a model of what moderate governments ought to be. "A realistic analyst," Thomas Nugent writes, "may have come to the conclusion that the constitutive principle of England was money and not honor or virtue."[49]

Montesquieu's purpose in writing *The Spirit of the*

Laws was to create ideal types of governments, not to describe conditions in England or elsewhere. Montesquieu's analysis in *the Spirit of the Laws* was a prescriptive model of different forms of government. This explains the interest James Madison and Alexander Hamilton had in his work. They, too, were searching for a model of what a republican government should be.

Jefferson's constitutional argument in his doctrine "The Earth Belongs In Usufruct to the Living, and not the Dead" represents a paradigmatic shift in his thinking from the constitutionalism of Montesquieu and Sir Edward Coke and the constitutional reasoning of Madison, Hamilton and Adams. The legacy of ancient constitutionalism, represented by Coke and Montesquieu in the eighteenth century, relied on four main points: First, "a very clear sense that a state's constitution provided binding normative constraints on state action...."[50] Second, the understanding of a constitution as established by written documents, contracts, or covenants at a particular moment in historical time...."[51] Third, "republican forms of government, resting as they did on virtue and homogeneity, were only suited to small states...."[52] Fourth: An "institutionally complex and diverse kingdom might offer its subjects more freedom than other forms of government, provided that intermediate powers and bodies—especially aristocratic ones (parlements and the House of Lords) were respected and not suppressed; and that the uniformity of the law was no great virtue in a free society, and was typically aimed at by men who would suppress liberty for the sake of it..."[53]

Political liberty, Montesquieu argued, is not to be

found in democratic or aristocratic states, but in moderate monarchical states with a system of checks and balances and a division of power between the executive, legislative and judiciary branches of government. "In short, freedom was best to be protected by a constitution in which provincial or cultural diversity, institutional variety, and a range of degrees of privileges and immunities could check the tendencies of a monarch to centralize and self-aggrandize...."[54] Montesquieu's theory of government is one in which factional interests, social orders and economic classes are balanced in a "quasi-Newtonian equilibrium serving man's desire for liberty, tranquility and peace."[55]

Montesquieu's "Newtonian equilibrium" between rival economic, social, and religious sects in society was echoed in both Madison's and Hamilton writings in the *Federalist Papers* "The diversity in the faculties of men," Madison wrote,

"from which the rights of property originate, is...an insuperable obstacle to uniformity of interests. From the protection of different and unequal faculties of acquiring property, the possession of different degrees and kinds of property immediately results; and from the influence of these on the sentiments and views of the respective proprietors, ensues a division of the society into different interests and parties...The latent causes of faction are thus sown in the nature of man...."[56]

Madison's constitutional thought, as that of Locke, Hobbes and Montesquieu, recognized that man will always "judge in his own cause, because his interest would certainly bias his judgment, and, not improbably, corrupt his integrity."[57]

Madison, Hamilton and Adams all agreed that man's

passions, prejudices and private interests, and not his love of virtue and equality, required, not only a system of checks and balances, but a confederate republic large enough to prevent, as Madison put it, "a rage for paper money, for an abolition of debts, for an equal division of property..." by factional leaders in any given state of the Union. Although factious leaders may "kindle a flame within their particular States," Madison wrote, "they are not likely to "spread a general conflagration through the other States."[58] "The entire design of the governmental edifice," Richard Matthews recognizes, "pitted power against power, ambition counteracting ambition. It gave the advantage to those who wanted to keep the status quo, to stop change...."[59] The chief concern of Hamilton and Madison was the protection of private property.

Adams made it very clear that he rejected Montesquieu's argument that the virtue of a republic requires its citizens to make sacrifices for the good of the community. "It is not true," he says:

that any people ever existed who loved the public better than themselves...and therefore this kind of virtue, this sort of love, is as precarious a foundation for liberty as honor or fear; it is the laws alone that really love the country, the public, the whole better than any part...[60]

There is "no such passion as a love of democracy, stronger than self-love, or superior to the love of private interest...."[61] If there were citizens who preferred the public to their private interest...it would not be from any such passion as love of the democracy, but from reason, conscience, a regard to justice, and a sense of duty and moral obligation; or else from a desire of fame, and the applause, gratitude, and rewards of the public."[62]

"The love of democracy," Montesquieu writes, "is that of equality." "Every man hates to have a superior," Adams writes, "but no man is willing to have an equal; every man desires to be superior to all others."[63] "The love of equality," Adams says, "at least since Adam's fall, ever existed in human nature, any otherwise than as a desire of bringing others down to our own level... That the real friends of equality are such from recollection, judgment, and a sense of duty, not from any passion, natural or artificial."[64]

"The love of democracy," Montesquieu writes, "is likewise that of frugality." "A passion for frugality," Adams says, "perhaps, never existed in a nation, if it ever did in an individual...it is sufficient to observe that no nation ever practiced it but from necessity. Poor nations only are frugal, rich ones always profuse...."[65] "That no love of frugality ever existed," he says, "as a passion; but always as a virtue, approved by deep and long reflection, as useful to individuals as well as the democracy. That, therefore, the democracy of Montesquieu, and its principles of virtue, equality, frugality...are all mere figments of the brain, and delusive imaginations."[66]

Jefferson felt Adams' praise of the English constitution in his *Defense of the Constitution* and his denunciation of Montesquieu's principles of a republic were further signs of a monarchical spirit in America and a retreat from the principles of the American Revolution. Jefferson also disagreed, not only with Adams, but with Hamilton's and Madison's concept of human nature; that man is governed by "the desire for recognition," "a

passion for distinction," by his selfish passions which,"
Adams wrote, "God and nature planted there, and
which no human legislator ever can eradicate..." were
not accurate descriptions of man."[67] He did not
conceive of people, as "timid and cautious," as Madison
did, or "as separate beings with no natural connection
to each other...."[68]

Among the Founding Fathers Jefferson was the only
adherent to the principles of Scottish moral sense
philosophy. He believed, as they did, that man was born
with a moral faculty which allowed him to distinguish
instinctively between just and unjust acts, between what
is wrong and what is right. Man is an animal with selfish
desires and appetites, but he is also a rational animal,
and his reason, which distinguishes him from the brutes
of nature, commands him to regard the interests of
others as his own. Man's sense of moral duty is, in fact,
a part of the very constitution of man, and is as
instinctively compelling as man's selfish instincts.

Education and the laws of civil society may strengthen
man's natural instinct for justice and truth, but man's
natural sociability and sense of duty is truly the
foundation of man's rights in civil society. The laws
enacted by governments, especially republican governments, must conform, he believed, to man's
benevolent nature and not to his selfish instincts, desires
and passions. Jefferson did not share Hamilton's,
Madison's and Adams' fears that, without the laws of
civil society, man would lapse into a state of anarchy.

Jefferson rejected the constitutional reasoning of
Coke, Montesquieu, Madison, Hamilton and Adams
and embraced instead the political arguments of his
friend, Desttut de Tracy, whose book, Commentary and

Review of Montesquieu's *Spirit of Laws*, he later edited and translated. He considered Tracy's Commentary "the most valuable work of the present age," forming a new "epoch in the science of government."[69]

Tracy believes that when the positive laws of society reflect man's nature, they are just and good, and when they do not, they are unjust and evil. "Justice and injustice, therefore, had an existence before any positive law; although it is only to laws of our own creation we can apply the epithets of just and unjust; since the laws of nature being simply necessary in the nature of things...."[70]

Like Madison and Hamilton, Tracy believes that representative democracies are not limited by the size of their territories, as Montesquieu assumed, but have "the property of being applicable to all political societies from the smallest to the greatest...."[71] They have the advantage that "neither internal troubles nor external aggression, can impede the political machine, because the evil cannot arise in every place, at the same time; there always remains some sound part, whence succor may be obtained for the assailed part."[72] There is, however, one "principle consideration which should set bounds to the territory of a nation." A representative democracy, he says, should not "contain within itself, people differing too much in manners, character, and particularly language, or which may have particular or opposite interests."[73]

Tracy rejects Adams' argument in the *Defense of the Constitution*, that those with the greatest advantages in life should exercise proportional advantages in the legislation of the state. Family, wealth and honors should not confer additional rights and privileges upon those who already enjoy advantages over the rest of the members of their society. Their wealth is guaranteed by the laws that relate to property, and their family name, reputation and honor will always depend on the judgment of their fellow citizens; no law can dispose of or enhance the splendor and consideration which is attached to birth, fortune, or personal glory. It is therefore always useless or injurious that those who already possess great advantages in society, should also be invested with a superiority of power, which, under the pretext of defending themselves, would be the means of social oppression.

Tracy's Commentary and Review, and Condorcet's unpublished essay on the "Observations on the Twenty-Ninth Book of *The Spirit of the Laws*," which is appended to it, is an indictment of two main points. First, Montesquieu's defense of a plurality of systems of weights and measures and second, the decentralized institutions that encourage and empower diversity in society; special interests competing against the general will of the nation or, what Rousseau referred to as the "General Will" in his *Social Contract*. Contrary to Montesquieu, Tracy believed that civil or criminal laws should be the same in every province of every state, without exception.

There are, Tracy says, three laws of rational government: The first is that laws should be "declared to be formed for the governed, not the governed for them; consequently they only exist in virtue of the will of the majority of those governed, and should change when the will changes...."[74] This law prevents the establishment of hereditary powers with exclusive privileges and honors.

The second is that "there should never be a power in society which cannot be changed without violence, nor any such that when it is changed all must change with it...."[75] The second law preserves the separation of the executive, legislative and judiciary, preventing "one man from being entrusted with the entire disposal of the power of a nation..."[76]

The third is a law which describes a "rational government to always have in view the conservation of the independence of the nation, the liberty of its members, and such security for every individual as to supercede the idea of fear internal or external."[77] This last law "implies the necessity of a proper extent of territory; but that the nation should not be composed of parts too much diversified...."[78]

Tracy's constitutionalism "is grounded in a radically individualistic social contract theory which envisions the deliberate creation of political institutions on a rational basis and leaves no room for institutional plurality of the ancient constitutional sort."[79] Madison, Adams and Hamilton's constitutionalism "recognized the need for jurisdictional pluralism and institutional accommodation to cultural differences...."[80] Adams, unlike Hamilton and Madison, however, was more "squarely within the mixed-constitutional, ancient-constitutional tradition, one that required seeing bicameralism as the institutional recognition of class differences."[81]

In his doctrine, "the earth belongs to the living and not the dead," Jefferson's reasoning is more closely associated with the thinking of Tracy and the French school than it is to the constitutionalism of Montesquieu, Hamilton, Madison and Adams. Jefferson's doctrine leaves no room for "jurisdictional pluralism and institutional accommodation to cultural differences." He no longer believed, as did Madison, that laws must reflect the cultural, social and economic diversity in society. Madison argues, contrary to Jefferson, that constitutions derive their legitimacy and permanence from the sentiments that attach people to their local traditions, customs and social manners, no matter how irrational some of those traditions and customs may be.

Jefferson's radical constitutional argument reflects his long-standing concern that the "Pseudo-aristocracy," which he said was "founded on wealth and birth without either virtue or talents," would, in good time, reestablish their political and economic control over the American republic and continue to plunder the bulk of its inhabitants for profit and gain. He disagreed with Adams who thought "it best to put the Pseudo-aristoi into a separate chamber of legislation where they may be hindered from doing mischief by their coordinate branches, and where also they may be a protection to wealth against the Agrarian and plundering enterprises of the Majority of the people."[82] He feared that the real danger was not from the majority but from the wealthy "because enough of these will find their way into every branch of the legislation to protect themselves... Legislatures of our own, in action for 30 years past, have proven that no fears of an equalization of property are to be apprehended from them."[83]

Jefferson observed in the states of Massachusetts and Connecticut "a traditionary reverence for certain families, which has rendered the offices of the government nearly hereditary in those families."[84] The danger, Jefferson believed, was not from the propertyless masses Adams, Madison and Hamilton feared would deprive the wealthy of their private property rights by a simple majority vote, but the wealthy aristocratic families in the United States who would trample on the rights of man, as they did in Europe. These families, almost hereditary in many states, perpetuate themselves through "the transmission of property from generation to generation."[85] "He knew in such a society, men of 'virtue and talent' who were not well-born might never reach their full potential." These Pseudo-aristocratic families could only be prevented from imposing their will and self-serving interests against the legitimate interests of the majority by periodically rewriting the laws of the nation. The Pseudo-aristocracy, he fervently believed, were enemies of equality and ill-disposed to the political virtues so critical to the health and vitality of a democratic society.

CHAPTER 6

PARTY AND POLITICS

When Jefferson returned from France after his five-year ministry to the Court of Louis XVI to become George Washington's secretary of state his perspective of the political climate of opinion in the United States was very different from other national leaders; it was a French perspective of America's political culture in the 1790's. The French Revolution and French revolutionary thought became Jefferson's point of reference for judging, not only the political authenticity of one's republicanism, but the direction and evolution of political developments in the United States. He believed the United States should support the French Revolution, a nation that had supported the American people in their War of Independence. He later expressed his astonishment to William Short,

at the change which I found had taken place in the United States in that time. No more like the same people; their notions, their habits and manners, the course of their commerce, so totally changed, that I, who stood in those of 1784, found myself not at all qualified to speak their sentiments, or forward their views in 1790...We return like foreigners, and, like them, require a considerable residence here to become Americanized.[1]

He left France, he said, "in the first year of her revolution, in the fervor of natural rights, and zeal for reformation. My conscientious devotion to these rights could not be heightened, but it had been aroused and excited by daily exercise."[2] He was mortified to discover, however, that the political conversations and debates in New York were a daily exercise in monocratic philosophy. There was a decided preference "of kingly over republican government...," and that he was the "only advocate on the republican side of the question...."[3]

After dining with Adams and Alexander Hamilton in the spring of 1791, he became convinced that Hamilton was the leader of an anti-republican, counter-revolutionary movement in the United States. Both Adams and Hamilton had, in fact, expressed the view that the British constitution was "the most perfect which ever existed," and both favored the Senate of the United States to be composed of the rich and well-born as a counter-weight to the democratic aspirations of the American people. "All men of respectability and genius," Hamilton said, "must for their own defense, unite to overset radical, egalitarian democrats. They must ensure the power of the government is entrusted to proper hands." [4]

Jefferson's pro-French egalitarian views was not lost on Hamilton. "Mr. Jefferson is at the head of a faction decidedly hostile to me and my administration

and...subversive of the principles of good government."[5]
"Mr. Jefferson has thrown censure on my principles of
government...He has predicted that the people would
not long tolerate my proceedings, and that I should not
maintain any ground."[6]

Hamilton not only complained of Jefferson's narrow
disposition toward federal authority and the funding
system, but of his "womanish attachment to France and
a womanish resentment against Great Britain."[7]
Hamilton believed the source of Jefferson's mis-
understandings and opposition was the result of his
experiences and associations in France where he saw
government from the side of its abuses. "He drank freely
of the French philosophy, in religion, in science, in
politics. He came from France in the moment of a
fermentation which he had a share in exciting, and in
the passions and feelings of which he shared both from
temperament and situation."[8]

It may have been Jefferson drank too freely of French
philosophy, but to Jefferson, Hamilton was intoxicated
with monarchist principles and a love of everything
English. In a 1792 letter to George Washington,
Jefferson expressed his disapproval and inability to
cooperate with Hamilton. "His system flowed from
principles adverse to liberty, and was calculated to
undermine and demolish the Republic, by creating an
influence of his department over the members of the
Legislature."[9]

The Hamiltonians were "strengthening all the features
of the government which gave it resemblance to an
English constitution, of adopting the English forms and
principles of administration."[10] From this moment on

the French Revolution and French revolutionary thought became Jefferson's point of reference for judging, not only the political authenticity of one's republicanism, but the direction and evolution of political developments in the United States. He believed the United States should support the French Revolution, a nation that had supported the American people in their War of Independence.

The French Revolution's Impacts on America

The divide between Jefferson and Hamilton ran far deeper than their disagreements over the funding system or commercial policy. It reached the core of their philosophies of government. Each considered the other's principles to be dangerous and subversive, tending to undermine the foundations of the American republic.

The conflict between Jefferson and Hamilton was heightened further by their attitudes toward the French Revolution. Although most conservative Americans, like Hamilton, welcomed the news of the French Revolution in its earliest stages, they became fierce critics of it by 1790. Colonel Higginson wrote: "The French Revolution not only divided parties, but moulded them; gave them their bitterness. The home issues were for a time subordinate; the real party lines were established on the other side of the Atlantic."[11] Jefferson and Madison believed the French Revolutionary debate established, without doubt, that political sentiments in the towns were pro-English, and in the country pro-French.

The conservative reaction to the French Revolution found a virulent spokesman in John Adams. As early as

April 19, 1790, John Adams expressed his misgivings about the French Revolution. He wrote:

> I know that the encyclopedists and economists, Diderot and D'Alembert, Voltaire and Rousseau have contributed to this great event more than Sidney, Locke, or Hoadley, perhaps more than the American Revolution; and I own to you, I know not what to make of a republic of thirty million atheists.[12]

He believed the political and economic principles of the French Revolution were essentially different from the principles of the American Revolution.

In the first year of his Vice-Presidency, Adams published a series of letters in the Gasette of the United States entitled "Discourses on Davila." In these letters he stated his objections to the French Revolution. Inveighing against the fashionable republican circles in France and the United States who wanted to abolish all distinctions and titles, Adams said of man that the "desire to be observed, considered, esteemed, praised, beloved, and admired by his fellows is one of the earliest as well as the keenest dispositions discovered in the heart of man."[13] Even beauty, riches and honor are "not so much desired for the pleasure they afford as the attention they command." According to Adams, every man, including the poorest mechanic, the common beggar, pirates, highwaymen and common thieves "court a set of admirers and plume themselves upon that superiority which they have or fancy they have over some others."[14]

In defense of holding merit as a quality likely to ensure a superior form of rule, Adams admitted merit should govern the world, but he wondered how merit can be discovered, and who shall judge it. Shall the whole nation vote for senators? Thirty millions of votes, for example, for each senator in France? It is obvious that this would be a lottery of millions of blanks to one prize, and that the chance of having wisdom and integrity in a senator by hereditary descent, would be far better.[15]

Adams wrote the French had mistakenly assumed the interests of the people would be better served and represented by collecting the sovereignty of the nation into a single, national assembly. He believed a single assembly would "act as arbitrarily and tyrannically as any despot" and unless there is a balance of powers, "the present struggle in Europe will...produce nothing but another fanaticism under new and strange names."[16] The National Assembly could not abolish man's "passion for distinction."

If all decorum, discipline, and subordination are to be destroyed and...anarchy, and insecurity of property are to be introduced, nations will lapse into fanaticism, darkness and superstition and will follow the standard, of the first mad despot who, with the enthusiasm of another Mohomet, will endeavor to obtain them.[17] He believed it was essential for every man to know his place in society, and be made to keep it.

Adams was sure there would always be rivalries between the rich and the poor, the industrious and the idle, the learned and the ignorant. No degree of philosophy or legislative enactments could eliminate such differences. If France were to place unlimited power of disposing property in the hands of the dis-enfranchised, she will find "the lamb committed to the custody of the wolf." Property must be secured, or

liberty cannot exist. The publication of Adams'
Discourses on Davila was favorably received by the
American conservatives who feared the egalitarian and
atheistic tendencies of the French Revolution.

Ideological differences between pro-French and pro-
English factions in the United States were further
inflamed by Edmund Burke's scathing criticism of the
French Revolution in his *Reflections on the Revolution
in France* and the reprinting of Thomas Paine's *Rights
of Man*. "American opinion of the French Revolution,"
Merrill Peterson observed

favorable at the outset, had already begun to divide when
the English polemics reverberated across the Atlantic in the
early months of 1791. Burke's *Reflections on the Revolution
in France* captured conservative feelings for the cause of
order, tradition, church, privilege, and royalty in France.[18]

Jefferson immediately recognized there were not one,
but two prominent voices in the country, Adams' and
Burke's, which were hostile to the French Revolution.

"The Revolution of France," Jefferson wrote:

does not astonish me so much as the revolution of Mr. Burke.
I wish I could believe the latter proceeded from pure motives
as the former. But what demonstrations could scarcely have
established, before, less than the hints of Dr. Priestly and Mr.
Paine establish firmly now. This is evidence of the rottenness
of his mind.....[19]

Jefferson believed Thomas Paine's *Rights of Man* was
the proper antidote to the political heresies of Burke and
Adams. Thomas Paine shared Jefferson's enthusiasm for

the French Revolution and his anger toward Burke. He wrote the *Rights of Man*, in part, as a refutation of Burke's *Reflections*. In contrast to Burke and Adams, Paine was firmly convinced the French Revolution was a harbinger of liberty throughout the world.

Although the ideas expressed in the *Rights of Man* are remarkably similar to Jefferson's doctrine "the earth belongs to the living and not the dead," the similarities between them have been denied by Jefferson's biographer, Dumas Malone. Malone argues that Jefferson's "commendation of Paine's work may...be regarded as a spontaneous outburst rather than a studied act."[20] In the *Rights of Man*, Paine wrote:

Every age and generation must be as free to act for itself, in all cases, as the ages and generations which preceded it.... man has no property in the generations which are to follow...It is the living, and not the dead that are to be accommodated. When a man ceases to be, his power and his wants cease with him; and having no longer any participation in the concerns of this world, he has no longer any authority in directing who shall be its governors, or how its government shall be organized, or how administered.[21]

These, of course, were the exact sentiments expressed by Jefferson his document "the earth belongs to the living and not the dead." Jefferson and Paine were both sympathetic to the French Revolution, and both agreed upon nearly all of the causes contributing to it. Jefferson's praise of the *Rights of Man* was evident in a letter he wrote to Thomas Paine on June 9, 1792:

Would you believe that in this country there should be high and important characters who need your lessons in republicanism, and do not heed them? It is but too true that we have a sect preaching up and pouting after an English constitution of King, lords, and commons, and whose heads are itching for crowns, coronets and mitres.[22]

Jefferson was sure that Americans were firm and unanimous in their principles of republicanism because "they love what you write and read it with delight."

Jefferson was even more convinced in 1791 that the success of the French Revolution was critically necessary, not only for the triumph of republicanism in the United States, but in Europe. "I look with great anxiety," Jefferson wrote,

for the first establishment of the new government in France, being perfectly convinced, that if it takes place there, it will spread sooner or later all over Europe. On the contrary, a check there would retard the revival of liberty in other countries.[23]

To Edmund Pendleton in 1791, Jefferson wrote:

The Success of the French Revolution will ensure the progress of liberty in Europe and its preservation here. The failure of that would have been a powerful argument with those who wish to prove that there must be a failure here.[24]

By 1793 the French Revolution became the paramount political issue in the United States. The first French republic was founded on September 22, 1792, by the newly established National Convention. The Jacobin Party had triumphed over the more moderate Girondins, and immediately stripped the king of his political powers, subsequently convicting Louis XVI of treason.

The Jacobin ascendancy to power in France, and the popular ferment it produced in the creation of secretive pro-French democratic societies hardened conservative opposition to the French Revolution. By September 1794 Washington concluded "these 'self-created societies'...represented a tyranny of the minority against the will of the majority, and that their only revolutionary principle was that 'every man can cut and carve for himself.'"[25] Jefferson was grieved by the administration's denunciation of pro-French sentiments in these democratic societies and continued to sympathize with France's revolutionary efforts

Although other prominent Americans—George Washington, John Adams, General Knox and Alexander Hamilton—were infuriated by the news of the August Days, the September Massacres, the triumph of the Jacobins and the execution of the King, Jefferson continued to justify the extremism of the French revolutionaries.

In a letter to William Short, on January 3, 1793, Jefferson wrote;

I considered that sect (Jacobins) as the same with the Republican patriots...both having in object the establishment of a free constitution...The Jacobins (as since called) yielded to the Feuillants, and tried the experiment of retaining their hereditary Executive. The experiment failed completely, and would have brought on the reestablishment of despotism had it been pursued.[26]

The Jacobins had no choice but to execute the King. In this historical struggle for human rights and liberties, Jefferson was aware

> many guilty persons fell without the forms of trial, and with them some innocent. These I deplore as much as anybody... [Yet it] was necessary to use the arm of the people, a machine not quite so blind as balls and bombs... But time and truth will rescue and embalm their memories, while their posterity will be enjoying that very liberty for which they would never have hesitated to offer up their lives.27

Jefferson recognized that the stakes were high: "The liberty of the whole earth was depending on the issue of the contest."

As the war progressed, he continued to hear of the many martyrs who fell to the cause, "but rather than it should have failed I would have seen half the earth desolated; were there but an Adam and an Eve left in every country, and left free...."28

Jefferson was not troubled when he heard news of the execution of Louis XVI in 1793. His death, he wrote, if it does not

> produce republics everywhere, it will at least soften the monarchical governments by rendering them amendable to punishments like other criminals, and doing away that rage of insolence, and oppression, the inviolability of the King's person.29

The Jay Treaty

Political passions within the American republic were further estranged by the publication of the Jay Treaty.

John Jay was sent to Great Britain in the autumn of 1794 to ease the tensions between America and Great Britain. He returned with a treaty that enraged pro-French and republican factions in the country. In this treaty, Britain demanded four major changes: First: It required America to concede its rights as a neutral country to trade freely with belligerents in non-contraband goods. Second: It required the United States to close its ports as a base of operations to England's enemies. Third: Britain agreed to pay the claims of the British creditors against American citizens. Britain abandoned its claim for compensation of slaves belonging to American citizens emancipated by the British Army in 1783. Fourth: Americans were still subject to impressment by the British Navy. In exchange for these concessions, Britain promised to surrender the Northwest posts by 1796 and agreed to pay for the spoliations upon American commerce while granting the right of American vessels to trade with India.

The news of the Treaty could not have come at a worse time. France had opened her markets to the United States as never before and gave her free access to the West Indies. It was only Britain's obstinacy which prevented further expansion of American trade.

The Republicans claimed that the Treaty put us completely in the hands of Great Britain, that it was a betrayal of the Revolution; the Federalists claimed that opposition to the Treaty came only from those who were tools of France.

The widening chasm between Republicans and Federalists was reflected in Jefferson's letter to Christoph D. Ebeling on July 20, 1795. Replying to Ebeling's inquiries about American politics, Jefferson said the nation was comprised of two parties—the Republicans and the Federalists. Speaking of the Federalists, Jefferson said:

The Anti-Republicans consist of (1) The old refugees and tories. (2) British merchants.... (3) American merchants trading on British capital.... (4) Speculators and holders in the banks and public funds. (5) Officers of the federal government with some exceptions. (6) Office-hunters, willing to give up principles for places... (7) Nervous persons, whose languid fibers have more analogy with a passive than [an] active state of things.[30]

"The Republican sector of the Union" he observed,

was comprised of: "1. The entire body of landholders throughout the United States. 2. The body of laborers, not being landholders, whether in husbandry or the arts." Outnumbered "500 to one," Jefferson says, and "Trifling as are the numbers of the Anti-republican party, there are circumstances which give them an appearance of strength and numbers. They all live in cities, together, and can act in a body readily and at all times; they give chief employment to the newspapers, and therefore have most of them under their command." The Agricultural interests, on the other hand, "are dispersed over a great extent of country, have little means of intercommunication with each other..."[31]

Jefferson later wrote that political dispositions in America were also rooted in man's nature. To Lafayette he wrote:

The parties of Whig and Tory are those of nature. They exist in all countries, whether called by these names, or by those of aristocrats and democrats, côté droite and côté gauche...The sickly, weakly, timid man fears the people, and is a Tory by nature. The healthy, strong and bold, cherishes them, and is formed a Whig by nature.[32]

It seemed obvious to Jefferson that the historic struggle for liberty between democrats and aristocrats was being reenacted in the United States.

The growing monarchical spirit in the United States was a source of intense anxiety for Jefferson. In a letter to Phillip Mazzei dated April 24, 1796, he described the changes which had taken place in the political landscape of America.

"In place of that noble love of liberty and republican government which carried us triumphantly through the war," he wrote,

an Anglican monarchical aristocratical party has sprung up, whose avowed object is to draw over us the substance, as they have already done the forms, of the British government... It would give you a fever were I to name to you the apostates who have gone over to these heresies, men who were Samsons in the field and Solomons in the council, but who have had their heads shorn by the harlot England. In short, we are likely to preserve the liberty we have obtained only by unremitting labors and perils.[33]

The "Anglican monarchical aristocratical party" had triumphed in the councils of government, particularly the executive and judiciary. However, Jefferson still had faith in the main body of citizens, who remained "true to their republican principles." Jefferson feared

England's influence in the councils of government and its effect on American public opinion could destroy republicanism in the United States. Only a republican France could counteract England's sinister influence in the United States. In a letter from Jefferson to Madison on June 15, 1797, he expressed his hope that "the victories lately obtained by the French on the Rhine, were as splendid as Bonaparte's..."34

Jefferson was assured by Volney that France would not make peace with England "because it is such an opportunity of sinking her as she never had and may not have again." Bonaparte's army would have to march seven hundred miles to Calais. Therefore, it is imagined "that the armies of the Rhine will be destined for England." Jefferson had earlier tied the political fortunes of the United States with France, and was still confident the victory of French arms would secure liberty in America.

Jefferson wrote to M. Odit on Oct. 14, 1795, the interests of both republics were alike. "Two people whose interests, whose principles, whose habits of attachment...have so many points of union, cannot but be easily kept together." Jefferson assured Odit that his countrymen took great interest in the success of the French republic, and that no one was more enthusiastic for France than himself. Grateful for France's assistance during the American Revolution, Jefferson wished to see France victorious in her war against England.

It was becoming apparent to Jefferson the political liberties of both France and the United States were threatened by counter-revolutionary forces at home and abroad. In both nations, conservatives regained political power in the executive branch of government. Although the political situation in France was far worse, both nations were facing a monarchist resurgence.

While Jefferson was counting on French arms to save the day, the French Directory began to step up its seizure of American ships and the confiscation of its neutral cargo. Angered by the ratification of the Jay Treaty and the election of John Adams to the presidency in 1797, France demanded the enforcement of their treaty of commerce of 1778 with the United States. In this treaty both nations pledged themselves "to uphold the doctrine of free ships, free goods in their relations with each other."

Hoping to alleviate tensions between the two countries, President Adams sent a mission to France to resolve Franco-American grievances. The three American plenipotentiaries, who were sent to negotiate a more favorable treaty, were forced to wait for three weeks in the anterooms of the Directory before they were approached by aides from Periogord Talleyrand, the Minister of Foreign Affairs. These aides suggested a cash payment to Talleyrand would pave the way toward negotiations between the two nations. Reports of Talleyrand's impertinence and indiscretion, the famous XYZ Affair, soon reached the capital where Adams, pressured by the anti-French faction in his administration to take action against France, began to prepare for war.

Jefferson never believed the stories he heard and read about Talleyrand's intransigence. Instead, he believed the Adams administration and the Hamiltonians were waging a campaign against the liberties of the American people. To Edmund Pendleton on January 29, 1799, Jefferson said, "a wicked use has been made of the

French negotiations and particularly the X. Y. Z dish cooked up by Marshall where the swindlers are made to appear as the French government."[35] Jefferson was certain the French government was "sincere in their dispositions for peace, not wishing us to break the British treaty, and willing to arrange a liberal one with us...."[36] The people, he warned, soon would realize they were being duped by the administration, and would then rally behind republican principles.

The Federalists were quick to take advantage of a growing anti-French sentiment in the country and passed the first Alien Act on June 27, 1798. This Act empowered the President to order "dangerous aliens to be deported from the United States territory."[37] The President had the prerogative of deciding what was dangerous and, in the event of a declaration of war, had the power to have the subjects of a hostile government "apprehended, restrained, secured and removed, as alien enemies." The Sedition Act, or the Act for the Punishment of Certain Crimes, declared it an offense for anyone conspiring "with the intent to oppose the government, to incite riots or insurrections against the laws of Congress, or to publish false and malicious writings against the government, either House of Congress, or the President...."[38] The Alien Act was contingent on a declaration of war, and never went into effect.

Jefferson believed that the Alien and Sedition Acts were aimed at both the Republicans and French sympathizers in the United States. These acts were designed to suppress lawful opposition to the government. He wrote:

The Alien and Sedition bills were just a beginning. If the people did not revolt against them, the next step would be to persuade Congress that the President should continue in office for life, reserving to another time the transfer of the succession to his heirs and the establishment of the Senate for life.[39]

The Kentucky Resolutions

In response to these odious and dangerous measures, Jefferson penned his draft of the Kentucky Resolutions, 1798. This document was introduced in the House by John Breckenridge on November 10, 1798 and became the rallying cry for many Republicans. The Kentucky Resolutions formulated the doctrine that "the powers not delegated to the United States by the Constitution nor prohibited by it to the states, are reserved to the states respectively or to the people...."[40]

According to Jefferson, the Constitution was founded on a compact amongst the states. Each state retained the right to judge for itself its mode and method of redress. The Government, created by this compact, was not made the exclusive nor final judge of the extent of the powers delegated to itself. Whenever the general Government assumes undelegated powers, "its acts are unauthoritative, void, and of no force."[41] Jefferson believed the conspiracy against the civil liberties of the American people could only be redressed by empowering the states to judge the constitutionality of Federal laws.

The Kentucky Resolutions formulated the doctrine stating, by compact, several states composing the United States constituted a general government for special purposes—delegated to that government certain definite powers, reserving, each State to itself, the residuary mass of rights to their own self-government; and that whenever the general government assumes undelegated powers, its acts are unauthoritative, void, and of no force...42

Jefferson wrote the several states which were party to this compact, did not accede to the principle of the general government created by the Constitution. The federal government did not have the exclusive power to judge the extent of the powers delegated to itself; since that would have made its discretion, and not the Constitution, the measure of its powers; but that, as in all other cases, of compact among powers having no common judge, each party has an equal right to judge for itself, as well of infractions as of the mode and measure of redress.

He argued one of the amendments to the Constitution specifically expresses the general principle articulated in the Kentucky Resolutions; "the powers not delegated to the United States by the Constitution, nor prohibited by it to the States, are reserved to the States respectively, or to the people..." The States did not accede to, nor delegate to the general government, under the Constitution, any of their powers over the freedom of religion, freedom of speech or freedom of the press. Each State retains the right to judge for itself

how far the licentiousness of speech and of the press may be abridged without lessening their useful freedom, and how far those abuses which cannot be separated from their use should be tolerated, rather than the use be destroyed.

The Constitution clearly states that "Congress shall make no law respecting an establishment of religion, or prohibiting the free exercise thereof, or abridging the freedom of speech or of the press."[43] Jefferson firmly believed the Constitution "throws down the sanctuary which covers" the freedoms of religion, speech and the press, and also that of "libels, falsehoods, and defamation, equally with heresy and false religion." These powers were expressly "withheld from the cognizance of federal tribunals."[44]

Jefferson stood firm in his conviction that every person has the right, under the Constitution,

to enjoy the right to public trial by an impartial jury, to be informed of [t]he nature and cause of the accusation, to be confronted with witnesses against him, to have compulsory process for obtaining witnesses in his favor, and to have the assistance of counsel for his defense...[45]

The Alien and Sedition Acts deprived American citizens of their right to due process under the law, rights guaranteed under the Constitution. The Alien Act authorizes the President to remove a person out of the United States who is under the protection of the law, on his own suspicion, without accusation, without jury, without public trial, without confrontation of the witnesses against him, without hearing witnesses in his favor, without defense, without counsel.[46]

The Alien Act is

contrary to the provision also of the Constitution, (and) is therefore not law, but utterly void, and of no force... that transferring the power of judging any person, who is under the protection of the laws, from the courts to the President of the United States, as is undertaken by the same act concerning aliens, is against the article of the Constitution which provides 'the judicial power of the United States shall be vested in courts....47

The Sedition Act, for similar reasons, violated the provisions in the Constitution which guaranteed free speech. Jefferson wrote the federal government was not authorized to judge a person's views, regardless of how obnoxious their views may be to another individual, "or be thought dangerous, to his or their election, or other interests, public or personal..."48

The Congress of the United States was never a party to the compact, but merely a creature of it, limited to the enumerated powers of the Constitution. The Congress has assumed, in their passage of the Alien and Sedition Acts, a right of enlarging its own powers by constructions, inferences, and indefinite deductions from those directly given, which this assembly does declare to be usurpations of the powers retained to the independent branches, mere interpolations into the compact, and direct infractions of it.

Jefferson warned the Congress and the President, as he once warned the British Parliament and the King,

that these and successive acts of the same character, unless arrested at the threshold, necessarily drive these States into revolution and blood, and will furnish new calumnies against republican government, and new pretexts for those who wish it to be believed that man cannot be governed but by a rod of iron....49

Jefferson stressed congressional representatives must show more respect for the rights of innocent aliens, "the claims of justification, the sacred force of truth, and the forms and substance of law and justice" than for "the bare suspicions of the President..."[50]

The Kentucky Resolutions represent an important stage in Jefferson's constitutional thought. During his ministry to France, Jefferson spoke of the imperfections of the Confederate government. In August of 1787 Jefferson wrote, "Its greatest failure is the imperfect manner in which matters of commerce have been provided for."[51] He recognized, as did other national leaders, the federal government needed the power and authority to negotiate treaties of commerce and to speak for the American people with one voice to foreign powers. However, he also clearly stated he was not "a friend to a very energetic government. It is always oppressive. It places the governors indeed more at their ease, at the expense of the people."[52] He told Madison that the states, although imperfect and in want of uniformity, were the "sacred palladium of liberty." In a letter to Madison, he further insisted a Bill of Rights was a necessary supplement to the Federal Constitution, and a "declaration of rights will be the text, whereby they (the states) will try all the acts of the federal government."[53]

Jefferson viewed the government of the United States in the Kentucky Resolutions to be, "as a true federal system, with a clear-cut division between the state, or domestic sphere, and the national, or foreign sphere," each "equally independent and supreme, in its own sphere of action." To the state governments were reserved 'all legislation and administration, in affairs which concern their citizens only'; to the federal government was given 'whatever concerns foreigns, or the citizens of the other states.' The 'foreign,' or federal sphere, moreover, was strictly limited to the few functions enumerated in the Constitution.[54]

Jefferson's logic in the Kentucky Resolutions is also reminiscent of his "Summary View of the Rights of British America" and his Declaration of Independence. Within these documents he listed the "train of abuses" by the Parliament and Crown which caused the American colonists to rebel. In the Declaration of Independence the enemy was a foreign power denying the American people their natural rights. In the Kentucky Resolutions, the enemy was no longer an external enemy, but an internal enemy with the same views and objectives as the British monarchy. The path to freedom against an external enemy was war, while the path to reclaiming the rights of the American people against an internal enemy was secession.

Jefferson's French Perspective

Jefferson's French perspective of the factional and regional political disputes in the United States reached its zenith in the Kentucky Resolutions. Republican forces in the United States, like those in France, were now waging a battle against counter-revolutionary forces within their own countries. He believed monarchist and aristocratic factions in the United States were determined to subvert the freedoms and liberties of the American people. It was left to him, the apostle of republicanism, and those loyal to the republican cause, to mount a campaign against the growing monarchical spirit in the United States.

He wrote to James Madison during his ministry to France in March of 1789, "there are some among us, who would now establish a monarchy. But they are inconsiderable in number and weight of character. The rising race are all republicans. We were educated in royalism; no wonder, if some of us retain that idolatry still."[55]

Jefferson's experience, during his years of opposition to Washington and Adam's presidential administrations, convinced him the tide was turning against republicanism in the United States.

State governments, he wrote in 1791, "will tend toward an excess of liberty...I would rather be exposed to the inconveniences attending too much liberty than those attending too small a degree of it."[56] State governments were the only true barriers against the encroachments of a central government, and the only powers capable of preserving the dynamic constitutional equilibrium between the federal and state governments.

In a 1799 letter to Jonathan Dayton, Hamilton presented a program of four measures designed to destroy the effect of the Kentucky Resolutions in the United States. First: He wanted to extend and promote the popularity of the government by extending the judiciary system, improving communications, granting funds for "new inventions, discoveries and improvements in agriculture and in the arts." Second: He wanted to increase the revenue of the government. He believed additional revenue would support a larger naval force and standing army. Third: He sought methods to enlarge the legal powers of the government.

He wanted laws to authorize "the calling out of the militia to suppress unlawful combinations and insurrection."

He also wanted laws to empower congress to "open canals in all cases in which it may be necessary to conduct them through the territory of two or more States...." He considered the subdivision of the great states indispensable to the security of the United States. Fourth: Hamilton wanted "laws for restraining and punishing incendiary and seditious practices."[57]

Hamilton's four-point program was designed to consolidate all powers in the federal government and suppress, with force of arms if need be, any opposition he considered to be subversive to the principles of good government. Although Hamilton's program was never enacted or even discussed in public, on January 29, 1791, the Federalists passed the Logan Law. This law prohibited any citizen of the United States "to carry on any verbal or written correspondence or intercourse with any foreign government..."[58] Dr. George Logan had seen representatives of the French Directory and brought back news of the pacific disposition of the French Government towards the United States.

Because Dr. Logan received his certificate for travel from Jefferson, Federalists immediately began to blame Jefferson for aiding and abetting Logan's mission to France. They believed Logan was a secret agent of American Jacobins, and with Jefferson's approval, was concocting invasion plans of the United States with the French army.

Jefferson believed the Logan Law was directed at him. Because these accusations came just before the presidential elections, Jefferson found it necessary to clarify his own political principles and practices. In a letter to Edmund Pendleton on January 29, 1799, he said the part ascribed to him was "entirely a calumny. Logan called on me, four or five days before his departure, and asked and received a certificate...of his citizenship and circumstances of life, merely as a protection, should he be molested in the present turbulent state of Europe."[59] Jefferson explained he had already given a hundred others without discriminating between Tories and Whigs.

Jefferson's Political Principles

In a letter to Eldridge Gerry on January 26, 1799, Jefferson proclaimed his faith in the "preservation of our present federal Constitution, according to the true sense in which it was adopted by the States...."[60] In this extensive letter, he reaffirmed his support for the French Revolution, although he was "not insensible under the atrocious depredations they have committed, on our commerce."[61]

Jefferson had four major concerns about the government under John Adams. His first concern was

to the monarchising of [the Constitution's] features by the forms of its administration with a view to conciliate a first transition to a President and Senate for life, and from that to an hereditary tenure of these offices, and thus to worm out the elective principle.[62]

Jefferson initially expressed his concern over the perpetual eligibility of the President for reelection, while he was minister to France. His opposition was founded in his fear that perpetual eligibility would undermine the very foundations of the American republic. Hamilton, who was now the acknowledged spokesman of the Federalist Party, had favored life tenure for the President.

Jefferson's second concern was with Hamilton's willingness to use force to suppress any opposition he considered a threat to the stability of the federal government. Jefferson preferred to rely on the militia solely in matters of internal defense and "for such a naval force only as may protect our coasts and harbors from such depredations as we have experienced."[63] A large naval force or standing army in time of peace would "overawe the public sentiment."

His third concern lay in his conviction of freedom of commerce. "I am for free commerce with all nations: political connection with none and little or no diplomatic establishment..."[64] There could be no cooperation or treaties with nations whose form of government was radically different from the American republic. Finally, Jefferson proclaimed his faith in the freedom of religion "and against all maneuvers to bring about a legal ascendancy of one sect over another; for freedom of the press, and against all violations of the Constitution to silence by force and not by reason the complaints...of our citizens against the conduct of their agents."[65]

Jefferson's concise and comprehensive statement of his political principles was necessary for two very important reasons. First, he was aware the Federalists were on a witch-hunt for political malcontents and would use their influence in newspapers to discredit him. Second, he wanted the American people to know, before the presidential election of 1800, his loyalties to the government of the United States were beyond reproach.

Jefferson's Support for the French Revolution

During his years of opposition to the presidential administrations of George Washington and John Adams, Jefferson relied on the success of French arms to save the American republic from monarchy, at home and abroad. Jefferson hoped the revolutionary spirit in France would find a home in the rapidly decaying political atmosphere of the United States. "I still hope," he wrote in 1791, "the French Revolution will issue happily. I feel that the permanence of our own leans in some degree on that, and that a failure there would be a powerful argument to prove that there must be a failure here."[66]

Throughout his years of opposition to the philosophy and policies of the Federalists, Jefferson saw parallels between political struggles in France and the conflict between political parties in the United States. He understood there were social, religious and economic differences between France and the United States, but he believed the contest for political liberty and a republican form of government was fundamentally the same in both countries. The French revolutionaries, at least, knew their enemies. Monarchists in France did not pretend to be Republicans, as they did in the United States.

Jefferson's personal commitment to the French Revolution and his profound faith in the ideology of the French revolutionaries blinded him to the truth that the principles and practices of the Federalist Party in the

United States were fundamentally different from the principles of the monarchists in France. From his perspective, the political conflicts and rivalries between Republicans and Federalists in the United States were a re-enactment of the struggles between republicans and monarchists in France.

When Jefferson returned from Paris, he believed he was fighting an epic battle against the entrenched forces of monarchism in America. He believed the future course of the American Republic, whether it was to become a monarchy or continue as a representative democracy, depended primarily upon his defiance and leadership.

Jefferson was not alone, of course, in his enthusiastic support for the French Revolution. "The French Revolution was for several years "the great dominant fact in American political life. It furnished issues, watchwords, and leaders, and was an important agent in determining the alignment and construction of parties ..."[67]

It was not, then, Jefferson's enthusiastic support for the French Revolution that distinguished him from other Americans in this period. What did distinguish Jefferson from other national leaders and his countrymen in the 1790's, however, was his active participation in the French Revolution during his ministry to France and his French revolutionary philosophy.

Jefferson was the only American to propose a ten-point charter of constitutional reform to Lafayette and St. Etienne on June 3, 1789, while he was the ambassador to France, and the only American who attempted to resolve the differences between the members of the Patriot Party at a meeting at his house to advance the cause of the French Revolution. He was also the only American who helped the French revolutionaries compose the French Declaration of the Rights of Man and of the Citizen.

Jefferson's enthusiasm for the French Revolution, in contrast to other American national leaders, was more profoundly rooted in the French revolutionary experience. His knowledge of the French Revolution did not come by way of newspapers, magazines, plays or toasts to the French Revolution in the self-created democratic societies throughout the country, as it did for his countrymen.

Jefferson had a more intimate and emotional reaction to class divisions and the poverty he witnessed in England and France than Adams, Madison and Hamilton who may have read about it but did not feel it. "With truths of a certain kind," Usbek said in Montesquieu's Persian Letters, "it is not enough to make them appear convincing; one must also make them felt."68 Jefferson was clearly moved by the poverty, social inequalities and class divisions he saw in France

The increasingly violent and egalitarian tendencies of the Jacobins also did not cause Jefferson to reevaluate his support for the revolution, as did some of its most avid supporters in the United States. On the contrary, Jefferson continued to justify the excesses of the revolution. He was even willing to rationalize the imprisonment and execution of some of his dearest friends in Paris. Lafayette was persecuted by the Jacobins in 1791 and imprisoned after trying to escape by the Austrians. Brissot de Warville was arrested by the Jacobins on June 2, 1793 and then guillotined the next day. Condorcet was arrested and imprisoned in 1794 and then died mysteriously in prison. And Destutt de Tracy was imprisoned for a year during the Reign of Terror, narrowly escaping execution. Revolutions, he had earlier said, were not made on "feather beds."

Scholars have expressed bewilderment at Jefferson's uncritical and unwavering support for the French Revolution during the Reign of Terror. Jefferson was, evidently, like so many other Americans in the 1790's, simply caught up in the revolutionary fever spreading over every geographic region of the country. "At that moment," Jefferson's biographer, Dumas Malone wrote, "he was in line with the predominant opinion of his countrymen. He indulged to some degree in what in our own day is called 'rationalization'...."[69] Jefferson's "Adam and Eve" letter, Malone asserts,

should be understandable in any society threatened by any form of political absolutism, he was saying that despotism had been over-thrown in France, that, therefore, it would eventually be overcome everywhere, and that in the light of this vast triumph for the cause of human liberty the losses must be regarded as slight...This lifelong champion of freedom could not lay first emphasis on security.[70]

In fact, it was not a fever at all that came over Jefferson but a recognition and understanding that the egalitarian and constitutional principles of the Jacobins were almost identical to his own. The French Declaration of Rights of 1793, which so outraged Hamilton and Adams, and other national leaders in the United States, articulated not only the radical doctrines of the Jacobin sect, but Jefferson's reasoning and principles in Jefferson's revolutionary doctrine, "the earth belongs to the living, and not the dead."

Jefferson agreed with the most radical articles of the French Declaration of Rights of 1793, a critical fact neglected entirely by scholars. Article 21 of the Declaration stated that "Society owes maintenance to unfortunate citizens, either procuring work for them or in providing the means of existence for those who are unable to labor."[71] Jefferson had earlier written to the Reverend James Madison, as we have already seen, that "whenever there are in any country uncultivated lands and unemployed poor it is clear that the laws of property have been so far extended as to violate natural right. If for the encouragement of industry we allow it to be appropriated, we must take care that other employment be provided to those excluded from that appropriation."[72] He wrote, in yet another letter during his travels in France, as we have also seen, that "legislators cannot invent too many devices for subdividing property, only taking care to let their subdivisions go hand in hand with the natural affections of the human mind."[73] The egalitarianism of Article 21 satisfied Jefferson's sense of social justice, providing for the unemployed poor a "means of existence."

Article 28 of the Declaration of Rights expressed Jefferson's constitutional principles in his own revolutionary document of 1789 that people always have "the right to review, to reform, and to alter its constitution. One generation cannot subject to its law the future generations."[74] It should not be surprising, then, that Jefferson embraced the Jacobin program for reform because it embodied his own revolutionary principles.

Clearly, Jefferson's support for the French Revolution

was not like every other American's, and his perspective of American political society was more French than American. Jefferson was, in his years of opposition to Washington and Adams, a dominating political leader who "looked upon the people as a multitude without a political shepherd, likely to go astray amidst the wastes of anarchy, or to fall into the pit of monarchy. With scrip and staff and as astute political policy, he became their shepherd...."[75] A shepherd, it must be said, who believed he possessed the revolutionary insights from his experiences in France to lead the American people toward a more democratic and egalitarian future.

Chapter 7

Jefferson's Mature Political Philosophy

After eleven years of opposition to the administrations of George Washington and John Adams, Jefferson was elected to the presidency of the United States in 1800. As he assumed office, he expressed his sentiments to John Dickinson about the new political climate in the country. "The storm through which we have passed has been tremendous indeed. The tough sides of our Argosy have been thoroughly tried. Her strength has stood the waves into which she was steered, with view to sink her. We shall put her on her republican tack, and she will now show by the beauty of her motion, the skill of her builders."[1]

Jefferson hoped to soon see "a perfect consolidation to effect which, nothing shall, be spared on my part, short of the abandonment of the principles of our revolution. The American republic would now shine like a beacon across the clouded horizons of man and would thereby serve as a standing monument and example for the aim and imitation of the people of other countries."[2]

Jefferson took great pride in comparing his ideas and practices with those of the other side:

who have discountenanced all advances in science as dangerous innovations, have endeavored to render philosophy and republicanism terms of reproach, to persuade us that man cannot be governed but by the rod, etc. I shall have the happiness of living and dying in the contrary hope.[3]

The government would no longer be in the hands of the monarchical-aristocratical party, as Jefferson earlier wrote. It would now serve the republican interests of the American people. His election, he proclaimed was "as real a revolution in the principles of our government as that of 1776 was in its form."[4]

The Argosy may have survived the "boisterous ocean" of domestic politics, but the tide of history had turned against the French Revolution and with it, Jefferson's hopes that a republican France would save the American republic from the monarchists in the United States and from England's ambitions to destroy her.

Jefferson's victory in the 1800 election coincided with Napoleon's ascendancy to power in France on the 18th Brumaire of the new French republican calendar, November 9, 1799. Jefferson immediately realized that the French Revolution had failed. Before his election to the presidency, Jefferson believed the example of a republican France, and French arms would change the face of Europe from its monarchist past to a republican future. "I considered a successful reformation of government in France as insuring a general reformation through Europe, and the resurrection to a new life of their people, now ground to dust by the abuses of the governing powers."[4]

The success of the French Revolution would insure "a general reformation through Europe, but a failure there," he wrote to Edward Rutledge in 1791, "would be a powerful argument to prove that there must be a failure here."[5]

The turning point in Jefferson's perspective of the French Revolution occurred with Napoleon's rise to power. When he first heard about a revolution in Paris on January 23, 1800, he said he did not know the specific causes for the uprising, but speculated that Bonaparte was at its head. Jefferson wrote: "After eight or nine years of perpetual broils and factions in their Directory, a standing division of three against two...it is possible...that Bonaparte may be for a single executive ...and that to this change the nation may rally itself ... ."[6]

Like so many votaries of learning in France, Jefferson believed Napoleon would terminate the misrule and confusion of the Directory and stabilize the liberal gains made by the Revolution. However, by February 2, 1800 Jefferson had already expressed his misgivings about Napoleon. He was not sure if he had the necessary skills in "forming governments friendly to the people. Wherever he has meddled we have seen nothing but fragments of the Old Roman government stuck into materials with which they can form no cohesion: we see the bigotry of an Italian, to the ancient splendor of his country, but nothing which bespeaks a luminous view of the organization of rational government."[7]

On February 26, 1800 a month after first hearing of the revolution, Jefferson concluded France's revolutionary experiment in representative government had failed. Jefferson hoped Napoleon would lead rationally, that "he would calculate truly the difference between the fame of a Washington and a Cromwell."[8]

Napoleon's rise to power had two important consequences for Jefferson's political theories and practices during his presidency. First, it signaled the failure of the French Revolution to secure liberty for its own people and other European countries; and second, it convinced Jefferson that the United States would have to face the anti-republican forces of the Old World alone. He was now convinced that the United States, instead of France, was to become the standard-bearer and example of republicanism in the world. Jefferson's nationalism has its origins, as Peter Onuf suggests, in "the crisis of the 1790's" and becomes "self-conscious," in a "principled form" in 1800, the year of Jefferson's election.[9] There were certainly many factors at home that contributed to Jefferson's nationalism, but the failure of the French Revolution, although not considered by historians to be such, must also be considered as one of them.

The Republican Party was created, in large measure, by the disposition of America's national leaders and parties toward the French Revolution and the Jay Treaty. A political leader's support for, or opposition to the French Revolution became for Jefferson the litmus test for one's loyalty to the "principles of 1776" and commitment to a republican form of government.

Jefferson's election to the presidency in 1800, coinciding as it did with Napoleon's ascendancy to power in France, signified in Jefferson's mind that the French Revolution failed, leaving him no choice but to pursue nationalistic policies and programs in the United States. Jefferson's nationalism, in this respect, was a consequence of the failure of the French Revolution and represented a decisive shift in his thinking from radical enlightenment internationalism, as Jonathan Israel defines it, to the camp of the moderate Enlightenment thinkers "who were willing to work within one country."[10]

During Jefferson's years of opposition to the Washington and Adams' administrations he paid close attention to the party struggles in France and the United States. He believed both countries were fighting for their liberty against monarchist forces at home and abroad. The American and French Revolutions were only the beginning of a long and arduous struggle for political liberty. He was aware, however, as he later expressed it to John Adams:

> The generation which commences a revolution rarely completes it...A first attempt to recover the right of self-government may fail, so may a second, a third, etc. But as a younger and more instructed race comes on, the sentiment becomes more and more intuitive, and a fourth, a fifth or some subsequent one of the ever renewed attempts will ultimately succeed. [11]

Considering the frequent political setbacks of revolutionary France, he surmised that revolutions do not end with the establishment of new laws and constitutions. It also required the vigilance and active participation of a free people to secure the blessings of liberty for themselves and for posterity. The American Revolution of 1776 was only the beginning of the revolutionary process.

The United States Constitution was meant to be republican according to every candid interpretation, he said, and "Yet we have seen it so interpreted and administered as to be truly what the French have called, a monarchie masque."[12] Jefferson always believed the Federalists were monarchists, disguising themselves as republicans. He was blinded by the example of revolutionary France and was unable to grasp the differences between the struggle for political liberty in France and the struggle for political liberty in the United States.

Because Jefferson could no longer rely on a republican France to protect the United States from monarchical governments in Europe, especially the English, it was necessary to consolidate and strengthen the gains made by the American Revolution and his own "Revolution of 1800." During his presidential administrations, Jefferson's struggles with the Federal Judiciary, his acquisition of the Louisiana territories, and his notorious Embargo Acts reflect his new nationalistic perspective of America's role in the world.

Jefferson's First Historic Battle: Federal Judiciary and the Supreme Court

Jefferson believed the Federal courts were bastions of Federalist principles and monarchist sentiments. The Judiciary Act of February 13, 1801, passed only a few weeks before the Federalists lost control of the Presidency and the Congress, authorized the creation of sixteen new circuit court judges to relieve Supreme Court Justices from circuit court duties. It also reduced the membership of the Supreme Court from six to five Justices. In political terms, this meant Jefferson would not be able to appoint a new Justice to the Supreme

Court, and he was faced with a Federal judiciary void of Republicans.

In an 1801 letter to Stuart, Jefferson revealed his immediate aims to remedy this situation.

Mr. Adams, who continued filling all the offices till nine o'clock of the night, at twelve of which he was to go out of office himself...The judges, of course, stands till the law shall be repealed, which we trust will be by the next Congress. But as to all others I made it immediately known that I should consider them nullities and appoint others, as I think I have a preferable right to name agents for my own administration. 13

Before the repeal of the Judiciary Act and the appointment of new judges, Jefferson believed: "The only shield for our republican citizens against the federalism of the courts is to have the attorneys and marshals republicans."14 There was, in Jefferson's mind, a program of resistance to "the federalism of the courts." This resistance would quickly culminate in the repeal of the Judiciary Act and the removal of certain Federal judges; thus reversing the injustices of the Adams' administration.

Jefferson's conflict with the Federal judiciary, and the rumors suggesting he was attempting to remove Federal judges, called up bitter retaliations by the Federalist press. The press accused him of depriving a minority of their just rights and rewards. They claimed Jefferson had become a political executioner of those who held opinions contrary to his own. In response to these charges, Jefferson accused the late administration of excluding republicans from all offices with the steady pursuit of monopolizing power for the Federalists.

Now that public sentiment declared its approval of a different political party, Jefferson questioned: "was it to be imagined that this monopoly of office was to be continued in the hands of the minority? Does it violate their equal rights, to assert some rights in the majority also....Can they not harmonize in society unless they have everything in their own hands?"[15] The will of the nation, demonstrated by the several elections, called "for an administration of government according with the opinions of those elected," and it was his responsibility to fulfill their expectations even if displacements and removals were required.

The bill authorizing Marbury's commission was left behind, and Jefferson contended, "for ...a deed, a bond, delivery is essential to give validity. Until, therefore, the commission is delivered out of the hands of the executive and his agents, it is not his deed. He may withhold or cancel it at pleasure...."[16] In retaliation, a writ of mandamus was issued on behalf of Marbury, along with three others, in an effort to compel Secretary of State James Madison to delivery their commissions. This conflict resulted in the historic case of *Marbury vs. Madison*.

Chief Justice Marshall ruled in *Marbury vs. Madison* that the Supreme Court had no jurisdiction in this case, and any Congressional grant of such jurisdiction was therefore void. Having denied Marbury's petition, Marshall surreptitiously established a new legal precedent. Although not specifically granted in the Constitution, the Supreme Court could pass judgment upon the validity of Congressional legislation and Executive actions.[17]

Jefferson contested this new Supreme Court right. He argued the principle of judicial review could not be established in this case, and that it did not have the constitutional right to pass judgments on congressional and executive actions.

In contrast to Marshall's interpretation of the Constitution, Jefferson believed the Constitution allowed for all three branches of government to participate equally in the adjudication of constitutional issues. He expressed his constitutional views in a letter to Abigail Adams in 1804, arguing:

> That instrument (Constitution) meant that it's co-ordinate branches should be checks on each other. But the opinion which gives to the judges the right to decide what laws are constitutional, and what not, not only for themselves in their own sphere of action, but for the legislature and executive also in their spheres, would make the judiciary a despotic branch. [18]

Jefferson always favored an independent judiciary but was careful to limit its jurisdiction. Even in 1776, when he declared "judges should hold estates for life in their offices, or, in other words, their commissions should be made during good behavior," he wanted their actions to be checked by the legislative and executive branches of government. In July of 1776 he wrote the judicial power "ought to be distinct from both the legislative and executive, and independent upon both, that so it may be a check upon both, as both should be a check upon that."[19] By 1789 Jefferson was even more specific. "The Judiciary if rendered independent, and kept strictly to their own department, merits great confidence for their learning and integrity."20

Jefferson did not believe the principle of judicial review was compatible with the principles of a democratic republic. He feared the Supreme Court had assigned unconstitutional prerogatives to its exercise of power with the intention of erasing republicanism in the United States. The principle of judicial review, according to Jefferson, empowered the Supreme Court to check the powers of the two other branches of government. However, the Supreme Court was not subject to a similar counter-check. Jefferson believed his "tripartite theory" would offer a more vital role of constitutional interpretation to the Congress, and in turn would be more representative of the people's will.

As Jefferson argued against the principle of judicial review on constitutional ground, he reflected upon the monstrous abuses the French people had suffered due to the unaccountability of the Parlements for their decisions. He later wrote of this in his *Autobiography*. The French Parlements were hereditary bodies which sought, through judicial decrees, to legislate obedience from the public as it enriched itself with public taxes. Jefferson wrote:

venality of the judges and their partialities to the rich" would result, as it did in France, in the Court's assumption of despotic powers. Sensitive to the injustices committed against the French people by the Parlements, Jefferson was determined to prevent a similar body, with life-tenure, to take root in the United States.21

To counteract the Federalist strongholds in the judiciary and their pernicious influence on the body politic, Jefferson sought legal expedients to remove

Federalist judges. The Republicans succeeded in impeaching Judge John Pickering in 1803 on highly questionable grounds. Judges could be removed only if they committed treason, bribery, or other high crimes and misdemeanors. Even though Justice Pickering was hopelessly insane, he had not committed any such crimes.

However, after an aborted attempt to impeach the intransigent Justice Samuel Chase, impeachment as a mode of redress and removal soon proved to be too cumbersome and ineffective. Realizing impeachment was a blunted instrument for removing judges, Jefferson hoped "the Constitution should be so amended to remove any judge from office." He recommended, in later years, all "future appointments of judges be for four or six years, and removable by the President and Senate. This will bring their conduct, at regular periods, under revision and probation, and may keep them in equipoise between the general and special governments."22 Jefferson thought it was beneficial for the judiciary to be independent of the Executive, but never from the will of the people.

Jefferson's conflict with the Supreme Court and Federal Judiciary emerged from three core beliefs: First: The Courts were hostile to the principles of a republican government. Second: The Supreme Court was trying to assume unconstitutional and despotic powers through the principle of judicial review over the other branches of government. Third: The Constitution empowered all branches of government to judge the constitutionality of acts within the boundaries of their jurisdiction.

Because the United States was the last bastion of liberty in the world, Jefferson found it necessary, as he wrote to John Dickinson on Dec.19, 1801 "to avail ourselves of our ascendancy to establish good principles and good practices; to fortify republicanism behind, as many barriers as possible, that the outworks may give time to rally and save the citadel, should that be again in danger."[23] Jefferson reasoned the French Revolution failed because republicans in France did not take the necessary precaution to consolidate and fortify the liberal gains made by their revolution in its earliest stages. He was not going to repeat those mistakes in the United States.

Jefferson's Second Historic Battle: The Louisiana Purchase

The second major issue in Jefferson's first presidential administration was the acquisition of the Louisiana Territory from France on May 2, 1803. Jefferson was eager to purchase this territory, and adroitly avoided Napoleon's desperate need for cash to pursue war with Great Britain. The purchase of the Louisiana territory, Jefferson wrote to Horatio Gates on July 11, 1803, could not simply "be ascribed to the accident of war," as his critics supposed, since he began plans for its acquisition in May, 1801. "They would see that though we could not say when war would arise, yet we said with energy what would take place when it should arise. We did not, by our intrigues, produce the war, but we availed ourselves of it when it happened."[24]

The Louisiana territory more than doubled the area of the United States. It added eight hundred seventy-five thousand square miles, eventually creating thirteen new states to the north and west of New Orleans "ascending from the Gulf of Mexico to the Canadian border, are Louisiana, Arkansas, Oklahoma, Missouri, Kansas, Iowa, Nebraska, Minnesota, South Dakota, North Dakota, Colorado, Wyoming, and Montana."[25] The lands acquired through the Louisiana Purchase, at the cost of eighty million francs or fifteen million dollars, would provide generations of Americans to come with the economic prerequisite for Jefferson's one-class republican dream: sufficient lands to live free and independent lives which would have the additional benefit of strengthening and securing the future of republicanism in the United States.

From the very beginning of his administration, Jefferson recognized the purchase of the Louisiana territory from France was an economic and political necessity for the United States. Federalists and Republicans from all regions of the country understood America's right to navigate the Mississippi River and control the port of Mississippi was essential to commerce and trade in the United States. The presence of a foreign power, France, England or Spain, in control of the port of Mississippi and the navigation of the Mississippi River would forever shape the political destiny of the United States. Jefferson was acutely aware of Napoleon's political ambitions for empire, and he knew the United States "had almost no defense in place to oppose such a Napoleonic adventure-less than a thousand men in uniform and no navy."[26]

The purchase of the Louisiana territory, however, raised serious constitutional issues for Jefferson. A strict constructionist, Jefferson knew that the Constitution did not expressly empower the President to admit new States into the Union. He expressed his reservations to Wilson Nicholas in 1803.

I am aware of the force of the observation you make on the power given by the Constitution to Congress, to admit new states into the Union, without restraining the subject to the territory then constituting the United States. But when I consider that the limits of the United States are precisely fixed by the treaty of 1783, that the Constitution expressly declares itself to be made for the United States, I cannot help believing the intention was not to permit Congress to admit into the Union new States...27

Instead of broadly interpreting the Constitution to justify his actions, Jefferson sought to rectify the situation with an amendment to the Constitution

I had rather ask an enlargement of power from the nation where it is found necessary, than to assume it by a construction which would make our powers boundless. Our peculiar security is in the possession of a written Constitution...Let us go on then perfecting it, by adding, by way of amendment to the Constitution those powers which time and trials show are still wanting. 28

When James Madison realized that Jefferson was seriously leaning toward a constitutional amendment, requiring ratification by the states, he warned Jefferson "that any hint of a long constitutional impasse could cause the impatient French ruler to renounce the treaty and revive the whole specter of a French move to retake New Orleans, perhaps blocking U.S. navigation of the Mississippi."29 Jefferson was persuaded by Madison's argument, and promptly moved to gain support for the agreement. He worried, however, that because he "had stretched the Constitution until it cracked," that "he would be impeached because his treaty-making powers did not specify the acquisition of territory.[30]

Jefferson's agony over the purchase of the Louisiana territory and his reluctance to exercise the "implied powers" of the Constitution, as Hamilton had interpreted them, was a lesson learned from the imprudence of the French Revolutionaries to build on the gains they had already achieved in the early phase of the revolution.

On February 14, 1815 he reminded the Marquis de Lafayette

how earnestly I urged yourself and the patriots of my acquaintance, to enter then into a compact with the king, securing freedom of religion, freedom of the press, trial by jury, habeas corpus, and a national legislature, all of which it was known he would then yield, to go home, and let these work on the amelioration of the condition of the people, until they should have rendered them capable of more, when occasions would not fail to arise for communicating to them more.[31]

The failure of the French Revolution served as a sobering example of the dangers imprudent and intemperate political actions could have on the course of human liberty. He preferred an amendment to the Constitution as opposed to a justification of the purchase of Louisiana under broad constitutional construction. He favored this because he did not want "to give up the certainty of such a degree of liberty" which obtained in the American republic. Jefferson knew, "A departure from principle in one instance, becomes a precedent, for a second; that second for a third; and so on, till the bulk of society is reduced to be mere automatons of misery, as they had become under the rule of Napoleon Bonaparte."32

Jefferson revealed his practical disposition toward political change when he wrote on March 31, 1801, after he was sure that the French Revolution was betrayed by Napoleon:

how far I should fall short of effecting all the reformation which reason would suggest, and experience approve, were I free to do whatever I thought best; but when, we reflect how difficult it is to move or inflect the great machine of society, how impossible to advance the notions of a whole people suddenly to ideal right, we see the wisdom of Solon's remark, that no more good must be attempted than the nation can bear. ... 33

Like Montesquieu before him, Jefferson believed the Constitution should be amended and revised by popular mandate, and only when time and circumstances demanded it. "But I know also," he wrote,

that laws and institutions must go hand in hand with the progress of the human mind... as that becomes more developed, more enlightened, as new discoveries are made, new truths disclosed, and manners and opinions change with the change of circumstances, institutions must advance also, and keep pace with the times.34

Jefferson had little patience for those who held a

"sanctimonious reverence" for constitutions and "deem them like the ark of the covenant, too sacred to be touched. They ascribe to a wisdom more than human, and suppose what they did to be beyond amendment."[35] His fair-minded logic resulted in an intolerant view of those who found solace in man's past achievements, and he was equally disapproving of those who supported sudden changes without sufficiently taking into consideration the customs, habits and manners of a people.

Unwilling to risk the republican consensus he helped to forge in the United States in the vain hope of radical reformation of the nation's laws and constitution Jefferson abandoned his radical republican agenda of 1789. The path he chose instead was one of reform and not revolution. His general reasoning in the purchase of the Louisiana territory, as it was in his constitutional struggle with the Supreme Court and the Federal Judiciary, was to fortify and strengthen republicanism in the United States without risking unnecessarily, by imprudent actions, the gains already won.

Jefferson's Third Historic Battle: Embargo

Jefferson's constitutionalism would be challenged once again with the most defining decision of his second Presidential term, the notorious Embargo Act of 1807. This act, submitted to the Senate on December 18, 1807 and to the House the next day, was approved by both Houses without floor debate in a closed door session of the House of Representatives. The Embargo Act was intended by its authors, Jefferson and Madison, to coerce the British and French governments into recognizing the commercial rights of a neutral country. This was to be accomplished by denying France and Britain safe haven in its ports while revoking their trading rights with the United States. The embargo was Jefferson's alternative to war.

After the failure of the Peace of Amiens in 1802, and the outbreak of war between England and France, American commerce was subjected to arbitrary rules and restrictions governing her access to distant markets. "New principles," he wrote in his fifth annual message to Congress, "have been interloped into the law of nations, founded neither in justice nor the usage or acknowledgment of nations. According to these, a belligerent takes to himself a commerce with its own enemy which it denies to a neutral, on the ground of its aiding that enemy in the war."[36]

Jefferson was acutely aware that Britain's "order interdicting all trade by neutrals between ports not in amity with them; and being now at war with nearly every nation on the Atlantic and Mediterranean seas," requiring "our vessels to sacrifice their cargoes at the first port they touch, or to return home without the benefit of going to any other market..." would destroy America's trade with the world.[37]

After the attack of the frigate Chesapeake on June, 22, 1807, by the British man-of-war, H.M.S Leopard, leaving behind twenty-one dead and removing four alleged deserters, Jefferson proposed three courses of action to deal with Britain's intransigence at sea. "1. Embargo. 2. War. 3. Submission and tribute...The first, he believed, would most likely prevail.[38]

The Embargo Act, generally considered a temporary and precautionary measure and not a permanent ban on all trade between the United States, Britain and France, was tolerated only by commercial interests in the North and East after its initial enactment. However, when it became apparent that it was a permanent ban on trade, resulting in enormous financial hardship for commercial interests in the North and the East, the measure was frequently and blatantly violated.

Jefferson was aware, as he later wrote to William Giles, "that eastern States were...in negotiation with agents of the British government, the object of which was an agreement that the New England States should take no further part in the war...that, without formally declaring their separation from the Union of the States, they should withdraw from all aid and obedience to them....."[39] It seemed to him that the resistance to the Embargo in the Northern and Eastern States was largely the work of monarchists in the Federalist Party who were committed, heart and soul, to England and monarchy.

The Embargo Act not only failed to force Britain and France to rescind their orders against neutrals, but hardened their resolve. This resulted in even more severe orders against American shipping. Jefferson's obstinacy in the enforcement of the Embargo Acts, after it became apparent the measure lost the support of the people it was intended to serve, destroyed both the political consensus he achieved in his first presidential term and the confidence and esteem he had earned. The Embargo Acts also raised serious questions about the constitutionality of his actions, and the sincerity in which he frequently espoused the principles of states' rights in favor of his own actions and measures.

The Embargo Act was intended to be an alternative

to a devastating war with England and France. Jefferson had earlier discussed this option, economic coercion, as an alternative to war with James Madison. He recognized then, as he did during his presidency, that there were higher principles to consider in a moment of crisis: "A strict observation of the written laws is doubtless one of the highest duties of a good citizen," he wrote to J. B. Colvin in 1810,

but it is not the highest. The laws of necessity, of self-preservation, of saving our country when in danger, are of higher obligation! To lose our country by a scrupulous adherence to written law, would be to lose the law itself, with life, liberty, property and all those who are enjoying them with us; thus absurdly sacrificing the end to the means. 40

Throughout his presidential administrations, 1801-1809, Jefferson's political philosophy was designed to exercise the theory and practice of good government. With the failure of the French Revolution, Jefferson found it necessary, as he later wrote to the Marquis de Lafayette, "to read a lesson in the fatal errors of the republicans" so that similar mistakes would not be repeated in the future."41 Unwilling to hazard the republican consensus in the United States for his ideal vision of a republic, as he had earlier suggested to James Madison, Jefferson followed a moderate course of action to further strengthen and consolidate republicanism in America.

Jefferson's departure from his radical views of 1789 was not a betrayal of his earlier beliefs, but a reasoned and pragmatic response to new realities. Jefferson's efforts to strengthen republicanism in the United States did not end with his departure from public office. He continued to examine, clarify and redefine in his retirement the principles of a republican form of government, and the measures which were necessary for its survival.

Jefferson's Republicanism

Although Jefferson's political strategies were designed to accommodate changes in the political landscape in Europe and in the United States, his principles of republicanism remained relatively intact throughout his public and private life. He may have departed from the constitutionalism of Montesquieu in his Paris years, but he remained loyal, nonetheless, to Montesquieu's principles of republicanism.

"A love of the republic in a democracy," Montesquieu wrote:

is a love of the democracy; as the latter is that of equality. A love of the democracy is likewise that of frugality. Since every individual ought here to enjoy the same happiness and the same advantages, they should consequently taste the same pleasures and form the same hopes, which cannot be expected but from a general frugality. The love of equality in a democracy limits ambition to the sole desire, to the sole happiness, of doing greater services to our country than the rest of our fellow citizens. They cannot all render her equal service, but they all ought to serve her with equal alacrity.[42]

Jefferson may have disagreed with Montesquieu about the geographic size of a republic, and for his apparent love of everything English, but he never forgot or tired of trying to implement Montesquieu's principles of republicanism—democracy, equality and frugality.

During his presidency Jefferson applied Montesquieu's prescriptive principles for a democratic republic. He believed public debts are a tax on "our meat and in our drink, in our necessaries and our comforts, in our labors and our amusements," and "if we are not frugal in the conduct of our public affairs, we will be like the people of England who

must come to labor sixteen hours in the twenty-four, give the earnings of fifteen to these to the government for their debts and daily expenses; and the sixteenth being insufficient to afford us bread, we must live, as they now do, on oatmeal and potatoes; have no time to think, no means of calling the mismanagers to account; but be glad to obtain subsistence by hiring ourselves to rivet their chains on the necks of our fellow-sufferers.43

Frugality in government, he believed, was synonymous with one's freedom and independence. He wrote in his doctrine, "the earth belongs to the living," governments do not have the right to burden the next generation with their own intemperate and imprudent behavior. Unsurprisingly, Jefferson retired the national debt in his second presidential administration.

Jefferson also proposed two bills in his own state of Virginia which, as he said, "laid the axe to the root of Pseudo-aristocracy." The accumulation of wealth in the hands of the few, as Montesquieu believed, tends to turn the minds of the people...toward their particular interests. Those who are allowed only what is necessary having nothing but their own reputation and their country's glory in view. But a soul depraved by luxury has many other desires, and soon becomes an enemy to the laws that confine it.[44]

Jefferson warned an American student about to travel abroad of Europeans' "fondness for luxury and dissipation and a contempt for the simplicity of his own country" lest they become "fascinated with the privileges of the European aristocrats, and [see] with abhorrence the lovely equality which the poor enjoys with the rich in his own country...."[45]

Ward Republics

Central governments, Jefferson always warned, tend to encroach upon the rights of individuals and states, no matter how well intentioned or honest its public officers. It was necessary, then, to create a countervailing force, a political infrastructure on local and state levels of government, to check the power and influence of the central government. Jefferson wanted to make it possible for every American to participate actively in the affairs of state, on all levels of government. He proposed, therefore, to democratize the institutions of government by sub- dividing every county into wards about six miles square. In each of the wards, he says, there should be a free school for reading, writing and arithmetic; "a company of militia...{and} justice of the peace and constable... Each ward was also responsible for the care of their own poor... roads... police... {and} elect within themselves one or more jurors...." Wards "would thus be a small republic within itself, and every man in the State would thus become an acting member of the common government, transacting in person a great portion of its rights and duties...."[46]

The ward republics, he informed Kerchival, "by making every citizen an acting member of the government, and in the offices nearest and most interesting to him, will attach him by his strongest feelings to the independence of the country, and its republican constitution.[47] He believed ward republics, like the townships in New England, were "the wisest invention ever devised by the wit of man for the perfect exercise of self-government."[48]

Ward republics, however, were a necessary, but not a sufficient condition for self-government in the United States. Jefferson also proposed we marshal our government into, 1. the general federal republic for all concerns foreign and federal; 2. that of the State, for what relates to our citizens exclusively; 3. the country republics, for the duties and concerns of the county; and 4. the ward republics...."[49]

In sum, he wrote, these proposals would provide for "general suffrage, equal representation, an executive chosen by the people, judges elective or amovable, justices, jurors, and sheriffs elective, ward divisions and periodical amendments of the constitution."[50] "The elementary republics of the wards, the county republics, the state republics, and the republic of the Union," he wrote to Joseph Cabell in 1816, "would form a graduation of authorities, standing each on the basis of law, holding everyone its delegated share of powers, and constituting truly a system of fundamental balances and checks for the government."[51]

The elementary republics, Jefferson reasoned, will empower every man to share "in the direction of his ward-republics" and make him feel "that he is a participator in the government of affairs, not merely at an election one day in the year, but every day." When every man is "a member of some of its councils, great or small, he will not let the heart be torn out of his body sooner than his power be wrestled from him by a Caesar or a Bonaparte."[52]

In his letter to Cartwright about ward republics, Jefferson also reiterated his belief in the principle of state's rights, articulated in the Kentucky Resolutions, and the doctrine of "the earth belongs to the living." State governments are not subordinate to the federal government, he wrote, but a "co-ordinate department of one simple and integral whole...The one is the domestic, the other the foreign branch of the same government; neither having control over the other, but within its own department."[53] In the event, he says, both parties cannot resolve their jurisdictional disputes, "a convention of the States must be called, to ascribe the doubtful power to that department which they may think best."[54] Our constitution, he says, is changeable only "by the authority of the people, on a special election of representatives..."[55]

Ward republics, state's rights and his doctrine of "the earth belongs to the living" are the fundamental principles of Jefferson's republicanism. Among the Founding Fathers, Richard Matthews wrote, "Jefferson alone wishes to institutionalize general education, participatory democracy, and permanent revolution through the establishment of ward republics."56 Jefferson's system of ward republics coupled with his doctrine of the earth belongs to the living, Matthews believes,

is also a symbolic national recommitment of each citizen to every other citizen, as well as to the citizenry as a whole. Through the daily action in the ward-republics, then, Jefferson thinks he has found a permanent check to tyranny, a way to keep alive the revolutionary ardor of the founding era, and a mechanism to allow the citizens truly to govern themselves.57

"Jefferson's fascination with ward republics," Matthews also contends, "was undoubtedly influenced by his own observations and knowledge of the American Indians."58 He notes the similarity between Jefferson's writings on ward republics and Charles Thompson's editorial commentary on tribal governments which Jefferson published in his *Notes on the State of Virginia*.

Jefferson was impressed with the Aborigines of his native state who, he said "never submitted themselves to any laws, any coercive power, any shadow of government. Their only controuls are their manners, and that moral sense of right and wrong, which, like the sense of tasting and feeling, in every man makes a part of his nature...." No law, "as among the savage Americans," he believed, was preferable to "too much law, as among the civilized Europeans...It will be said, that great societies cannot exist without government. The Savages therefore break them into small ones."59

Jefferson's sympathy for and knowledge of tribal society among the Native Americans may have had some influence on his understanding of the structure of ward republics, but it was more likely the political sociology of Montesquieu which shaped his philosophy of republicanism and his ideas about ward republics, or "small republics," as he also called them. The ward republics, in fact, represent yet another "Montesquieuian moment" in Jefferson's political philosophy, a progressive return to Montesquieu's principles of democracy.

It should not be surprising, then, that in the same letter he expressed his ideas about ward republics to Joseph Cabell, he also recommended the reading of Tracy's "Review of Montesquieu, printed at Philadelphia a few years ago. It has the advantage, too, of being equally sound and corrective of the principles of political economy...."[60] Chipman's, Priestley's *Principles of Government*, and the *Federalist Papers* were "excellent in many respects but for fundamental principles not comparable to the Review."[61]

Montesquieu's definition of a republic in *The Spirit of the Laws* reappears in his concept of ward republics. "It is natural for a republic," Montesquieu wrote:

to have only a small territory; otherwise it cannot long subsist. In an extensive republic there are men of large fortunes, and consequently of less moderation; there are trusts too considerable to be placed in any single subject; he has interests of his own; he soon begins to think he may be happy and glorious, by oppressing his fellow-citizens; and that he may raise himself to grandeur on the ruins of his country. In an extensive republic the public good is sacrificed to a thousand private views...[62]

In a small republic, he says, "the interests of the public

is more obvious, better understood, and more within the reach of every citizen; abuse have less extent, and, of course, are less protected."63

Jefferson now realized that the principle of democracy, that is, the principles of self-government and popular sovereignty were only truly possible in "small republics." Ward republics, unlike Montesquieu's small republic, were part of "a system of fundamental balances and checks," "a graduation of authorities" from the "elementary republics of the wards, the county republics, the state republics, and the republic of the Union..."64 In this graduated system of republics, Jefferson was able to retain, first, the social and political structure of Montesquieu's small republics with all the advantages of a confederate republic, espoused by Hamilton, Madison and Destutt de Tracy; and, secondly, it allowed him to avoid the two excesses of democracy, "the spirit of inequality, which leads, Montesquieu wrote, to aristocracy or monarchy, and the spirit of extreme equality, which leads to despotic power..."65 Jefferson copied these passages from Montesquieu's *Spirit of the Laws* in his *Commonplace Book*.

In the ward republics, like New England townships, Montesquieu's small republics and Greek city-states, citizens would participate directly in the affairs of the state. In the other republics, county, state and federal, citizens would elect officials to represent their interests. The representatives, in turn, were subject to rotation in office and removal by the will of the majority of the citizens in each district. Even judges, Jefferson believed, were to be treated no differently than any other public servant.

The ward republics became the foundation of Jefferson's political philosophy. They fulfilled, Matthews argues, four critical functions. First, "to check the petty tyrants at home; second, to maintain the revolutionary spirit of 1776; third, to provide a base for general education; and fourth, to ensure a space in which the citizens can become proficient in the art of politics."[66] Jefferson also believed that the practice of democracy in ward republics would infuse the spirit of republicanism at every other level of government, thereby insuring the success of republicanism in one state.

Jefferson's progressive return to the principles of democracy and republicanism as set forth in Montesquieu's *Spirit of the Laws* and his continuing interest in Montesquieu's work was also reflected in his translation of Destutt de Tracy's *Commentary and Review of Montesquieu's Spirit of the Laws* in 1811 and de Tracy's *A Treatise on Political Economy* in 1817.

In his Preface to the Commentary, Tracy explained that Montesquieu's *Spirit of the Laws* was so useful and influential in the affairs of the new republic that he was submitting his study "to a man who is well skilled in both languages."[67] In his Commentary, Tracy criticized Montesquieu's praise of English laws and carefully amended his statement concerning the extent of territory required for a republic. In his *Treatise on Political Economy,* Tracy also expressed his endorsement of Jefferson's doctrine "the earth belongs to the living."

Jefferson expressed these same ideas in his letters to Samuel Kercheval, Joseph Cabell, Pierre Samuel Du Pont de Nemours, and Isaac H. Tiffany in 1816. In 1817, the same year Tracy's *Treatise* was published, he wrote to Francois de Marbois that he "had much confidence that we shall proceed successfully for ages to come, and that, contrary to the principle of Montesquieu, it will be seen that the larger the extent of country, the more firm its republican structure, if founded, [not] on conquest, but in principles of compact and equality."68 Montesquieu defined a confederate republic in almost exactly the same language. A confederate republic, Montesquieu wrote, can be successful if founded on compact and not conquest.

De Tracy's Commentary, Jefferson wrote to John Adams in 1816, was never published in the original, because it was not safe; but translated and published in Philadelphia (1811), yet without the author's name. He had since permitted his name to be mentioned. Although called a Commentary, it is in truth an elementary work on the principles of government...He has lately published a third work on Political Economy...in which all it's principles are demonstrated with the severity of Euclid, and, like him, without ever using a superfluous word...I have been 4 years endeavoring to get it published."69 Jefferson first acquired Montesquieu's *Spirit of the Laws* in 1769 and remained interested in, and influenced by, Montesquieu's constitutionalism throughout his life.

During his presidency and in his years of retirement, therefore, Jefferson pursued a political course of action to counteract "the abuses of monarchy" which "filled all the space of political contemplation" in the United States, by pursing his political philosophy based on the synthesis of his doctrines "the earth belongs to the living," the Kentucky Resolutions and ward republics, to build a republican consensus in the United States. Too many martyrs had already sacrificed their lives to the cause of republicanism and, he was determined, by any means necessary, to prevent the spirit of monarchism from resurfacing in his own country.

The failure of the French Revolution and international republicanism made it imperative to develop new systems of representation in the United States. In his draft of the Constitution for the State of Virginia, "the doctrine of the earth belongs to the living," the Kentucky Resolutions and his system of ward republics, Jefferson was influenced by the constitutionalism and political sociology of Montesquieu's *Spirit of the Laws*. Montesquieu's analysis provided him with a prescriptive model of a democratic republic. Jefferson did not agree with all of Montesquieu's ideas, but he did agree with Montesquieu's analysis of the internal dangers facing a democratic republic and the safeguards needed for a republic to survive and to prosper.

Jefferson used the lessons he learned from *The Spirit of the Laws* in his draft of the state constitution of Virginia and then modified Montesquieu's system of checks and balances to account for the dynamic relationship between the states and the federal government in the Kentucky Resolutions. In his doctrine "the earth belongs to the living and not the dead," he departed from the constitutionalism of Montesquieu only later to institutionalize it in his system of ward republics. The system of ward republics democratized and radicalized Montesquieu's system of checks and balances to accommodate the dynamic equilibrium between different republics within the same state. In ward republics citizens have the right and the duty to change the laws and institutions to accommodate the interests, aspirations and needs of each new generation.

The changes instituted by each new generation are the product of a democratic consensus, a generational consensus; they are not changes imposed on the people by a central government, national leaders or political parties. This consensus is not, as some scholars have suggested, the "General Will" in Rousseau's *Social Contract* but the will of an electoral majority. Jefferson's Kentucky Resolutions, the doctrine the earth belongs to the living, and his system of ward republics reflects, therefore, the evolutionary development of Jefferson's political philosophy within the general framework of Montesquieu's philosophy of a democratic republic. There were many "Montesqueuian Moments," and not a "Machiavellian Moment," as P.G.A. Pocock has argued in Jefferson's political philosophy.

Conclusion

Jefferson's intimate associations with the French *philosophes* in their celebrated salons during the French Revolution, and his active participation in their revolution transformed his thinking about government, economics, science and ethics. He retained many of the liberal and republican features of his earlier thought but invested them with new content and meaning.

In the tradition of the Scottish and English republican writers, politics remained for Jefferson "the vehicle for the practice, and a means to the promotion of the moral virtues," from which it follows that clearest title to participate in rule belongs to those who demonstrate the most virtue or the most potential for virtue or the greatest concern for virtue.[1]

In the classical republican tradition, J.G.A. Pocock says "the alternative to a hereditary, entrenched, or artificial aristocracy was a natural aristocracy-an elite of persons distinguished by natural superiority, leisure and learning...."[2] Jefferson believed, as he expressed it to John Adams, in a natural aristocracy based exclusively on an individual's talents and genius, and not, as it was in England and France, on inheritance, rank and title. A natural aristocracy that was more interested in promoting the general welfare of their communities and nation than in the pursuit of their selfish passions and ambitions. It was this natural aristocracy wanted to create and nurture at the University of Virginia, Mr. Jefferson's university, to compete with Harvard, Yale and Princeton, whom he believed were more elitists and less democratic.

Jefferson agreed with the republican writers that a nation of small propertied farmers, some with household manufactures, were uniquely qualified, because of their independence and self-reliance, to manage and administer the affairs of state. Their political participation, he believed, was necessary on all levels of government-local, state and national-for a republican government to flourish and succeed; a citizenry "restrained by the fact that they cannot afford to spend too much time away from their farms, but who are wealthy enough and in close enough proximity to the city, to attend the militia, assembly, and committee or other meetings on a periodic basis."[3] "Republics were also supposed to have citizens who were more or less equal to one another... A republican state required a general equality of property-holding among the citizens."[4]

Most of the revolutionary leaders conceived of property "as a source of authority and independence, not as a commodity or as the source of productivity and capitalistic investment."[5] Even Adam Smith claimed in the *Wealth of Nations* "that businessmen could not be good political leaders."[6] Smith thought that businessmen in a modern complicated commercial society were too engaged in their occupations and the making of money to be able to make impartial judgments about the varied interests of their society."7

In this respect, Jefferson's republicanism was quite different from Hamilton, Adams and other Federalists who believed that only America's wealthiest families were uniquely qualified to govern and administer the affairs of state. They believed the agricultural class lacked the education, manners, wealth, independence and the impartial disposition of a classical gentleman.

In the liberal tradition of Hobbes and Locke it is not the virtuous or the exemplary life that concerns them but man's security, in his person and property. In man's natural state, his perfect equality and liberty were causes of conflict and war. "Each man," Hobbes wrote,

"has the liberty to use his own power for the preservation of his. . .own life, and consequently, of doing anything which in his own Judgment, and Reason, he shall conceive to be the aptest means thereunto. . .and there is nothing he can make use of, that may not be a help unto him, in preserving his life against his enemyes; it followeth, that in such a condition, every man has a right to every thing. . .therefore, as long as this natural Right of every man to every thing endureth. Can be no security to any man."8

During this time, he continues, "men live without a common Power to keep them all in awe, they are in a condition...of War, and such a war, is as of every man, against every man."9

"Humans are social in the sense they need the assistance of one another to survive," Hume argues, " and are drawn to one another by impulsive passions of tenderness and lust, envy and triumph, fear and dominion;

but they lack any pattern or order for their sociability...
confronting the chaos and driven by fear the chaos naturally
induces, can with great pains construct rules and patterns that
reduce natural freedom and equality (to achieve)some
modest degree of social order and security."10

Man's liberty and equality are then principal causes
of quarrel. Hobbes imagines a state of nature in which
each person is free to decide for himself what he needs,
what is owing to others, and what is just and right.

Locke's concept of human nature, although seemingly
less dystopic than Hobbes,' also considered man to be
isolated, acquisitive and selfish, incapable of judging
impartially and fairly the interests of others. "Men living
together according to reason," Locke writes, "without
a common superior on earth with authority to judge
between them, is properly the state of nature..." In such
a condition, with no possibility to appeal "to our
common judge, nor the decisions of law, for remedy in
a case...puts all men in a state of nature, force without
right upon man's person makes a state of war."11 To
avoid this state, wherein there is no appeal but to
heaven, is one great reason of men's putting themselves
into society and quitting the state of nature."12

Madison, Hamilton and Adams rejected Hobbes'
view of the state of nature, but agreed, as Madison put
it, that man was "actuated by some common impulse of
passion, or of interest, adverse to the rights of other
citizens, or to the permanent and aggregate interests of
the community."13 "The latent causes of faction,"
Madison believes, "is sown in the nature of man."14

"Why has government been instituted at all?"
Hamilton asks, "because the passions of men will not

conform to the dictates of reason and justice without restraint. Self-government is not instituted for its own sake but in order to constrain the natural bent of the passions."[15]

Man has a desire to be observed," Adams observed, "considered, esteemed, praised, beloved, and admired by his fellows...a passion for distinction...."[16] "There is," he admits, "in human nature...simple Benevolence or an affection for the good of others; but alone it is not a balance for the selfish affections. Nature then has kindly added to benevolence the desire for reputation in order to make us good members of society."[17]

Jefferson disagreed with the liberal concept of human nature expressed by Thomas Hobbes that "humans lack any pattern or order for their sociability, of the sort discernible in beehives or wolf packs or bison herds or bird nests. In fact, some of their strongest and most frequent passions...led human(s) to threaten one another and endanger themselves for no beneficial purpose."[18]

Jefferson believed man was made for society and that his moral sense of duty to others was as powerful an instinctual force in human nature as man's selfish passions. It was this sense of God's benevolence, and a moral instinct implanted in man by God, "that finally gave the Jeffersonians their sense of community, and prevented an emphasis on 'rights' from becoming anarchy, or from making society seem a hopeless jungle."[19]

Jefferson's doctrine of politics was "always directed toward the formation and cultivation of character; it proceeded pedagogically and not technically."[20] He was opposed to the liberal theory where "politics is separated from ethics, and legislation no longer serves to enlighten the citizenry but to inculcate rules of order for a well-regulated social existence."[21] Jefferson did not accept Locke's rational justification for the gross inequalities he witnessed in England and France. Inequality was not a natural right; it was rather a violation of man's natural rights.

Jefferson believed that every individual was entitled, by the laws of nature, to the goods he produced through his industry and labors. He did not believe, however, that man had a natural right to private property in perpetuity. Jefferson, like the Jacobins whose principles he considered "noble and pure," was an enemy of those very inequalities in wealth and property sanctioned by Hobbes, Locke, Adams, Madison and Hamilton as natural rights.

The French Revolution, the revolution that molded human society in accordance with human reason and not historical precedent, caused Jefferson to reevaluate and redefine his principles of republicanism. Jefferson did not disagree with Locke that government is constituted "for the preservation and advancement of civil goods," but he did not believe republican governments were instituted to protect "the few most rational and industrious" who "become far wealthier than the majority," as Locke, Adams, Madison and Hamilton did.[22]

Jefferson's concept of limited government was grounded in man's moral instinct, not his selfish passions. Man was already a socialized being with an inner sense of duty and respect for the rights of others. He was not dependent on the state for the realization of his human nature, as it was for the classical republicans.

In this sense, Jefferson was neither an English liberal nor a republican.

Jefferson's economic model of society was simple; it reflected the thinking of the classical economists of his day, Adam Smith, J.B. Say, Destutt de Tracy, Malthus and Ricardo. Individuals were free to pursue their own interests and use their energies and skills as they saw fit. This belief was predicated upon the assumption that all individuals had possession, or could easily have possession, of land or other resources from which they could make a living from their labors. Every individual had the opportunity of becoming a proprietor in the United States.

Jefferson's economic thought, therefore, depended on an abundance of cheap land and scarcity of labor. The high wages afforded labor and the plentiful supply of western lands in America seemed to guarantee that Americans could avoid the physical deprivations and hunger of Europe's working class. American families would form self-sufficient units, each associating with others to augment their supply of goods and services. He foresaw a nation of agriculturalists with household manufactures to supplement their incomes and wages. The purchase of the Louisiana territories and the western expansion of the country, he hoped, would secure these blessings for generations yet unborn.

Jefferson embraced Smith's, Tracy's and Say's labor theory of value, the laws of supply and demand, and free and unfettered markets for producers and consumers, but he was, like them, critical of finance capitalism. Investors in public securities and the national debt, he believed, were swindlers who "not only encouraged speculations on fictitious capital, but seduced those of real capital, even in private life, to contract debts too freely...."23 Banks "were doing business," he wrote, "on capitals, three-fourths of which were fictitious; and to extend their profit they furnished fictitious capital to every man, who having nothing and disliking the labors of the plow, chose rather to call himself a merchant...."24 He was "an enemy of banks, not of those discounting for cash, but of those foisting their own paper into circulation, and thus banishing our cash."25 He inveighed against these tendencies in his own day but feared, that

like a dropsical man calling out for water, water, our deluded citizens are clamoring for more banks, more banks. The American mind is now in that state of fever which the world has so often seen in the history of other nations. We are under the bank bubble, as England was under the South Sea bubble, France under the Mississippi bubble, and as every nation is liable to be, under whatever bubble, design or delusion may puff up in moments when off their guard.26

By 1820, Jefferson observed, the deluge of paper money from the banks "reduced the prices of property and produce suddenly to one-third of what they had been."27 He expressed fear and concern that men "enriched by the dexterity of a leader, would follow... the chief who was leading them to fortune, and become the zealous instruments of that enterprise."28 He remained cautiously optimistic, however, that with their financial ruin, Americans would finally recognize the folly of their ways and embrace the sound economic reasoning of Tracy and Say.

Jefferson was a tireless advocate for equality and an enemy of inequality. He drafted legislation in 1776 to repeal of the laws of primogeniture and entail in the state of Virginia, laws he believed contributed to the concentration of wealth in the hands of fewer and fewer families. In revolutionary France, Jefferson witnessed the extremes of poverty and wealth, a monarchy and aristocracy with absolute power over millions of inhabitants who had no rights and were entirely dependent for the livelihood on the good graces of their masters. These extremes, politically and economically, radicalized him. He saw that reforms alone, although preferable to doing nothing at all, would not uproot the deeply entrenched interests that had a stranglehold on the French people. His doctrine The Earth Belongs In Usufruct to the Living, and not the Dead was a reaction to those social and economic conditions. He believed that political, social and economic equality was one of the main pillars in the foundation of every democratic republic and that gross inequality in income and wealth posed a threat to its survival.

"Jefferson's desire to keep the republic virtuous," Richard Matthews reasons,

by creating a state of permanent revolution... represents a radical notion of politics. Jefferson's idea of permanent revolution, when tied to his unorthodox views of property and his politics of the heart, places his political theory beyond the boundaries of even bourgeois radicalism. It presents a radical alternative to the rest of mainstream American political thought.[29]

Jefferson's faith in nature's God, and the laws of nature, as he stated it in the Declaration of Independence can be understood, Jurgen Habermas says, as a general physics of sociation. With its knowledge concerning the basic character and constitution of human nature, it specifies those institutional arrangements...which can be expected to produce the natural modes of reaction that will lead to an orderly cohabitation of human beings.[30]

Jefferson believed, that under the right conditions— economic equality, universal education, and participatory democracy-the human species itself was capable of unbounded improvement in its march toward liberté, egalité, fraternité.

NOTES

INTRODUCTION

1 Jurgen Habermas, *Theory and Practice* (Boston, 1973), p. 108
2 Peter Gay, The Enlightenment: An Interpretation (New York, 1967), p. 17
3 Ibid.
4 Ibid.
5 Thomas Jefferson, *Notes on the State of Virginia*, ed. William Peden (Chapel Hill, 1955), p. 87.
6 Gordon S. Wood, *Friend Divided* (New York, 2017), p. 17. To William Short, Apr. 2,1785, *Thomas Jefferson Travels*, ed., Anthony Brandt (Washington, D.C, 2006), p. 24.
8 Thomas Jefferson Travels, loc.cit., p. 24.
9 William Howard Adams, *The Paris Years of Thomas Jefferson* (London, 1997), p. 77.
10 Ibid.
11 Henry Adams, *History of the United States of America during the Administration of Thomas Jefferson*, (New York, 1986), p. 101.
12 To Charles Bellini, Sept. 30, 1785, *The Writings of Thomas Jefferson*, ed. H.A.Washington, vol.1 (Cambridge, 1853), p. 444.
13 Adams, *Paris Years*, loc.cit., p. 59.
14 To Madame Tesse, March 20, 1787, Writings, vol.2, loc.cit., p. 132.
15 Ibid.
16 To James Madison, Sept. 20, 1785, Writings, vol. 1, p. 432.
17 To Samuel H. Smith, Sept. 21, 1814, Writings, loc.cit., vol. 6, p. 383.

18 To Mr. Bellini, Sept. 30, 1785, Writings, vol. 1, p.445.
19 To Peter Carr, Aug. 19, 1785, ibid., p. 399.
20 To Charles Bellini, Sept. 30, 1785, Writings, ibid., vol. 1, p. 445.
21 To Mrs. Trist, Aug. 18,1785, ibid., p. 394.
22 To Chastellux, Sept. 2,1785, Jefferson Abroad, ked., Douglas L. Wilson and Lucia Stanton (New York, 1999), p. 30.
23 Ibid.
24 Writings, op.cit., p. 445.
25 Henry Adams, loc.cit., p. 84.
26 Ibid., p. 67.
27 Kingsley Martin, *French Liberal Thought in the 18th Century* (New York, 1962), p. 104.
28 Ibid.
29 Ibid.
30 Adams, *Adams, Paris Years, lo.cit., p.74*
31 Dumas Malone, *Jefferson and the Rights of Man* (Boston, 1951), p. 16.
32 O'Brien, loc.cit., p. 34.
33 By Louis Uchitelle, Feb. 21, 1998.
34 Catherine Kerrison, *Jefferson's Daughters* (New York, 2018), p. 99.
35 Joseph J. Ellis, *American Sphinx* (New York, 1998), p. 129.
36 Wood, loc.cit., p.226.
37 Jonathan Israel, *A Revolution of the Mind* (Princeton, 1010), p. 38.
38 Dorinda Outram, *The Enlightenment* (New York, 2013), p. 15.
39 Ibid., p. 16.
40 Ibid.
41 Ibid., p. 17
42 Israel, loc.cit., p. 14.
43 Ibid., p. 17.
44 Ibid.
45 Israel, loc.cit., p. 19.

46 Ibid.
47 Ibid., p. 21.
48 Ibid., p. 46.
49 Ibid., p. 95.
50 Lester J. Cappon, *The Adams Jefferson Letters*, (University of North Carolina), p. 332.
51 William Howard Allan, *The Paris Years* (London, 1997), p. 7.
52 Ibid.
53 To Eliza Trist, Writings, loc.cit., vol. 1, p.394.
54 Ibid.
55 To Bellini, Writings, loc.cit., vol. 1, p. 444.
56 To Dr. Cooper, Sept. 10, 1814, Writings, vol. 6, p. 377-378
57 Ibid.
58 Ibid.
59 To J. Bannister, Jr., ibid., p. 467
60 Ibid.
61 Lester J. Cappon, ed., *The Adams-Jefferson Letters* (New York, 1959), p. 492.
62 Saul Padover, ed, *The Complete Jefferson* (New York, 1943), p.1033
63 Padover, loc.cit. p. 1033.
63 Padover, loc.cit. p. 1033.

CHAPTER ONE

1 To Benjamin Rush, January 16, 1811, *The Writings of Thomas Jefferson*, H. A. Washington, ed. vol. 5 New York, 1856), p. 559.
2 Carl Becker, *The Declaration of Independence* (New York, 1922), p. 51.
3 Thomas L. Hankins, *Science and the Enlightenment* (Cambridge, 1985), p. 3.
4 David Hume, *A Treatise of Human Nature* (Oxford, 1888), Introduction, XIX
5 Ibid., p. XXI
6 To the University of Virginia, Aug. 1-4, 1818, *The Complete Jefferson*, Saul K. Padover, ed. (New York, 1943), 1099.
7 Ibid.
8 Ibid..
9 Lester J. Cappon,, ed., *The Adams-Jefferson Letters* (New York, 1959), p. 458.
10 "*The Autobiography of Thomas Jefferson*" Adrienne Koch and William Peden, ed., *The Life and Selected Writings of Thomas Jefferson* (1944), p. 4
11 Dumas Malone, *Jefferson the Virginian* (Boston, 1948), p. 388.
12 *The English Philosophers from Bacon to Mill*, Edwin A. Burtt, ed. (New York, 1939), p. 6.
13 Edwin A. Burtt, ed., *The English Philosophers from Bacon to Mill* (New York, 1939), p. 34.
14 Ibid.
15 Ibid,. p. 35.
16 Ibid.
17 Ibid.
18 Thomas Jefferson, *Notes on the State of Virginia* (Chapel Hill, 1955), p. 46.
19 Ibid., p. 46.
20 Ibid., p. 47.
21 Ibid., p. 49.
22 Jefferson, Notes, p. p. 53.
23 Ibid., p. 53.
24 Ibid.
25 Ibid., p. 63.
26 Ibid., p. 56.
27 Burtt, loc. cit., p. 15
28 Martin, loc. cit., p. 34.
29 Jefferson, op. cit., p. 64
30 Russell Nye, *The Cultural Life of the New Nation* (New York, 1960) p. 58.
31 Jefferson, op.cit., p. 121.
32 Charles A. Miller, *Jefferson and Nature* (Blatimore, 1988), p. 157
33 Hankins, loc.cit., p. 6.
34 Bernard Cohen, *Science and the Founding Fathers* (New York, 1995), p.42.
35 Saul K. Padover ed. The Complete Jefferson (New York, 1943), p. 977.
36 Ibid., p. 979.
37 Ernest Dilworth, ed., *Voltaire's Philosophical Letters* (New York, 1961), p. 70.
38 Charles Coulton Gillispie, *The Edge of Objectivity* (Princeton, 1960), p. 163
39 Paul Hazard, European Thought in the Eighteenth Century (New York, 1963), p. 41.

40 Ibid., p. 43.
41 Degenaar, Marjolein and Lokorst, "Molyneux's Problem," *Stanford Encyclopedia* of Philosophy (Fall 2011 Edition), Edward N. Zalta, ed.
42 Dilworth, *Voltaire's Philosophical Letters*, loc. cit., p. 70.
43 Ibid., p. 71.
44 Ibid., p. 73.
45 Ibid., p. 79
46 Ibid., p. 54.
47 Ibid., p. 55.
48 Richard N. Schwab, ed., *Preliminary Discourse to the Encyclopedia of Diderot* (New York, 1963), p. 5.
49 Ibid., p. 6.
50 Ibid., p. 7.
51 Ibid., p. 14.
52 *Encyclopedia*, ed., Nelly Hoyt and Thomas Cassirer (New York, 1965), p. 5.
53 Ibid., p. 6.
54 Ibid.
55 Ibid.
56 To Thomas Cooper, Aug. 14, 1820, *The Writings of Thomas Jefferson*, H.A. Washington, ed., vol. 7 (New York, 1854), p. 170.
57 To Adams, Aug. 15, 1820, Cappon, loc. cit., p. 567.
58 Ibid., p. 568.
59 Hankins, loc.cit., p. 127
60 Ibid., p. 119-120.
61 Ibid., p. 127.
62 Clark Chelsey, *Dugald Stewart: Historian of the Enlightenment*, Dissertation (UCSB, 1976), p. 46.
63 Ibid.
64 Ibid., p. 50.
65 Ibid., p. 44.
66 Ibid.
67 Ibid., p. 46.
68 Ibid.
69 Ibid.
70 Ibid., p. 50.
71 Ibid.
72 Ibid.
73 Adrienne Koch, *The Philosophy of Thomas Jefferson* (Chicago, 1943), p. 75.
74 To Adams, Aug. 15, 1820, Cappon, loc. cit., p. 569.
75 To Thomas Cooper, July 10, 1812, Writings, loc. cit., vol. 6, p. 73

76 To John Adams, March 14,1820, Ibid., p. 562.
77 To Thomas Jefferson, May 12, 1820, ibid., p. 564.
78 Ibid., p. 565.
79 Ibid.
80 To John Adams, Jan. 8, 1825, ibid., p. 605.
81 To John Adams, Jan. 8, 1825,Cappon, loc. cit., p.606
82 To John Adams, loc.cit., p. 606.
83 To Thomas Jefferson, Jan. 22, 1825, ibid., p. 607.
84 To John Adams, April, 11,1823, Cappon, loc. cit., p. 592.
85 Ibid.
86 Alexandre Koyré, From the Closed World to the Infinite Universe (Baltimore, 1957), p.122.
87 Ibid., p. 138.
88 To John Adams, April, 11,1823, Cappon, loc. cit., p. 592.
89 To Andrew Ellicott, Nov. 24, 1808, Padover, loc. cit., p. 1030.
90 To John Adams, Mar. 21, 1819, Cappon, op. cit., p. 536
91 Baron D. Holbach, *The System of Nature*, vol.1, trans. (Paris, 1971), p. 68.

CHAPTER TWO

1 Malone, loc.cit., p. 156.
2 Ibid., p. 157.
3 Ibid.
4 To Edward Carrington, January 16, 1787, Writings, op. cit., vol. 2, p. 99.
5 To James Madison, January 30, 1787, ibid., p. 93.
6 To James Madison, December 20, 1789, ibid., p. 331.
7 To Madison, loc.cit., p. 332.
8 Montesquieu, Baron de, *Oeuvres de Montesquieu*, vol. 1 (Amsterdam, 1758), p. 271.
9 To William Smith, November 13, 1787, Writings, op. cit., vol. 2, p. 319.
10 T. V. Smith, "Thomas Jefferson and the Perfectibility of Man," Ethics, vol. LIII (July, 1943), p. 301.
11 To James Madison, December 20, 1787, Writings,

op. cit., vol. 2, p. 329.
12 Ibid.
13 Ibid., p. 330.
14 John Locke, *Second Treatise on Government* (London, 1690), p. 94.
15 Ibid.
16 To John Adams, Nov. 13, 1787,The Writings of Thomas Jefferson, ed. H.A. Washington, vol. 2 (New York, 1853), p. 317.
17 To James Madison, July 31, 1788, ibid., vol. 3, p. 445.
18 To John Jay, Aug. 6, 1787, loc.cit., vol. 2, p. 231.
19 To John Jay, loc.cit., p. 231.
20 To Edward Rutledge, July 18, 1788, Writings, loc. cit., vol. 2, p. 435.
21 To Richard Price, January 8, 1789, ibid., vol. 2, p. 553.
22 Ibid., p. 554.
23 To Richard Price, loc.cit., p. 554.
24 Ibid., p. 556.
25 Ibid..
26 To Madame de Brehan, March, 14, 1789, ibid., vol. 2, p. 591.
27 To Edward Rutledge, Sept. 18, 1789, ibid., vol. 3, p. 111.
28 To John Jay, Sept. 19, 1789, ibid., vol. 3, p. 118.
29 To David Humphrey, March 18, 1789, ibid., p. 93.
30 To John Jay, Aug. 27, 1789, ibid., vol. 3, p. 10.
31 Ibid., p. 11.
32 To Rebault de St. Etienne, June 3, 1789, ibid., vol. 3, p. 46.
33 To Thomas Paine, July 11, 1789, ibid., vol. 3, p. 70.
34 O'Brien, loc. cit., p. 63.
35 Ibid., p. 42.
36 Ibid.
37 To John Adams, Aug. 30, 1787, Writings, op. cit., vol. 2, p. 259.
38 To Thomas Paine, July 11, 1789, Writings, loc. cit., vol. 3, p. 69.
39 James Morton Smith, ed., The Republic of Letters (New York, 1995), vol. 1, p. 624.
40 Ibid.
41 Ibid.
42 Smith, loc.cit., p. 624.
43 Ibid.

44 Ibid., p. 6
45 Ibid.
46 Ibid., p. 628.
47 Ibid.
48 Smith, Republic of Letters, loc.cit., p. 628.
49 Ibid., p. 629.
50 Ibid.
51 Jurgen Habermas, Theory and Practice (Boston, 1973), p. 88.
52 Ibid.
53 Ibid., p. 91.
54 Ibid., p. 91.
55 Ibid., p. 88.
56 http://www.Inscriptions Journal.org, "Social Class and Revolution," p. 1.
57 Ibid., p. 5.
58 Social Class and Revolution, loc.cit., p. 5.
59 Ibid.
60 Ibid.
61 Ibid., p. 7.
62 Martin, loc. cit., p. 83.
63 Ibid.
64 Ibid., p. 76.
65 Ibid., p. 152.
66 Ibid., p. 84.
67 Martin, loc.cit, p. 89.
68 Ibid., p. 118.
69 Adams to Jefferson, Mar. 2, 1816, Cappon, Adams-Jefferson Letters loc.cit., p. 465.
70 To Madison, July 29, 1789, Republic of Letters, loc.cit., p. 465.
71 Ibid., p. 632.
72 Henry Higgs, The Physiocrats (New York, 1897), p. 9.
73 Andrew Burstein, Jefferson's Secrets (New York, 2005), p. 57.
74 Ibid.
75 The Jeffersonian Cyclopedia,ed., John. P. Foley (New York, 1900), p. 456.
76 Smith, Republic of Letters, loc.cit., p. 632.
77 Ibid.
78 Ibid.
79 Ibid., p. 633.
80 Ibid.
81 Ibid.,
82 Smith, Republic of Letters, loc.cit., p. 634.
83 Ibid. p. 634.
84 Ibid., p. 634.
85 Ibid.
86 Ibid.

87John Adams, Prophets of Progress, loc.cit., p. 197.
88 Smith, op.cit., p. 635.
89 Ibid., p. 64
90 Ibid., p. 641.
91 Ibid.
92 Ibid.
93 John Locke, loc. cit., p. 68.
94 Ibid., p. 69.
95 Locke, loc.cit., p. 69.
96Algernon Sidney, Discourses Concerning Government (London, 1763), p. 15.
97 Herbert W. Sloan, Principle and Interest (Oxford University Press, 1995), p. 81.
98 Sloan, loc. cit., p. 82.
99 Ibid.
100 Ibid., p. 83.
101 Ibid., p. 82.

CHAPTER THREE

1 Michael P. Zuckert, The Natural Rights Republic (Notre Dame, 1996), p. 80.
2 John Locke, The *Second Treatise on Government* (London, 1690), p. 17.
3 Ibid.
4 Locke, loc. cit., p. 19.
5 Locke, loc.cit., p. 21.
6 Ibid., p. 22.
7 Ibid, 29.
8 Thomas L. Pangle, The Spirit of Modern Republicanism (Chicago, 1990), p. 163.
9 Henry Home Lord Kames, Essays on the Principles of Morality and Natural Religion, ed., Catherine Moan (Indianapolis, 2005), p. 54.
10 Francis Hutcheson, An Inquiry into the Original of Our Ideas of Beauty and Virtue, ed. Wolfgang Leidhold (Indianapolis, 2005), p. 187.
11 Kames, loc. cit., p. 47
12 Ibid.
13 Kames, loc. cit., p. 49.
14 Ibid.
15 Raul Perez Johnson, "Jean Jacques Burlamaqui and the Theory of Social Compact," (Historia Constitucional, 2005), p. 335.
16 Johnson, loc. cit., p. 336
17 Ibid.
18 Ibid., p. 338.
19 Ibid., p. 339.
20 Burlalmaqui, loc. cit., p. 62.

21 To Rev. James Madison, Oct. 28, 1785, Adrienne Koch and William Peden, eds., The Life and Selected Writings of Thomas Jefferson (Chapel Hill, 1954), p. 389.
22 Ibid.
23 Koch and Peden, loc. cit., p. 389.
24 Koch and Peden, Selected Writings, loc.cit., p. 389.
24 Ibid., p. 390.
25 Jean Jacques Rousseau, The First and *Second Discourse*s, ed., Roger D. Masters (New York, 1964), p. 141.
26 Ibid., p. 168.
27 To Isaac McPherson, Aug. 13, 1813. The Writings of Thomas Jefferson, H. A. Washington, ed. (New York, 1856), vol. 6, p. 180.
28 Lester J. Cappon, ed., The Adams-Jefferson Letters (New York, 1959), p. 467.
29 Ibid.
30 Ibid., p. 473.
31 Ibid., p. 474.
32 Thomas Jefferson, Notes on the State of Virginia, ed., William Peden (Chapel Hill, 1954), p. 93.
33 Rousseau, op. cit., p. 81.
34 Ibid.
35 Baron de Montesquieu, The *Spirit of Laws*, ed., Thomas Nugent (New York, 1966), p. 73.
36 Montesquieu, loc.cit.,p. 73.
37 To Rev. James Madison, Oct. 28, 1785, Selected Writings, Koch and Peden, loc.cit., p. 389.
38 Charles Wiltse, The Jeffersonian Tradition in American Democracy (New York, 1935), p. 72.
39 Wiltse, loc.cit., p.73.
40 Ibid
41 Madison and Jefferson, eds., Andrew Burstein and Nancy Isenberg (New York, 2010), p. 205.
42 Wikipedia, Usufruct, history, from Book II, Property, Ownership, and its Modifications, Republic Act No. 386, The Civil Code of the Philippines (June 18, 1949).
43 Burstein and Isenberg, op. cit.,

p. 53.
44 Ibid.
45 Burstein and Isenberg, loc.cit., p. 53..
46 Burstein and Isenberg, loc.cit., p. 53..

CHAPTER FOUR

1 Thomas Jefferson, Notes on the State of Virginia, ed., William Peden (Chapel Hill, 1955), p. 83.
2 Ibid., p. 85.
3 Ibid., p. 164.
4 Ibid.
5 Jefferson, loc. cit., p. 164.
6 Ibid., p. 165.
7 The Adams-Jefferson Letters, ed., Lester J. Cappon New York, 1959), p. 389.
8 Jefferson, loc. cit., p. 165.
9 Andrea Wulf, Founding Gardeners (New York, 2011), p. 10.
10 Wulf, loc. cit.,. p. 16.
11 Ibid., p. 160.
12 Franklin Writings, J.A. Leo Le May, ed. (New York, 1987), p. 368.
13 Ibid., p. 369.
14 Wulf, op. cit., p. 5.
15 Ibid., p. 7.
16 Ibid., p. 116.
17 Wulf, loc. cit., p. 84.
18 Alexander Hamilton, Hamilton Writings, Joanne B. Freeman, ed. (New York, 2001), p. 112.
19 To Joseph Milligan, Apr. 6, 1816, The Writings of Thomas Jefferson, e., H.A. Washington, vol. 6 (New York, 1854), p. 570.
20 Ronald Meek, The Economics of Physiocracy (Cambridge, 1963), p. 15.
21 Meek, op. cit., p. 69.
22 Higgs, loc. cit., p. 136.
23 Ibid.
24 Ibid.
25 Higgs, loc. cit., p. 136.
26 To Hogendorp, Oct. 13, 1785, 30.Writings, loc. cit., vol. 1, p. 465.
27 To Joseph Milligan, April 6, 1816, Ibid., vol. 6,. p. 570.
28 Ibid., p. 571.
29 To Milligan, Writings, loc. cit., p. 571.

30 Alexander Hamilton: Writings, ed., Joanne Freeman (New York, 2001), p. 537.
31 Ibid., p. 538.
32 Ibid., p. 563.
33 The Writings of Thomas Jefferson, H.A. Washington, ed. (New York, 1854), vol. 9, p. 92.
34 Smith, op. cit., p. 867.
35 Smith, loc.cit., p. 867.
36 Ibid.
37 To John W. Eppes, June 24, 1813, Writings, op. cit., vol. 6, p. 136.
38 Smith, loc. cit., p. 872.
44 Smith, loc.cit.,p. 872.
39 To J.W. Eppes, September 11,1813, Writings, loc. cit., vol. 6, P. 197.
40 To Samuel Kerchival, July 12, 1816, ibid., vol. 7, p. 235.
41 Letter to George Washington, Writings, loc. cit., vol. 3, p. 464.
42 "The Anas," The Jeffersonian Cyclopedia, ed., John P. Foley (New York, 1900), p. 68.
43 Hamilton, loc. cit., p. 576.
44 Ibid., p. 575.
45 Hamilton, loc.cit., p. 579.
46 Ibid.
47 Ibid. p. 580.
48 Ibid.
49 Smith, loc. cit., p. 313.
50 "Opinion Against the Constitutionality of a National Bank," Feb. 15, 1791, The Complete Jefferson, ed., Saul K. Padover (New York, 1943), p. 345.
51 "Ideas of Finance," Nov. 6, 1813, loc.cit., p. 359.
52 To John W. Eppes, Nov. 6, 1813, Writings, op. cit., vol. 6, p. 239.
53 Ibid., p. 241.
54 Ibid.
55 To Eppes, loc.cit, p. 234.
56 Ibid.
57 To George Washington, May, 23, 1792, ibid., vol. 3, p. 362.
58 Anas, Writings, loc. cit., vol. 9, p. 96.
59 Adam Smith, loc. cit., p. 355.
60 Drew R. McCoy, The Elusive Republic (Chapel Hill, 1980), p. 51.

61 Ibid., p. 54.
62 Ibid., p. 38.
63 McCoy, loc.cit., p. 39
64 Ibid., p. 68.
65 Lawrence Kaplan, Jefferson and France (London, 1967), p. 20.
66 To Dupont de Nemours on June 28, 1809, Writings, loc. cit., vol. 5, p. 456.
67 Ibid.
68 To Dupont, loc. cit., p. 457.
69 To Gov. James Jay, ibid., p. 440.
70 Smith, op. cit., p. 347.
71 To A. Penna, 1809, Cyclopedia, loc. cit., p. 529.
72 To DuPont, June 28, 1809, Writings, loc. cit., vol. 5, p. 457.
73 To J.B. Say, March 2, 1815, ibid., vol. 6, p. 431.
74 McCoy, loc.cit, p. 236-237.
75 Ibid., p. 62.
76 Gilbert Chinard, Jefferson et Les Ideologues (Paris, 1925), p. 26.
77 Tracy, loc. cit., p. iv.
78 Ibid.
79 Ibid., p. 240.
80 Ibid., p. 237.
81 Tracy, loc. cit.., p. iv.
82 Joyce Appleby, "Economics: The Agrarian Republic," Thomas Jefferson and the Politics of Nature, ed., Thomas Engeman (University of Notre Dame, 2000), p. 146.
83 Appleby, loc. cit., p. 153.
84 Ibid.
85 Ibid., p. 146.
86 To William Ludlow, Sept. 6, 1824, Writings, loc. cit., vol. 7, p. 378.
87 Ibid. p. 377.
88 To J.B. Say, Writings, loc. cit., vol. 4, p. 527.
89 To DuPont, 1811, Cyclopedia, loc. cit., p. 531.
90 To General Kosciusko, June 28, 1812, Writings, loc. cit., vol. 6, p. 69.
91 To John Melish, Jan. 1813, ibid., p. 94.
92 Thomas Piketty, Capital in the Twenty-First Century (London, 2014), p. 23.
93 Ibid., p. 152.
94 Michael O'Connor, Origins of Academic Economics in the United States (New York, 1974), p. 26.
95 Piketty, loc.cit., p. 25.
96 Ibid., p. 26.
97 Sloan, loc.cit., p. 61.
98 Ibid., p. 54.
99 Gordon Wood, Friends Divided, loc.cit., p. 186.
100 Ibid., p. 183.

CHAPTER FIVE

1 Adam Ferguson, Essay on the History of Civil Society, ed., Louis Schneider (London, 1995), p. 65.
2 Francis Newton Thorpe, The Constitutional History of the United States (Chicago, 1901), p.155.
3 Baron de Montesquieu, The Spirit of the Laws, ed., Thomas Nugent, vol. 1 (New York, 1966), p. 1.
4 Ibid.
5 Ibid., p. 2.
6 Ibid.
7 Montesquieu, loc. cit., p. 6.
8 Montesquieu, loc.cit.., p. 8.
9 Ibid.
10 Ibid., p. 9.
11 Ibid.
12 Ibid., p. 13.
13 Montesquieu, loc. cit., p. 28.
14 Draft Constitution,1776, Lillian Goldman Law Library , The Avalon Project (New Haven, CT.)
15 Ibid.
16 To Destutt de Tracy, Jan. 26, 1811, The Writings of Thomas Jefferson, ed., H.A. Washington (New York, 1854
17 Montesquieu, loc. cit., p. 126.
18 Alexander Hamilton, John Jay and James Madison, The Federalist Papers (New York, 1789), p. 50.
19 Ibid., p. 126.
20 Montesquieu, op. cit., p. 126.
21 To C.F.C. de Volney, Feb. 8, 1805, Writings, loc. cit., vol. 5, p. 570.
22 Gilbert Chinard, ed., The Correspondence of Jefferson and Du Pont de Nemours (London, 1931), LXIV.
23 Montesquieu, op. cit., p. 152.
24 Jefferson, Notes of the State of Virginia, ed., William Peden (Chapel Hill, 1954), p. 120.
25 Ibid.
26 Jefferson's Draft Constitution, loc. cit.
27 David N. Mayer, The Constitutional Thought of

Thomas Jefferson (London, 1997), p. 57,
28 Ibid.
29 Ibid.
30 John Roche, ed., Origins of American Political Thought, "The Origins of the Separation of Powers," Benjamin P. Wright (New York, 1967), p. 148.
31 Jefferson, Notes, op. cit., p. 118.
32 Jefferson, loc. cit., p. 119.
33 Montesquieu, loc. cit., p. 155.
34 Montesquieu, loc. cit., p. 248.
35 Jefferson, Notes., p. 162.
36 Montesquieu, loc. cit., p. 243.
37 Jefferson, op.cit., p. 162.
38 Ibid., p. 163.
39 Montesquieu, op.cit., p. 247.
40 Ibid., p. 248.
41 Jefferson, loc. cit., p. 137.
42 Montesquieu, Book XXVI, loc. cit., p. 65.
43 Jefferson, Notes, p. 159.
44 Daniel L. Dreisbach, Thomas Jefferson and the Wall of Separation (New York, 2002), p. 148.
45 The Republic of Letters, ed., James Morton Smith, vol. 1 (New York, 1995), p. 159.
46 To James Madison, ibid
47 Mayer, loc.cit., p. 59.
48 Ibid., p. 60.
49 Montesquieu, *Spirit of Laws*, loc.cit., p. iv.
50 Jacob Levy, "Ancient and Modern Constitutionalism Revisited," University of Chicago Political Workshop, November 18, 2002, p. 4.
51 Ibid., p. 15.
52 Ibid.
53 Ibid.
54 Ibid.
55 Paul Carrese, "Montesquieu's complex natural right and moderate liberalism: the roots of American moderation," Polity, January 1, 2004, p. 7.
56 Alexander Hamilton, John Jay, James Madison, The Federalist (New York, 1787), p. 55.
57 Ibid., p. 62
58 Ibid.
59 Richard Matthews, If Men were Angels (University Press of Kansas, 1995), p. 232.
60 The Selected Writings of John

and John Quincy Adams, ed., Adrienne Koch and William Peden (New York, 1946), p. 108.
61 Ibid., p. 110.
62 Ibid.
63 Ibid., p. 109.
64 Adams, Selected Writings, loc.cit., p. 110.00
65 Ibid., p. 109
66 Ibid., p. 110
67 Adams, His Political Writings, ed. George A. Peek, Jr. (New York, 1954), p. 133.
68 Matthews, loc.cit., p. 240.
69 Levy, loc.cit., p. 21.
70 Antoine Louis Claude Destutt de Tracy, Commentary and Review of Montesquieu's Spirt of Laws, trans. Thomas Jefferson (New York, 1811), p 7.
71 Ibid., p. 77.
72 Ibid.
73 Ibid., p. 117
74 Tracy, loc.cit., p. 154.
75 Ibid.
76 Ibid.
77 Ibid.
78 Ibid.
79 Levy, loc.cit., p. 25.
80 Ibid.
81 Ibid.
82 Adams-Jefferson Letters, loc.cit., p. 388.
83 Ibid.
84 Ibid, p. 389.
85 John Ferling, Jefferson and Hamilton (New York, 2013) p. 54.
86 Ibid.

CHAPTER SIX

1 To William Short, Oct.3, 1801, *The Writings of Thomas Jefferson*, ed. H.A. Washington, vol. 4 (New York, 1853), p. 413.
2 The Anas of Thomas Jefferson, Feb. 4, 1818, *Writings*, vol. 9, p. 91.
3 Ibid.
4 John Ferling, *Jefferson and Hamilton* (New York, 2013), p. 182.
5 Alexander Hamilton to Edward

Carrington, May 26, 1792, *The Papers of Alexander Hamilton*, ed., Harold C. Syrett, vol. XI (New York, 1966), p. 529

6 Hamilton, loc.cit., p. 439
7 Ibid.
8 Ibid.
9 Thomas Jefferson to George Washington, Sept. 9, 1792, *The Jeffersonian ann Hamiltonian Traditions in American Politics*, ed., Albert Fried (New York, 1968), p. 69
10 Ibid., p. 72
11 Charles Downer Hazen, *Contemporary Opinion of the French Revolution* (Mass. 1897), p. 153
12 John Adams to Richard Price, April 19, 1790, *The Works of John Adams*, ed., Charles Francis Adams, vol. IX (Boston, 1851), p. 563
13 John Adams, *Discourses on Davila*, loc. cit., vol. VI, p. 232
14 Ibid., p. 239
15 Ibid.
16 *Adams*, loc.cit., p. 239
17 Ibid., p. 275
18 Merrill D. Peterson, *Thomas Jefferson and the New Nation* (New York, 1970), p. 438
19 To Benjamin Vaughan, 1791, *The Jeffersonian Cyclopedia*, ed., John Foley, vol. 1 (New York, 1900), p. 111
20 Dumas Malone, *Jefferson and the ordeal of Liberty* (Boston, 1962), p. 357
21 Thomas Paine, *The Complete Works of Thomas Paine*, vol. 2 (London, 1791), p. 13
22 To Thomas Paine, June 9, 1792, Hazen, loc. cit., p. 186
23 To Colonel Mason, Feb. 4, 1791, The Writings of Thomas Jefferson, loc. cit., vol. 3, p.209
24 To Edmund Pendleton, 1791, The Jeffersonian Encyclopedia, loc. cit., vol. 2. p. 776
25 Joseph J. Ellis, *His Excellency George Washington* (New York, 2005), p. 224
26 To William Short, Jan. 3, 1793, Writings, loc. cit., vol. 3, p. 501
27 To Short, loc.cit., p. 502
28 Ibid.
29 Jeffersonian Cyclopedia,

March, 1793, loc. cit., p. 520
30 Thomas Jefferson, Notes on Christoph Ebeling's Leter of July 20, 1795, Writings, op. cit., vol. 3, p. 73
31 Ibid.
32 To Lafayette, November 4, 1823, Writings, loc. cit., vol. 7, p. 325
33 To Phillip Mazzei, April 24, 1795, *The Life and Selected Writings of Thomas Jefferson*, Adrienne Koch and William Peden, eds. (Chapel Hill, 1954), p. 537
34 To James Madison, June 15, 1795, The Republic of Letters, James Morton Smith, ed. (New York, 1995), p. 123
35 To Edmund Pendleton, January 29, 1799, Writings, loc. cit., vol. 4, p. 274.
36 Ibid. p. 275
37 Adrienne Koch, *Jefferson and Madison* (London, 1950), p. 178
38 Koch, loc.cit;, p. 178.
39 To Stephen t. Mason, Oct. 19, 1798, Writings, loc. cit., p. 258
40 Ethelbert Dudley Warfield, *The Kentucky Resolutions of 1798* (New York, 1894), p. 77.
41 Ibid., p. 76
42 *The Complete Jefferson*, ed., Saul K. Padover (New York, 1943), p. 129.
43 Padover, loc. cit., p. 129
44 Ibid., p. 130.
45 Ibid., p. 131.
46 Padover, loc.cit., p. 131.
47 Ibid.
48 Ibid., p. 133
49 Ibid.
50 Ibid.
51 To Edward Carrington, Aug. 4, 1787, Writings, op. cit., vol. 2, p. 21.
52 Comments on the Federal Constitution, Dec. 20, 1787, Padover, loc.cit., p. 122.
53 To James Madison, March 15, 1789, Smith, loc. cit., vol. 2, p.587.
54 David N. Mayer, *The Constitutional Thought of Thomas Jefferson (University of Virginia*, 1997), p. 186.
55 Padover, loc. cit., p. 124.
56 Mayer, op. cit., p. 187.

57 To Jonathan Drayton, 1799,
   The American Enlightenment,
   ed., Adrienne Koch (New
   York, 1965), p. 582.
58 Ibid., p. 584.
59 To Edmund Pendleton, Jan. 29,
   1799, Writings, loc.cit., vol. 4,
   p. 276.
60 To Eldridge Gerry, January 26,
   1799, ibid., vol. 4, 268.
61 Ibid.
62 To Gerry, loc.cit., p. 268.
63 Ibid.
64 Ibid.
65 Ibid.
66 To Edward Rutledge, Aug. 25,
   1791, Writings, loc.cit.., vol. 3,
   p. 286.
67 Hazen, loc. cit., p. 289.
68 *Montesquieu's Persian Letters,*
   ed. C.J. Betts (New York,
   1993), p. 53.
69 Malone, loc. cit., p. 48.
70 Malone, loc.cit., p. 49.
71 Frank Maloy Anderson, ed.,
   The Constitutions and Other
   Select Documents Illustrative
   of the History of France 1789–
   1901 (Minneapolis: H. W.
   Wilson, 1904), pp. 170–74.
72 To Rev. James Madison, Oct.
   28, 1785, Selected Writings,
   loc. cit., p. 389.
73 Ibid.
74 Anderson, op.cit., p. 171.
75 Francis Newton Thorpe, *The*
   Constitutional History of the
   United States (Chicago, 1901),
   vol. 1, p. 153.

CHAPTER SEVEN

1 To John Dickinson, Mar. 6,
   1801, The Writings of Thomas
   Jefferson, ed., H.A.
   Washington, vol. 4 (New York,
   1854), p. 366.
2 Ibid.
3 Ibid.
4 *"Autobiography"* The
   Jeffersonian Cyclopedia, ed.
   John P. Foley (New York,
   1900), p. 772.
5 To Edward Rutledge, Aug. 25,
   1791, The Writings of Thomas
   Jefferson, ed., H.A.
   Washington, vol. 3 (New York,
   1854), p. 286.
6 To Henry Innis, Jan 23, 1800,
   ibid., vol. 4 p. 316.
7 To N.R., Feb. 2, 1800, Ibid.,
   p. 319.
8 To Samuel Adams, Feb.26, 1800,
   ibid., p. 322.
9 Peter Onuf, Jefferson's Empire
   (University of Virginia, 2000),
   p. 83.
10 Jonathan Israel, A Revolution
   of the Mind (Princeton, 2010),
   p. 46.
11 To John Adams, Sept.4, 1823,
   Writings, loc. cit., vol. 7 p. 307.
12 To Robert Livingston, Dec/ 14,
   1800, ibid., vol. 4, p. 338
13 To A. Stuart, Esq., April. 8,
   1800, Writings, loc. cit.,, vol. 4,
   p. 393.
14 Ibid., p. 394.
15 To A. Stuart, Esq., April. 8,
   1800, Writings, loc. cit.,, vol. 4,
   p. 394.
16 To George Hay, June 2, 1807,
   Writings, op. cit., vol. 5, p. 84.
17 Dohald O. Dewey, Jefferson
   versus Marshall (New York,
   1970), p. 110.
18 To Abigail Adams, Sept. 11,
   1804, Writings, loc. cit., 561.
19 To George Wythe, July 1776,
   The Jeffersonian Cyclopedia,
   ed. John P. Foley, (New York,
   1900), p. 447.
20 To James Madison, March 15,
   1789, Writings, loc. cit., vol. 3,
   p. 3
21 "Autobiograhy," Cyclopedia,
   loc. cit., p. 447.
22 To William Barry, July 2, 1822,
   Writings, loc. cit., vol. 7,
   p. 256.
23 To John Dickinson, Dec. 19,
   1801, ibid., vol. 4, p. 424.
24 To Horatio Gates, July 11,
   1803, ibid., p. 495.
25 Charles A. Cerami, Jefferson's
   Great Gambit (Illinois, 2003),
   p. 258.
26 Cerami, loc. cit., p. 258.
27 To Wilson C. Nicolas,
   September 7, 1803, Writings,
   loc. cit., vol. 4, p. 506.
28 Ibid.
29 Cerami, loc. cit., p. 212.
30 Cerami, loc.cit., p. 220.
31 To Lafayette, Feb. 14, 1815,
   Writings, loc. cit., vol. 6,
   p. 421.
32 Ibid., p.422.
33 To Walter Jones, Marc 31,

1801, Writings, loc. cit., vol., 4, p. 393.

34 To Samuel Kerscheval, Jully 12, 1816, ibid., vol. 7, p. 14.

35 Ibid., p. 15.

36 "Fifth Annual Message," Dec. 3, 1805, The Complete Jefferson, ed. Saul K. Padover (New York, 1943), p. 416

37 Ibid., p. 436.

38 To Governor Pinckney, Nov. 8, 1808, Writings,, loc. cit., vol. 5, p. 384.

39 To William Giles, Dec. 25, 1825, ibid., vol. 7, p. 425.

40 To J.B. Colvin, Sept. 20, 1810, Writings, loc. cit., vol. 5, p. 542.

41 To Lafayette, Feb. 14, 1815, ibid., vol. 6, p. 422.

42 Montesquieu's Spirt of the Laws, translated by Thomas Nugent (New York 1966), p. 41

43 Montesquieu, loc. cit., p. 41

44 Montesquie, loc. cit., p. 41.

45 To J. Bannister, Oct. 15, 1785, Writings, op. cit., vol. 1, p. 468.

46 To John Cartwright, June 5, 1824, Writings, loc. cit., vol., 7, p. 358

47 To Samuel Kerchival, July 12, 1816, Ibid., p. 13.

48 Ibid.

49 To Samuel Kerchival, July 12, 1816, Writings, loc. cit., vol. 7, p. 13.

50 Ibid.

51 To Joseph Cabell, Feb. 2, 1816, Writings, loc. cit., vol 6, p. 544.

52 Ibid.

53 To John Cartwright, June 5, 1824, ibid., vol. 7, p. 353.

54 Ibid., p. 358.

55 Ibid., p. 359

56 Richard K. Matthews, The Radical Politics of Thomas Jefferson (Kansas, 1984), p. 81.

57 Matthews, loc. cit., p. 87.

58 Ibid., p. 148.

59 Thomas Jefferson, Notes on the State of Virginia, ed., William Peden (Chapel Hill, 1955), p. 93.

60 To Joseph Cabell, Feb. 2, 1816, Writings, loc. cit.;, vol. 6,

p. 542.

61 Ibid.

62 Montesquieu, loc.cit., p. 110.

63 Ibid.

64 Ibid.

65 Ibid.

66 Richard Matthews, loc. cit., p. 83.

67 Destutt de Tracy, Commentary and Review of Montesquieu's Spirit of the Laws, translated by Thomas Jefferson (Philadelphia, 1811), Preface.

68 To Marbois, June 14, 1817, Writings, loc. cit., vol. 7, p. 77.

69 To John Adams, Oct. 14, 1816, Adams-Jefferson Letters, loc. cit., p. 491.

CONCLUSION

1 Thomas Prangle, The Spirit of Modern Republicanism (University of Chicago 1988), p. 112.

2 P.G.A. Pocock, The Machiavellian Moment (Princeton, 1975), p. 515.

3 Prangle, ibid., p. 102.

4 Gordon Wood, Empire of Liberty (Oxford, 2009), p. 8.

5 Ibid., p. 9.

6 Ibid.

7 Wood, loc.cit., p. 24.

8 Thomas Hobbes, Leviathan, ed., Francis B. Randall (New York, 1964), p. 88.

9 Ibid., p. 84.

10 Pangle, loc.cit., p. 244.

11 John Locke, The Second Treatise on Government, ed., Thomas P. Peardon (New York, 195dd2), p. 13.

12 Ibid., p. 14.

13 The Federalist, Alexander Hamilton, John Jay, James Madison (New York, 1787), p. 54.

14 Ibid.92.

15 Ibid.

16 John Adams, His Political Writings, ed., George A. Peek Jr. (New York, 1954), p. 176

17 Adams,.Political Writings, loc.cit., p. 178.

18 Pangle, loc.cit., p. 244.

19 Daniel J. Boorstin, The Lost

World of Thomas Jefferson
(Boston, 1948), p. 245.

20 Jurgen Habermas, Theory and
Practice (Boston, 1973), p. 42.

21 Ibid.

22 Thomas I. Pangle, The Spirit of
Modern Republicanism
(University of Chicago, 1988),
p. 168.

23 To Albert Gallatin, Dec. 1820,
The Jeffersonian Cyclopedia,
ed. John P. Foley (New York,
1900), p. 78.

24 To Richard Rush, June, 1819,
ibid., 76.

25 To John Adams, Jan 1814,
ibid., p. 77.

26 To Charles Yancey, Jan. 1816,
ibid., p. 77.

27 To Albert Gallatin, Dec. 1820,
ibid., 78

28 Anas, The Writings of Thomas
Jefferson, ed., H.A.Washington,
vol. 9 (New York, 1854), p. 92.

29 Richard Matthews, loc.cit.,
p. 267-268.

30 Jurgen Habermas, Theory and
Practice (Boston, 1973), p. 71.

BIBLIOGRAPHY

PRIMARY SOURCES

Adams, John. *His Political Writings*, ed. George A. Peek Jr., New York, 1954.

Adams, John. *The Works of John Adams*, ed. Charles Francis Adams, Boston, 1851.

Alembert, Jean Le Rond. *Discours Preliminaire de l'encyclopedie*, Paris, 1919.

Bacon, Francis. *Works*, ed., Spedding, Ellis and Heath, London, 1857-59.

Brenner, Lenni. *Jefferson and Madison on the Separation of Church and State*, New Jersey, 2004.

Burlamaqui, Jean Jacques. *The Principles of Natural and Politic Law*, ed., Knud Haakonssen, Indianapolis, 2004.

Burtt, Edward A., ed. *The English Philosophers from Bacon to Mill*, New York, 1939.

Cappon, Lester J., ed. *The Adams-Jefferson Letters*, New York, 1959.

Chinard, Gilbert, ed. *The Correspondence of Jefferson and Du Pont De Nemours*, London, 1931.

Chinard, Gilbert. *Jefferson and Les Ideologues*, Paris, 1925.

Chinard, Gilbert, ed. The *Commonplace Book* of Thomas Jefferson, Paris, 1926.

Descartes, Rene. *Discourse on Method and Meditations*, ed., Laurence J. La Fleur, New York, 1960.

Dumbaud, Edward, ed. *The Political Writings of Thomas Jefferson*, New York, 1955.

Ferguson, Adam. *Principles of Moral and Political Sciences*, 2 vols., Edinburgh, 1992.

Ferguson, Adam. *Essay on the History of Civil Society*, ed. Louis Schneider, London, 1995.

Foley, John P., ed. *The Jeffersonian Cyclopedia*, New York, 1900.

Ford, Paul Leicester, ed. *The Works of Thomas Jefferson*, 12 vols., New York, 1904.

Freeman, Joanne B., ed. *Hamilton Writings*, New York, 2001.

Hamilton, Alexander. "The Farmer Refuted," *The Papers of Alexander Hamilton*, vol. 1. Ed., Harold C. Syrett, New York, 1961.

Hamilton, Alexander, John Jay and James Madison. *The Federalist*, New York, 1787.

Haraszti, Zoltan, ed., *John Adams and the Prophets of Progress*, New York, 1964.

Hobbes, Thomas. *Leviathan*, ed., Francis B. Randall, New York, 1651.

Home, Henry (Lord Kames). *The Principles of Morality and Natural Religion*, ed., Knud Haakonssen, Indianapolis, 2005.

Holbach, Baron D. The System of Nature, Vol. 1, trans. Paris, 1971.

Hutcheson, Francis. An Inquiry Concerning the Original of our Ideas of Beauty and Virtue, London, 1726.

Jefferson, Thomas. *Notes on the State of Virginia*, ed., William Peden, Chapel Hill, 1954.

Jefferson, Thomas. *The Garden and Farm Books*, ed., Robert C. Baron, Colorado, 1987.

Jefferson, Thomas. "A Summary View of the Rights of British America," *The Papers of Thomas Jefferson*, ed., Julian Boyd, Princeton, 1950.

Koch, Adrienne and William Peden, eds. *The Life and Selected Writings of Thomas Jefferson*, Chapel Hill, 1954.

Koch, Adrienne, ed. *The American Enlightenment*, New York, 1965.

Lee, Gordon C., ed. *Crusade Against Ignorance*, New York, 1961.

Le May, J.A. Leo, ed. *Franklin Writings*, New York, 1987.

Locke, John. The *Second Treatise on Government*, London, 1690.

Locke, John. An *Essay on Human Understanding*, 2 vols., ed., Alexander C. Fraser, New York, 1959.

Malone, Dumas, ed. *The Correspondence of Thomas Jefferson and Pierre Samuel Du Pont De Nemours, 1798-1817*, trans. Linwood Lehman, New York, 1930.

Montesquieu, Baron de. *Oeuvres de Montesquieu*, 2 vols., Amsterdam, 1758.

Montesquieu, Baron de. *The Persian Letters*, New York, 1964 (first published in 1721).

Montesquieu, Baron de. *The Spirit of the Laws*, ed., Thomas Nugent, New York, 1966.

Padover, Saul K. *Thomas Jefferson on Democracy*, New York, 1939.

Padover, Saul K. *The Complete Jefferson*, New York, 1943.

Paine, Thomas. *The Complete Works of Thomas Paine, London, 1791*.

Penniman, Howard, ed. John Locke, "A Letter Concerning Toleration," New York, 1947.

Reid, Thomas. *Essays on the Active Powers of the Human Mind*, ed., A.D. Woozley, London, 1969.

Rossi, Paolo. Philosophy, *Technology and the Arts in the Early Modern Era*, New York, 1970.

Roche, John, ed. *Origins of American Political Thought*, "The Origins of the Separation of Powers," New York, 1967.

Rousseau, Jean-Jacques. The First and *Second Discourse*s, ed., Roger D. Masters, New York, 1964.

Rousseau, Jean-Jacques. The *Social Contract* and Discourse on the Origin of Inequality, ed., Lester G. Crocker, New York, 1971.

Sanford, Charles B. *The Religious Life of Thomas Jefferson*, Charlottesville, 1984.

Say, Jean Baptiste. *A Treatise on Political Economy*, Philadelphia, 1880.

D'Alembert, Jean le Rond. Preliminary Discourse to the *Encyclopedia* of Diderot, Schwab, Richard N., ed., New York, 1963.

Smith, Adam. *The Wealth of Nations*, 2 vols., London, 1776.

Smith, James Morton, ed. *Republic of Letters*, 3 vols., New York, 1995.

Sowerby, Millicant E., ed. *Catalogue of the Library of Thomas Jefferson, 5 vols.*, Washington, 1952.

Spurlin, Paul M. *Montesquieu in America*, Baton-Rouge, 1940.

Stewart, Dugald, *Outlines of Moral Philosophy*, Edinburgh, 1801.

Stewart, Dugald. *The Philosophy of the Active and Moral Powers of Man, Part 1*, Edinburgh, 1828.

Stewart, Dugald. Collected Works, ed., *Sir William Hamilton, vols. 1-11*, Edinburgh, 1854-1858.

Sydney, Algernon. *Discourses Concerning Government*, London, 1763.

Thayer, H.S., ed. *Newton's Philosophy of Nature*, New York, 1953.

Tracy, Destutt de. *A Treatise on Political Economy*, ed., Thomas Jefferson, Georgetown, 1817.

Tracy, Destutt de. *Commentary and Review of Montesquieu's Spirit of the Laws*, ed., Thomas Jefferson, New York, 1811.

Warfield, Ethelbert Dudley. *The Kentucky Resolutions of 1798*, New York, 1894.

Washington, H.S., ed. *The Writings of Thomas Jefferson*, vols. 1–9, New York, 1856.

ARTICLES

Bassani, Luigi Marco, "Property and Happiness in Thomas Jefferson's Political Philosophy," 6th Australian Scholars Conference, Auburn, March 24-26, 2000.

Berman, Harold J., "The Origins of Historical Jurisprudence: Coke, Selden, Hale," *Yale Law Journal*, 1994.

Bryant, Barry, "The Pursuit of Happiness," *WPS Presidential Address*, 2005.

Carrese, Paul, "Montesquieu's complex natural right and moderate liberalism: the roots of American moderation," *Polity*, January 1, 2004.

Chinard, Gilbert, "Jefferson and the American Philosophical Society," *Proceedings*, vol. LXXXVII, July 1943.

David, Paul A., "The Growth of Real Product in the United States before 1840: New Evidence, Controlled Conjectures," *Journal of Economic History*, XXVII, 1967.

Degenaar, Marjolein and M. Lokhorst, "Molyneux's Problem," Stanford *Encyclopedia* of Philosophy, Fall, 2011 Edition, Edward N. Zalta, ed.

Dilworth, Ernest, ed., *Voltaire's Philosophical Letters*, New York, 1961.

Dorfman, Joseph, "The Economic Philosophy of Thomas Jefferson," *Political Science Quarterly*, Vol. 55, No. 1, 1940.

Galileo, math quote, *www.gogeometry.com.*

Gould, William D., "The Religious Opinions of Thomas Jefferson," *Mississippi Valley Historical Review,* XX, June 1933.

Johnson, Raul Perez, "Jean Jacques Burlamaqui and the Theory of Social Compact, *Historia Constitucional,* 2005.

Kimball, Marie, "Jefferson's Four Freedoms," *Virginia Quarterly Review,* April 1943.

Knoles, G.H., "The Religious Ideas of Thomas Jefferson," *Mississippi Valley Historical Review,* XXX, June 1943.

Koch, Adrienne, "Pragmatic Wisdom and the American Enlightenment," *William and Mary Quarterly,* XVIII, July 1961.

Main, Jackson T., "The Distribution of Property in Post-Revolutionary Virginia," *Massachusetts Valley Historical Review,* 41, 1954.

Palmer, R. R., "A Neglected Work: Otto Vosler on Jefferson and the Revolutionary Era," *William and Mary Quarterly,* April 12, 1962.

Schneider, Herbert, "The Enlightenment in Thomas Jefferson," *Ethics,* LIII, July 1943.

Smelser, Marshall, "The Jacobin Phrenzy: The Menace of Monarchy, Plutocracy and Anglophilia, 1789-1798," *Virginia Quarterly Review,* April 19, 1943.

Smith, T.V., "Thomas Jefferson and the Perfectibility of Man," *Ethics,* vol. LIII, no. 4, July 1943.

White, Andrew D., "Jefferson and Slavery," *Atlantic Monthly,* IX, January 1862.

Levy, Jacob, "Ancient and Modern Constitutionalism Revisited," *University of Chicago Political Workshop,* November 18, 2002.

Osborn, Henry F., "Thomas Jefferson as a Paleontologist," *Science,* vol. LXXXVII, December 1935.

Peterson, Merrill D., ed., "Thomas Jefferson and Commercial Policy, 1783-1793," New York, 1967.

Peterson, Merrill D., ed., "A Re-examination of Jeffersonian Economics," William D. Grampp, New York, 1967.

Setser, Vernon G., "The Commercial Reciprocity Policy of the United States, 1774-1829," New York, 1969.

Warfield, Ethelbert Dudley, *The Kentucky Resolutions of 1798,* New York, 1894.

Zook, George F. "Proposals for New Commercial Treaty Between France and the United States, 1778-1793," *South Atlantic Quarterly.*

SECONDARY SOURCES

Adams, Henry. *History of the United States,* vol. 1, New York, 1903.

Adams, William Howard. *The Paris Years of Thomas Jefferson,* London, 1997.

Appleby, Joyce. *Capitalism and a New Social Order,* New York, 1984.

Appleby, Joyce. Economic: *The Agrarian Republic*, Notre Dame, 2000.

Arrowood, Charles, ed. *Thomas Jefferson and Education*, London, 1930.

Bailyn, Bernard. *The Ideological Origins of the American Revolution*, Cambridge, 1973.

Banning, Lance. *The Jeffersonian Persuasion*, New York, 1978.

Beard, Charles A. *An Economic Interpretation of the Constitution of the United States*, New York, 1913.

Beard, Charles. *Economic Origins of Jeffersonian Democracy*, New York, 1915.

Becker, Carl. *The Declaration of Independence*, New York, 1922.

Becker, Carl. *The Heavenly City of Eighteenth Century Philosophers*, London, 1932.

Bedini, Silvio A. Thomas Jefferson, *Statesman of Science*, London, 1990.

Beer, M. *An Inquiry into Physiocracy*, London, 1939.

Berman, Eleanor D. *Thomas Jefferson Among the Arts*, New York, 1947.

Boorstin, Daniel. *The Lost World of Thomas Jefferson*, Boston, 1948.

Borden, Morton. *Political Parties in the Early Republic*, New York, 1967.

Bowers, Claude. *Jefferson and Hamilton*, New York, 1966.

Boyd, Julian, ed. *The Papers of Thomas Jefferson*, vol. 15, New York.

Bury, J.B. *The Idea of Progress*, New York, 1932.

Burstein, Andrew; Isenberg, Nancy. *Madison and Jefferson*, New York, 2010.

Burstein, Andrew. *Jefferson's Secrets*, New York, 2005.

Butterfield, Herbert. *The Origins of Modern Science*, New York, 1957.

Cassirer, Ernst. *The Philosophy of the Enlightenment*, Boston, 1951.

Ceaser, James. "Natural Rights and Scientific Racism," *Thomas Jefferson and the Politics of Nature*, ed., Thomas S. Engeman, Indiana, 2000.

Cerami, Charles A. *Jefferson's Great Gamble*, Illinois, 2003.

Chambers, William Nisbet. *Political Parties in a New Nation*, New York, 1963.

Chelsey, Clark. Dugald Stewart, *Historian of the Enlightenment*, Ph.D. dissertation, UCSB, 1976.

Chernow, Ron. *Alexander Hamilton*, New York, 2004.

Chinard, Gilbert. *Thomas Jefferson, Apostle of Americanism*, Ann Arbor, 1929.

Cohen, I. Bernard. *Science and the Founding Fathers*, New York, 1995.

Commager, Henry Steele. *Jefferson, Nationalism, and the American Enlightenment*, New York, 1975.

Commager, Henry Steele. *The Empire of Reason*, New York, 1978.

Cunningham, Noble E. *The Jeffersonian Republicans*, Chapel Hill, 1957.

Cunningham, Noble E. *In Pursuit of Reason: The Life of Thomas Jefferson*, Ballantine Books, 1987.

DeConde, Alexander. *The Quasi-War*, New York, 1966.

Dewey, Donald O. *Jefferson versus Marshall*, New York, 1970.

Downer, Charles. *Contemporary Opinions of the French Revolution*, Massachusetts, 1897.

Dreisbach, Daniel L. *Thomas Jefferson and the Wall of Separation Between Church and State* (Critical America), New York, 2003.

Ellis, Joseph. *American Creation*, New York, 2007.

Ellis, Joseph. *American Sphinx*, New York, 1998.

Ellis, Richard. *His Excellency George Washington*, New York, 2005.

Ellis, Richard. *The Jeffersonian Crisis*, New York, 1971.

Engeman, Thomas S., ed. *Thomas Jefferson and the Politics of Nature*, Notre Dame, 1999.

Ferling, John. *Jefferson and Hamilton*, New York, 2013.

Ferguson, Robert A. *The American Enlightenment*, 1750-1820, London, 1994.

Ferrone, Vincenzo, *The Enlightenment*, Princeton, 2015.

Fried, Albert, ed. *The Jeffersonian and Hamiltonian Traditions in American Politics*, New York, 1968.

Gillispie, Charles Coulston. *The Edge of Objectivity*, Princeton, 1960.

Gordon-Reed, Annette. *The Hemingses of Monticello*, New York, 2008.

Habermas, Jurgen. *Theory and Practice*, Boston, 1973.

Hauser, Marc. *Moral Minds*, New York, 2006.

Hazard, Paul. *The European Mind*, 1680-1715, New York, 1963.

Hazen, Charles Downer. *Contemporary American Opinion of the French Revolution*, Baltimore, 1897.

Israel, Jonathan. *A Revolution of the Mind*, Princeton, 2010.

Kerrison, Catherine. *Jefferson's Daughters*, New York, 2018.

Hankins, Thomas L. *Science and the Enlightenment*, New York, 1985.

Higgs, Henry. *The Physiocrats*, New York, 1952.

Honeywell, Roy J. *The Educational Work of Thomas Jefferson*, Cambridge, 1931.

Hofstadter, Richard. *The American Political Tradition*, New York, 1948.

Isenberg, Nancy; and Burstein, Andrew. Madison and Jefferson, New York, 2010.

Jackson, David, ed. *American Studies in Honor of William Boyd*, "The Political Economy of Jefferson, Madison and Adams." *Durham*, 1968.

Jones, Richard Foster. *Ancients and Moderns*. Berkeley, 1961.

Kaplan, Lawrence S. *Jefferson and France*, London, 1967.

Kingsley, Martin. *French Liberal Thought in the Eighteenth Century*, New York, 1962.

Koch, Adrienne. *Jefferson and Madison*, New York, 1972.

Koch, Adrienne. *The Philosophy of Thomas Jefferson*, New York, 1944.

Koyré, Alexandre. *From the Closed World to the Infinite Universe*, Baltimore, 1957.

Koyré, Alexandre. *Newtonian Studies*, Chicago, 1965.

Larson, Edward J. *A Magnificent Catastrophe*, New York, 2007.

Levy, Leonard W. *Jefferson and Civil Liberties*, New York, 1963.

Lipscomb, Andrew A. and Albert Ellery Bergh, eds. *Autobiography of Thomas Jefferson*, vol. 1, New York, 1950.

Lipscomb, Andrew A. and Albert Ellery Bergh, eds. *The Writings of Thomas Jefferson*, vol. 15, New York, 1975.

Lovejoy, Arthur O. *The Great Chain of Being*, Harvard, 1936.

Lynd, Staughton. *Intellectual Origins of the American Revolution*, New York, 1968.

Macintyre, Gordon. Dugald Stewart, *The Pride and Ornament of Scotland*, Brighton, 2003.

MacPherson, C.B. *The Political Theory of Possessive Individualism*, London, 1962.

McClellan, James. *Science Reorganized: Scientific Societies in the Eighteenth Century*, New York, 1985.

McCoy, Drew R. *The Elusive Republic*, Chapel Hill, 1980.

McCullough, John. *John Adams*, New York, 2001.

McLaughlin, Jack. *Jefferson and Monticello* (New York, 1988).

Malone, Dumas. *Jefferson and His Times*, 6 vols., Boston, 1948.

Malone, Dumas. *Jefferson and the Ordeal of Liberty*, Boston, 1962.

Malone, Dumas. Jefferson and the *Rights of Man*, Boston, 1951.

Martin, Edwin T. *Thomas Jefferson: Scientist*, New York, 1961.

Matthews, Richard K. *The Radical Politics of Thomas Jefferson*, Kansas, 1984.

Mayer, David N. *The Constitutional Thought of Thomas Jefferson*, London, 1994.

Meek, Ronald. *The Economics of Physiocracy*, Cambridge, 1963.

Miller, Charles A. *Jefferson and Nature*, Baltimore, 1988.

Miller, John. *The Federalist Era*, New York, 1960.

Mitchell, Broadus. *Alexander Hamilton*, New York, 1962.

Miller, John Chester. *The Wolf by the Ears*, New York, 1977.

Morrow, Glenn R. *The Ethical and Economic Theories of Adam Smith*, New York, 1969.

Nettels, Curtis B. *The Emergence of a National Economy*, London, 1962.

Nock, Albert J. *Jefferson*, New York, 1926.

O'Brien, Conor Cruise. *The Long Affair*, Chicago, 1996.

Onuf, Peter S. and Leonard J. Sadosky. *Jeffersonian America*, Oxford, 2002.

Onuf, Peter S. *Jefferson's Empire*, Charlottesville, 2005.

Onuf, Peter S. *The Mind of Thomas Jefferson*, Charlottesville, 2007.

Outram, Dorinda. *The Enlightenment*, Cambridge, 2013.

Pangle, Thomas L. *The Spirit of Modern Republicanism*, Chicago, 1990.

Parrington, Vernon L. *The Colonial Mind, 1620-1800*, vol. 1, New York, 1927.

Peterson, Merrill. *The Jefferson Image in the American Mind*, Charlottesville, 1998.

Peterson, Merrill, ed. *Thomas Jefferson, A Profile*, New York, 1967.

Peterson, Merrill, ed. Thomas Jefferson: *A Reexamination of Jeffersonian Economics*, William D. Grampp, New York, 1967.

Peterson, Merrill. *Thomas Jefferson and the New Nation*,
New York, 1970.

Pocock, J.G.A. *The Machiavellian Moment*, Princeton, 1975.

Riskin, Jessica. *Science in the Age of Sensibility*, University of Chicago,
2002

Robineau, L. *Administration et Oeuvres Economiques*, Paris, 1889.

Shacktman, Tom. *Gentlemen Scientists and Revolutionaries*, New York,
2014.

Smith, Preserved. *The Enlightenment*, New York, 1934.

Sloan, Herbert E. *Principle and Interest*, University of Virginia, 1995.

Talmon, J.L. *The Origins of Totalitarian Democracy*, New York, 1965.

Thorpe, Francis Newton. *The Constitutional History of the United States*,
vol. 1, New York, 1901.

Whatley, Richard, *Lectures on Political Economy*, New York, 1966.

White, Morton. *The Philosophy of the American Revolution*,
New York, 1978.

Wood, Gordon S. *Friends Divided*, New York, 2017.

Wiencek, Henry. *Master of the Mountain: Thomas Jefferson and his Slaves*,
New York, 2012.

Wilson, Douglas L. and Lucia Stanton. *Jefferson Abroad*, New York, 1999.

Williams, William Appleman. *The Contours of American History*,
New York, 1961.

Wills, Garry. *The Negro President*, New York, 2003.

Wills, Garry. *Inventing America*, New York, 1978.

Wiltse, Charles M. *The Jeffersonian Tradition in American Democracy*,
New York, 1935.

Woods, Gordon S. *The Empire of Liberty*, New York, 2009.

Zuckert, Michael P. *The Natural Rights Republic*, Notre Dame, 1996.

INDEX

The Author

Clark Chelsey received his BA in philosophy in 1968 from UCSB and his Ph.D in European and American intellectual history in 1976. Dr. Chelsey was an Associate of History at UCSB from 1970-1974, and was the recipient of the coveted Regents Fellowship in 1974. Dr. Chelsey's dissertation on Dugald Stewart and the Scottish Enlightenment was one of the first major philosophical studies on Dugald Stewart, the last representative of the Scottish school of Common Sense.

Clark Chelsey lives in Mill Valley in a house he designed and built with his wife, Gayle, and his son Julian, a student at UCSD. He continues to lecture on a wide range of philosophical and historical subjects at several philosophical societies in the Bay Area.

CPSIA information can be obtained
at www.ICGtesting.com
Printed in the USA
FSHW021013021019
62611FS